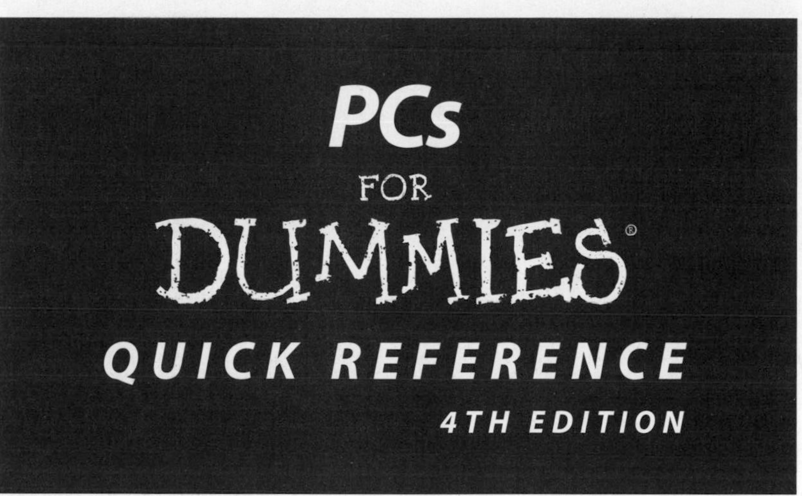

by Dan Gookin

Wiley Publishing, Inc.

PCs For Dummies® Quick Reference, 4th Edition

Published by
Wiley Publishing, Inc.
111 River Street
Hoboken, NJ 07030-5774

www.wiley.com

Published by Wiley Publishing, Inc., Indianapolis, Indiana

Published simultaneously in Canada

For general information on our other products and services, please contact our Customer Care Department within the U.S. at 800-762-2974, outside the U.S. at 317-572-3993, or fax 317-572-4002.

For technical support, please visit www.wiley.com/techsupport.

Wiley also publishes its books in a variety of electronic formats. Some content that appears in print may not be available in electronic books.

Library of Congress Control Number: 2007920020

ISBN: 978-0-470-11526-8

Manufactured in the United States of America

10 9 8 7 6 5 4 3 2 1

About the Author

Dan Gookin has been writing about technology for over 600 years. He has contributed articles to numerous high-tech magazines and written more than 100 books about personal computing technology, many of them accurate.

He combines his love of writing with his interest in technology to create books that are informative and entertaining, but not boring. Having sold more than 14 million copies translated into more than 30 languages, Dan can attest that his method of crafting computer tomes does seem to work.

Perhaps Dan's most famous title is the original *DOS For Dummies,* published in 1991. It became the world's fastest-selling computer book, at one time moving more copies per week than the *New York Times* number-one best seller (although, because it's a reference book, it could not be listed on the *NYT* best seller list). That book spawned the entire line of *For Dummies* books, which remains a publishing phenomenon to this day.

Dan's most recent titles include *Word 2007 For Dummies, Laptops For Dummies,* 2nd Edition; *Programmer's Guide to NCurses*, and many more! He writes a blog and maintains the Wambooli Forums on his vast and helpful Web page `www.wambooli.com`.

Dan holds a degree in communications and visual arts from the University of California, San Diego. He lives in the Pacific Northwest, where he enjoys spending time with his boys in the gentle woods of Idaho.

Publisher's Acknowledgments

We're proud of this book; please send us your comments through our online registration form located at www.dummies.com/register/.

Some of the people who helped bring this book to market include the following:

Acquisitions, Editorial, and Media Development

Senior Project Editor: Mark Enochs

Executive Acquisitions Editor: Greg Croy

Copy Editor: Becky Whitney

Technical Editor: James F. Kelly

Editorial Manager: Leah Cameron

Media Development Manager: Laura VanWinkle

Editorial Assistant: Amanda Foxworth

Sr. Editorial Assistant: Cherie Case

Composition Services

Project Coordinator: Kristie Rees

Layout and Graphics: Joyce Haughey, Barbara Moore, LeAndra Hosier, Ronald Terry, Erin Zeltner

Proofreaders: Laura Albert, Aptara

Anniversary Logo Design: Richard Pacifico

Indexer: Aptara

Publishing and Editorial for Technology Dummies

Richard Swadley, Vice President and Executive Group Publisher

Andy Cummings, Vice President and Publisher

Mary Bednarek, Executive Acquisitions Director

Mary C. Corder, Editorial Director

Publishing for Consumer Dummies

Diane Graves Steele, Vice President and Publisher

Joyce Pepple, Acquisitions Director

Composition Services

Gerry Fahey, Vice President of Production Services

Debbie Stailey, Director of Composition Services

Table of Contents

Part I: PC Overview 1

Part II: Connecting Stuff 23

Part VIII: Organizing Your Stuff 125

Part IX: Printing 141

Part I

PC Overview

Welcome to Part I, where I introduce you to the PC, piece by piece. Here you'll find a visual tour, personal introductions, basic understandings, and a hint of what's to come as you uncover the basics of the ever-useful personal computer.

In this part . . .

- Basic computer science
- PC types and models
- Hardware expansion
- The operating system
- The Internet
- Files, folders, and your stuff

What You See: Basic Hardware

A computer is really the sum of its parts more than it is a single gizmo. The parts all have official, technical names, which you may know already. Some parts live inside the box; some dwell outside. Connecting everything are cables — vast, tangled, and ugly. All together, the pieces, parts, and cables make up your computer system.

The central item in the computer system, the hive of high-tech wonderment, the PC's bosom (as it were), is the *console.* Other items surround the console and connect to it. Those things are *peripherals.*

Despite the common elements, each computer system is quite unique, sporting different internals, different types and amounts of storage, and different software to make things go. I suppose that's why the things are *personal* computers and not *generic* computers. The basic PC setup — console and peripherals — is illustrated in Figures 1-1 and 1-2.

Figure 1-1

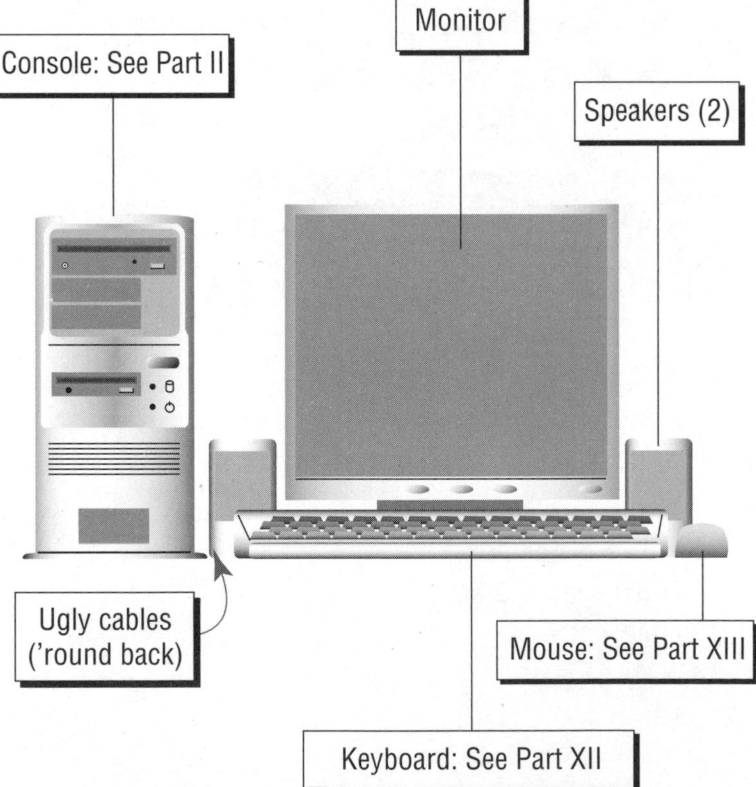

Figure 1-2

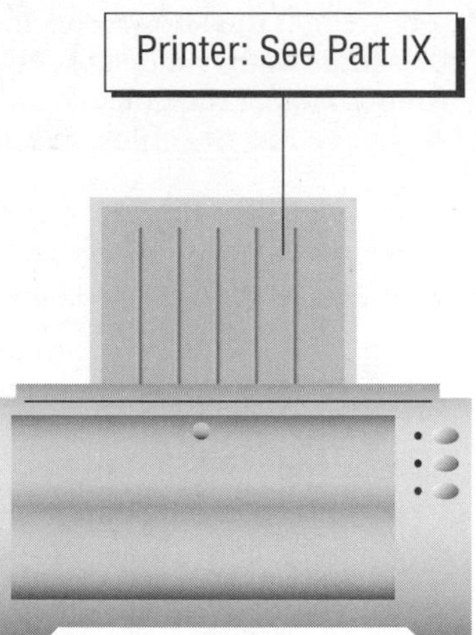

Here are some of the basic components you should recognize and know by their official names:

- **Console:** The centerpiece of any computer system. It's the box-o-guts! Also called the *system unit* and often mistakenly referred to as the CPU. ***See also*** Part II.
- **Monitor:** The computer's display. It can sit on top of or to the side of the console. This part of the basic computer system is necessary because it's how you see the information the computer displays, also known as *output.*
- **Keyboard:** The thing you type on, and one method for you to send information to the computer, also known as *input.* Despite all the computer's graphics, most of the time you spend using it involves typing. ***See also*** Part XII.
- **Mouse:** The gizmo that helps you work with graphical images that the computer displays on the screen. It's the second method you use for entering information (next to the keyboard), a second form of *input.* ***See also*** Part XIII.
- **Speakers:** The PC speaks! And squawks, and plays music, and often talks. To hear that stuff, you need speakers. They can be either external or part of the monitor. ***See also*** Part II.
- **Printer:** The device that puts your work down on paper — documents, copies of e-mail messages, charts, graphics, photos, or anything else your creative heart desires. The printer is the PC's second most popular gizmo for output. ***See also*** Part IX.

- **Lots of ugly cables:** Rarely seen in the showroom and never in ads, although they exist! Cables! Lots of ugly cables keep everything connected. They're usually found 'round back of the console and other components. Yes, even wireless systems have lots of cables. ***See also*** Part II.

A computer system can include a variety of other devices and gizmos beyond the basic items mentioned here. These *peripherals* include scanners, digital cameras, external disk drives, modems, and a host of other gadgets various and sundry.

What You See: Console — the Front

The *console* is the sun of your computer's solar system, the central hub of activity. Every other device, gizmo, or gadget in the computer system plugs into the console in one way or another. The console is also home to many of your PC's most important, secret, and forbidden parts.

Figure 1-3 shows important items on the front side of the console. These are things you should be able to locate and identify on your own computer, although their specific locations may be different from what you see here:

- **CD-ROM / DVD drive:** Part of the PC's storage system, and one of the main disk drives, the CD-ROM / DVD drive is designed for reading and, often, creating CDs and DVDs. Access to the drive may also be hidden behind a panel or door.
- **Future expansion:** You can add disk drives or devices to the console. They may be obvious or well hidden, thanks to a clever console design.
- **Floppy drive:** An ancient part of the PC's storage system, although rarely found on today's PCs, this drive is designed to read from and write to floppy disks. Not every PC sold today has a floppy drive, but if yours does, it appears somewhere on the front of the console.
- **Air vents:** The thing's gotta breathe!
- **Secret door/connectors:** Many consoles have special connectors on the front for USB, digital video (IEEE 1394), and audio devices. These may be obvious on the front of the console or concealed behind a door or panel.
- **Buttons and lights:** The console has at least one button and some lights. Additional buttons may appear on some consoles, as with additional lights. The following list highlights some of the more common buttons and lights:

  - **Power button:** This button is used to start up the computer, turn the computer off, or do other power-related things. ***See also*** Part IV.

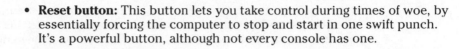

- **Reset button:** This button lets you take control during times of woe, by essentially forcing the computer to stop and start in one swift punch. It's a powerful button, although not every console has one.

- **Sleep button:** This button appears mostly on laptop PCs and is used to put the system into a special suspended, or Stand By, mode. Few consoles have such a button, yet the sleep icon may appear as a light on the console, to indicate that the computer is not off, but, rather, is "asleep."

- **Hard drive light:** This festive light flashes as the hard drive is being accessed. Because hard drives are often buried internally, the light provides a visual clue to whether the drive is alive or dead.
- **Power light:** This is merely a light on the console that is on when the computer is on. If your computer doesn't make much noise, this light is often your only clue that the sucker is turned on.

Figure 1-3

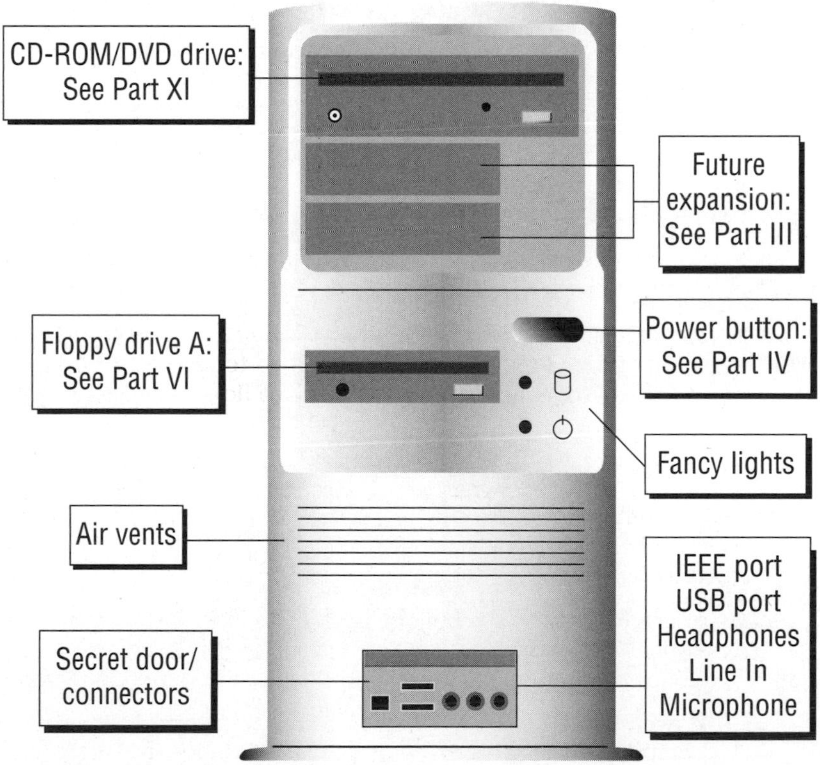

This list doesn't cover everything you could possibly find on the front of your computer. For example, your console may also have an infrared port for communicating with a laptop or handheld computer. Even so, become familiar with those few items mentioned in the list. Many computer manuals and software instructions assume that you know where everything is and what it's called.

What You See: Console — the Back

Forget the pretty face: When it comes to the important stuff, you need to look at the console's ugly rump (see Figure 1-4). That's where most of the computer's components connect to the console.

Figure 1-4

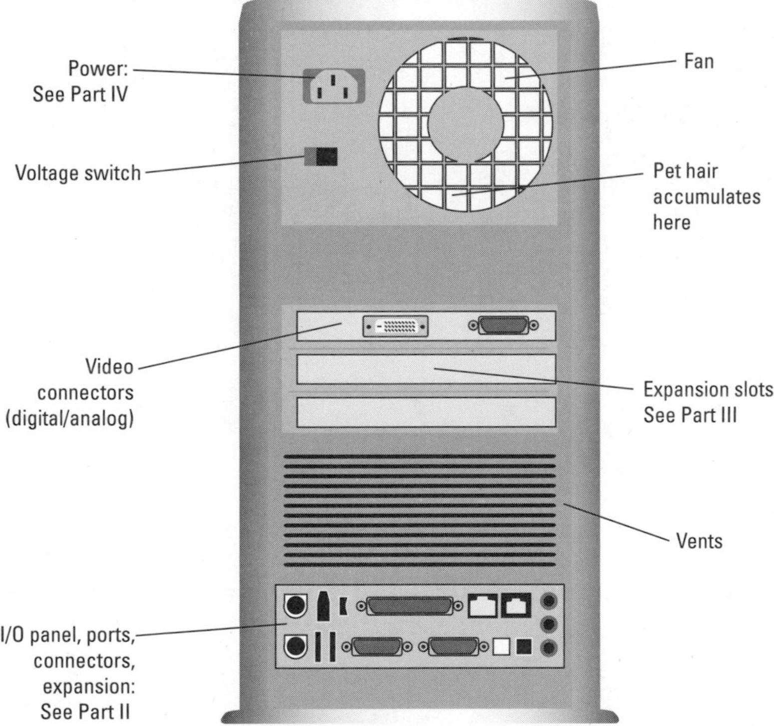

Other items are worth noting as well:

- **Power connector:** The power cord that plugs into the wall gazinta here.
- **Fan:** Air gets blown out here, to keep the inside of the console cool.
- **Voltage switch:** Some power supplies have two operating frequencies. This switch needs to be set only once to match the proper voltage for your country.
- **Expansion slots:** These slots are where add-on components and options are installed inside the console. You cannot see the slots directly, although the slot covers are visible on the back of the console, as shown nearby.
- **Expansion cards:** These items plug into the expansion slots and reveal a part of themselves on the console's rump, such as the digital video expansion card shown in Figure 1-4.
- **Vents:** That breathing thing again.
- **I/O panel:** Modern PCs put all their connectors in one central location, the I/O panel. It contains holes for plugging in a variety of goodies. ***See also*** Part II to find out what the holes are called and what plugs into them.

The I/O panel may be in one location, as shown in the illustration, or it may be split up into separate areas. For example, you can have one location for the mouse and keyboard connectors, plus another location for other items that attach to the console.

When the video connector (for the monitor) is on both the I/O panel and an expansion card, use the connector on the expansion card.

What You See: Console — the I/O Panel

I/O is computer-talk for input and output. The computer's world is all about input and output, and the console, because it's the center of your computer's world, plays a major role in that input/output thing. *To accommodate all that input and output, an I/O panel is provided, replete with a variety of connectors.* (See Figure 1-5.)

Here are a few items you can find on the I/O panel:

- **Keyboard connector:** Where the keyboard plugs into the console. A USB keyboard can plug into the USB port as well.
- **Mouse connector:** Where the mouse plugs into the console, although a USB mouse can plug directly into the USB port.
- **USB port:** The ever-versatile port for the multitude of USB devices to connect to your computer. ***See also*** Part III.

Figure 1-5

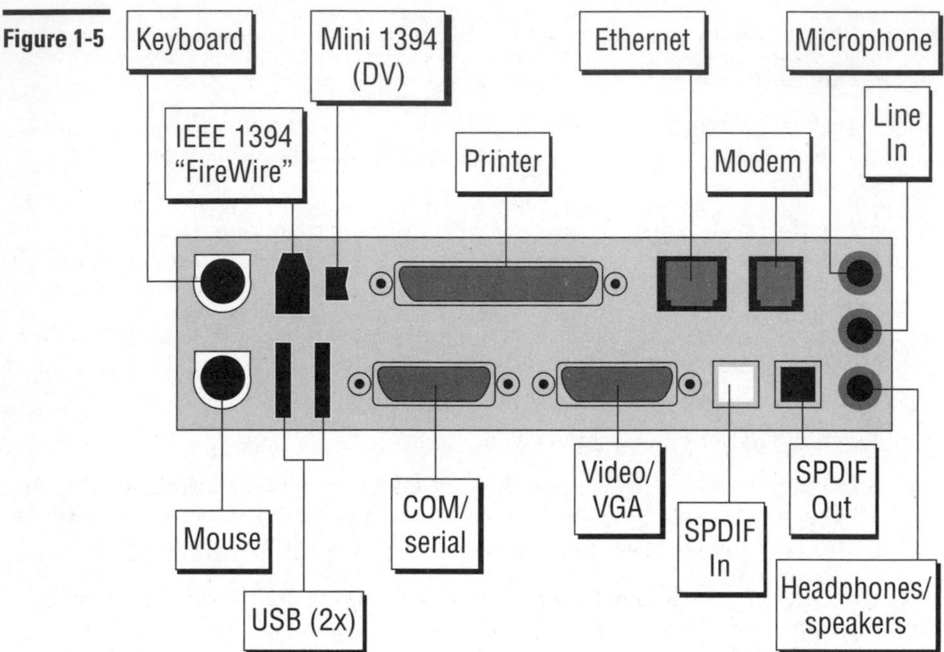

- **COM (or serial) port:** A once highly versatile connector that is now used primarily for ancient hardware — specifically, external modems and computer mice. Some consoles have two COM ports, labeled COM1 and COM2. In the olden days, it was called the RS-232C port. This port's connector has nine pins.
- **Video connector:** Where the monitor connects to the console. It's the same size as the COM port, but sports up to 15 holes. Use the I/O panel's connector only when you cannot find a second connector on an expansion card. (The expansion card connector indicates the presence of a much more powerful video adapter.) Note that newer digital monitors use a white, rectangular connector that may also be exclusive to an expansion card, not the I/O panel.
- **S-Video out:** A connector used for video output, primarily on PCs with high-end video. You use the S-Video out port to connect the PC to a TV set. (This port isn't shown in the illustration.)
- **SPDIF in/out:** A port that is used to connect the console to a high-end audio device, such as an external sound processor or a stereo system. The connector uses fiber optics to carry the sound signal, which is less

susceptible to outside noise than a traditional wire connector. SPDIF stands for Sony/Philips Digital Interconnect Format.

- **Microphone jack:** A jack that you can plug an optional microphone into for recording your voice or using voice-control software.
- **Line In jack:** An audio input used for connecting the PC's sound system to your stereo or VCR, for capturing audio and other sounds.
- **Headphones/speaker jack:** Where you plug in a set of headphones to listen privately to your computer, or plug in a set of speakers for more public listening.
- **Modem:** Where you plug in a standard phone cord, to connect your computer to the phone jack in the wall. That way, the computer's internal modem can use the telephone to contact the Internet. Modem holes can also be found on expansion cards in some PCs.
- **Phone:** A hole, if available, that's next to the modem jack. You can connect a standard telephone so that you can use a real phone on the same line as the computer.
- **Ethernet:** Where the computer connects to a network, or where you connect the computer to a cable or DSL modem. (Networking and the Internet are very similar things.) The hole for this port, also known as RJ-45, can also appear on the back of an expansion card. ***See also*** Part X.
- **Printer port:** Where the printer plugs in. This port is also called an LPT, or a Centronics, port. (That's for the old-timers.)
- **IEEE 1394 port:** A port that's similar to a USB port in that it accepts a variety of high-speed add-ons, such as an external disk drive, a scanner, or a videocamera. This port is also known as *FireWire.* The smaller of the IEEE 1394 ports, the 1394 *mini,* is used primarily to connect a digital video gizmo.
- **Joystick port:** A port that is found on some older PCs, used primarily to connect an old-style joystick or a MIDI musical device. Today, most of those gizmos are connected by using USB ports.

For more information on plugging stuff in, ***see also*** Part II.

I/O Symbol Table

Connectors, connectors everywhere! They can look similar, or they can be confusing as all get-out. Fortunately, the computer industry understands how confusing connectors can be. To make things easier, many connectors on a PC console not only have unique shapes, but are also color coded and often flagged with specific icons, as shown in the handy nearby table.

Note that the colors aren't an established standard, so some PCs may sport a different color scheme than what's indicated. Also, not every connector is color coded.

Also note that different icons or symbols may be used on different PCs.

Connector	*Symbol*	*Name*	*Color*
		COM or serial	Cyan
		Digital video	White
		Ethernet or RJ-45	None
		IEEE 1394	None
		IEEE 1394 mini	None
		Infrared	None
		Joystick	Mustard
		Keyboard	Purple
		Line In (audio)	Grey
		Microphone	Pink
		Modem	None
		Monitor	Blue
		Mouse	Green

Connector	Symbol	Name	Color
		Power	Yellow
		Printer	Violet
	IN	SPDIF In	Pink or white
	OUT	SPDIF Out	Black
		Speakers or headphones	Lime
		S-Video	Yellow
		USB	None

The Basics: What Is a PC?

PC is an acronym for *Personal Computer,* so any type of personal computer, from a handheld or palm computer to a laptop to a desktop and, yes, even the Apple Macintosh, is a personal computer. As long as one person is using the computer, it's a *personal* computer, or PC.

Specifically, the type of computer now labeled a PC is the direct ancestor of the original IBM PC, introduced back in the early 1980s. Although there were other personal computers at that time, they were referred to as *microcomputers* and were used mostly by computer enthusiasts and home hobbyists.

Microcomputer was a play on words for *mini-computer,* but also on the name of the main piece of hardware, the *microprocessor.* (More on that in the next section.) The largest, most powerful computers available were *mainframe* systems, used by the government and large corporations. Mini-computers were used by small businesses and universities. Both the mainframes and minis had one central computer with multiple people using the system at once. The microcomputer, on the other hand, lacked such power and therefore was a one-person system.

When IBM introduced its own version of the microcomputer, it legitimized the microcomputer, making it "safe" for use in a business environment. Because of the IBM PC's tremendous popularity, it became the standard for all microcomputers.

Knockoffs and imitations were referred to as PC *clones* or PC *compatibles.* Those systems could run the same programs as the original IBM PC, but because the hardware wasn't made by IBM, manufacturers dared not use the term PC by itself. Over time, however, the terms *clone* and *compatible* were dropped, and any microcomputer that could use the same hardware and run the same software as the IBM PC was dubbed a PC.

The PC is now the standard computer platform around the world, so much so that being PC- or IBM-compatible is no longer an issue. Unless the computer says Macintosh or Sun on its case, it's a PC.

All this fuss over the term PC is really a tempest in a teapot. A computer is nothing more than a very fast, expensive calculator with a larger display and far more buttons. To better understand the thing, you must think of a PC in terms of its two main parts: hardware and software.

Hardware

Hardware is the physical part of the computer. If you can touch it, it's hardware.

The main piece of hardware is the computer's microprocessor, also called the *c*entral *p*rocessing *u*nit, or CPU. All other hardware inside the computer (the *console*) is designed to support and serve the microprocessor.

Supporting the microprocessor is more hardware. For storage, there's computer memory, or RAM, as well as disk drives. There's also a chipset, which consists of various support hardware that helps control the computer's monitor, networking, power management, and other hardware. All this stuff exists inside the console and lives on a large sheet of green fiberglass called the *motherboard.*

Software

Hardware by itself is dumb. That's because computer hardware must be controlled by software. Contrary to popular myth, the computer's microprocessor (hardware) isn't the computer's "brain." The computer's brain (if any) is the software that controls and runs the hardware.

The main piece of software in a computer is its *operating system,* which is really the PC's brain. The operating system is the one program in charge, the head honcho, the big cheese. The most popular PC operating system is Windows, produced by Microsoft Corporation. Other operating systems, such as Linux, can also be used on PCs, but Windows is by far the most popular PC operating system.

Other software comes in the form of programs that carry out specific tasks. By using various programs, you can direct the computer to perform a variety of services. Indeed, it's this versatility that has kept the PC popular and useful over the past 25 years or so.

- Computer software is nothing more than instructions that tell the hardware what to do, how to act, or when to lose your data.

- Although computer software comes on CDs or DVDs, those discs aren't software. Software is stored on discs, just as music is stored on a CD or a video is stored on a DVD.
- You never have to learn about programming to use a computer. Someone else does the programming; then you buy the program (the software) to get your work done.

You

The last part of your computer system is you, the computer operator. Although software controls the hardware, it's you who controls the software, by telling it what you want done.

The computer does whatever you want it to do. Its flexibility and potential are really unlimited. If you want a system to help you compose music, you can assemble the proper hardware and software to make that happen. If you want to run a business, you can do that too. The flexibility and configuration possibilities of the PC are endless, which is why the PC has remained the best-selling, most useful computer platform in the universe.

The Basics: Types and Models of PCs

There's no such thing as the *typical* PC. Not only does each manufacturer add its own touches of design and style, but different and various configurations are also available. They're all PCs, but how they look and — most importantly — how they sit on your desk divides them into various subclasses. Here's the rundown:

- **Desktop:** The original IBM PC sat flat and square on top of a desk, which is why that model and similar ones are referred to as desktop computers. Typically, the monitor is set right on top of the slablike console.
- **Desktop (small footprint):** This arrangement is basically the same as the traditional desktop, although the console is considerably smaller — often, too small to set the monitor atop the console. The *footprint* refers to how much desk space the console occupies.
- **Minitower:** This PC configuration is the most popular. It's essentially a small-footprint desktop on its side, although the PC isn't really sideways. The console is small enough to sit on top of your desk, with the monitor sitting right next to it.
- **Notebook or laptop:** This portable version of the PC is usually the size of a typical three-ring binder or coffee-table book. Yes, they manage to squeeze everything in a desktop PC into a portable, battery-powered, convenient unit. Despite their heftier price tags, laptops are very popular and often outsell desktop PCs.

- **Tower:** This older style of PC is like the minitower, but considerably taller and with more room inside the console. This box is found mostly in the "back office" of a business, where it controls the network or is used to prop up one end of a wobbly table.

The Basics: Inside the Console

You find nestled inside the console the core elements of a computer, as shown in Figure 1-6. These are the basic elements of the computer system, the electronic orchestra through which the PC plays its tune.

Figure 1-6

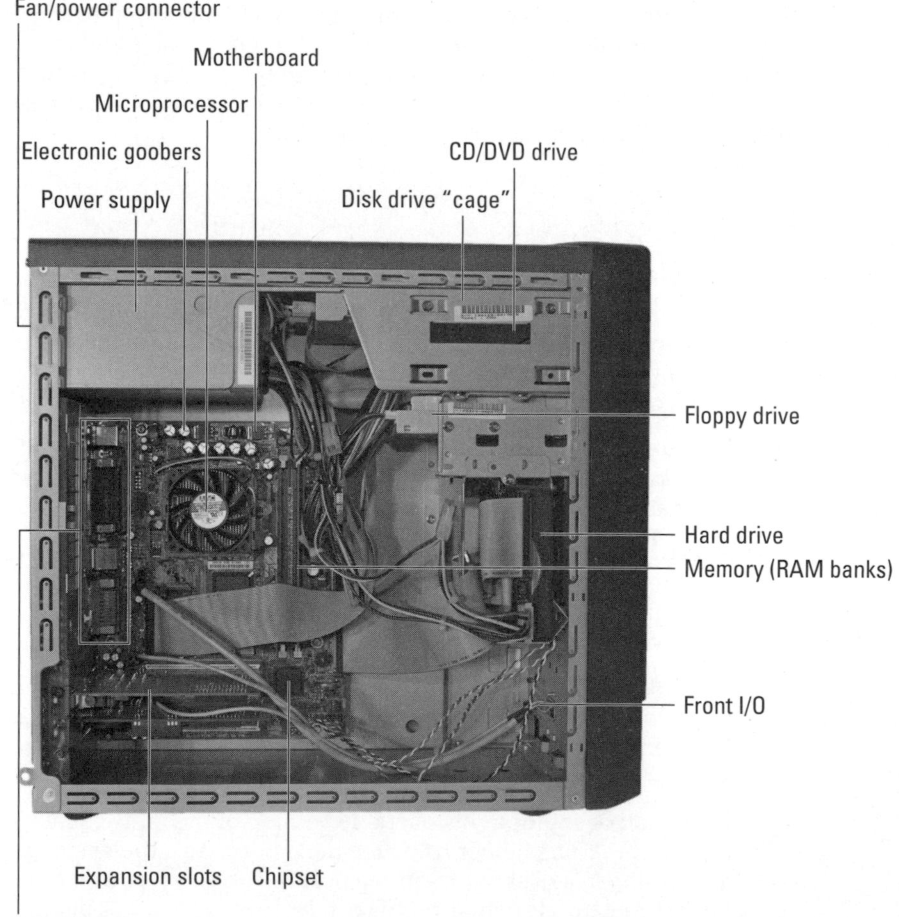

The location of these gizmos varies from computer to computer, but, if you're curious, the following list details some of the more important elements:

- **Power supply:** This doojobbie serves two purposes. First, it converts the AC current from the wall into DC current to drive the motherboard and devices inside the console. Second, the power supply houses the fan that keeps the console's insides cool. The power supply connects to each internal disk drive as well as to the motherboard and any expansion cards requiring extra juice. This item also connects to the power button.
- **Motherboard:** This main circuitry board inside the console is the home base for the PC's microprocessor, memory, chipset, and other vital components.
- **Disk drive cage:** This metal structure is used to hold the various disk drives installed in the console as well as provide space for more disk drives.
- **CD-ROM/DVD drive:** The drive is installed in the disk drive cage, in one of the places where the drive can be accessed from the front of the console (so that you can insert and remove CDs or DVDs). The drive also connects to the power supply and to a special connector on the motherboard.
- **Hard drive:** This drive lives inside the console's drive cage, but doesn't need to have access to outside the case. The hard drive is connected to the power supply and the motherboard.
- **Floppy drive:** Like the CD-ROM/DVD drive, this drive is installed in the console's drive cage with outside access. The floppy drive is connected to the power supply and the motherboard. Don't be surprised not to find one on your new PC; it's quickly becoming a relic.
- **Memory:** The computer's memory, or *RAM,* is installed into a series of banks on the motherboard. Memory comes in tiny expansion card modules called *DIMMs.* They plug into corresponding slots on the motherboard.
- **Microprocessor:** This is the main chip. The boss. The CPU. All the other electronics inside the console are designed to work well with, and serve, the microprocessor. Today's PCs come with high-speed, high-power microprocessors that require extra cooling; the microprocessor wears a special little fan like a hat, which helps keep it cool.
- **Chipset:** One or more computer chips on the motherboard supply the computer's basic personality (so to speak). These chips control input/output (I/O) as well as the basic configuration of the computer's monitor, keyboard, mouse, networking, and other main components.
- **Expansion slot:** Designed for internal expansion of the computer, this type of slot isn't as plentiful as in years past. This is because most of the features previously added by using an *expansion card* (video, networking, modem, more memory) are now part of the chipset on the motherboard.

Also, more and more devices that were once added internally (DVD drives, extra hard drives) can now be added externally, thanks to the USB port. Even so, expansion slots remain inside the console and allow you to further add to or configure your PC. Expansion cards plug into expansion slots, like adding new shelves inside a cupboard.

Depending on your PC's design, it can use any or all of the potential four types of expansion slots:

- **ISA:** The traditional type of expansion slot of ancient design (available on the first IBM PC, 25 years ago), and occasionally found in some PCs sold today. The main reason is for backward compatibility with older expansion cards. ISA stands for Industry Standard Architecture.
- **PCI:** A more advanced type of expansion slot than ISA. PCI stands for Peripheral Component Interconnect. Most PCs have at least one of these slots, if not more. (It depends on the size of the console.)
- **AGP:** An expansion slot designed specifically for advanced, high-end graphics cards. AGP stands for Accelerated Graphics Port. Not every motherboard has this slot. (Lesser graphics adapters plug into a PCI slot or are included in the chipset.)
- **PCI-Express** and **PCI-X:** Two new standards designed to replace the PCI expansion slot. Both are faster than PCI and, as you can guess, they're not compatible with each other. Still, they're presently the best solution for high-end graphic cards; both new PCI standards are much more efficient than AGP.

Your console's innards, and the motherboard specifically, have many more technical details, most of which aren't really necessary for the casual computer operator to know.

Be aware of your computer's microprocessor and its name and horsepower. Often, this information is displayed when the computer first starts — although you have to be quick to catch it.

You should also know the quantity of RAM installed in the console. Computers crave RAM, especially when they're running high-end graphics programs or complex computer games.

The expansion slots provide a way to add more internal components to your PC, although for starting out, the motherboard contains just about everything you need. Still, be aware that it's possible to add more features and abilities by simply purchasing and installing a new expansion card. ***See also*** "The Basics: Adding Hardware."

Please don't open your PC unless directed to by tech support or when you're installing or upgrading your computer. When you open your PC, be sure to turn off *and* unplug the console before opening it up and looking inside.

The Basics: Adding Hardware

The beauty of the computer is that it can be endlessly expanded or upgraded. The computer you own now probably won't look the same a month or a year down the road. It's the PC's ability to be expanded and improved on that has made it one of the most successful computer hardware designs ever.

You can add new hardware to your computer system in two ways: internally or externally.

Internal expansion

Internal hardware is added to the PC by plugging an expansion card into one of the expansion slots on the console's motherboard. At one time, this method was about the only way you could add more memory, better video, networking, or a special modem. Now, however, most of that stuff is included with the chipset on the motherboard. Even so, expansion slots remain for many purposes, which allows you to customize your PC any way you want.

Popular expansion cards let you add video support for a second monitor, a more advanced video adapter, a secondary network adapter, a custom sound card, a card to support extra internal disk drives, or a card to add another port (USB/IEEE) or accessory.

Beyond expansion cards, your console may have extra room for more memory or disk drives inside its drive cage. It may even be possible to replace the microprocessor with a better, faster version (although such an upgrade is often financially impractical).

Before going nuts, however, ensure that your PC has ample internal expansion options. The drive cage must have room for an extra hard drive, for example. And, you need to ensure that you have open expansion slots — and slots of the right type — for whatever expansion card options you crave.

If expansion is your goal, get a minitower or full-size tower PC. Those models often come with more expansion slots and drive cage "bays" than the smaller-format PCs.

External expansion

Everything that plugs into the console can be considered *external* expansion, although certain key parts of the PC aren't really expansion "options." The keyboard, mouse, and monitor are necessary to the PC's basic operations. Even the printer and modem can arguably be considered basic PC components and not expansion options.

Although the PC has specific places to plug in a mouse, a keyboard, a printer, a modem, a network, and audio devices, true expansion happens on the PC thanks to the USB ports. Although at one time the IEEE port was pretty fast, today's faster USB port standards make it the PC expansion option of choice. In fact, you can even find USB-compatible mouse, keyboard, printer, network, and audio devices. USB is consuming the world of external computer expansion!

The most popular external expansion options are described in this list:

- **Digital cameras:** You can connect a digital camera to your computer for copying, or *downloading,* images. After they're in the computer, you can photo-edit those images, e-mail them, create a slide show, print them, or do a number of miraculous things.
- **Digital media players:** These handy gizmos contain copies of music, pictures, and video already stored on your PC. You simply "beam" the media to the player, and you can take it with you.
- **Scanners:** The scanner lets you create a graphical image for the computer by using anything that's flat. You can scan old photographs or your kid's artwork or even use the scanner with special software to read text.
- **Videocameras:** You can connect a videocamera to your PC directly for use in online chats or for online meetings, by creating your own *webcam.* You can also connect a videocamera to transfer your home movies. Special software can be used to edit those movies and create your own DVDs.
- **External storage:** Possibly the handiest thing to add to your computer system is more storage. Unlike days of yore, when you needed to know which end of a screwdriver to use, now you can add extra storage to your computer system by plugging in an external USB hard drive, CD-ROM drive, or DVD drive.

Numerous other expansion options exist. In fact, the list is long enough that it would make quite a thick book by itself. For the variety, simply check a computer catalog, online store, or retail computer store near you. ***See also*** Part II for information on connecting things to the console.

The Basics: Windows

The computer's operating system, Windows, is in charge of the entire computer. It does things you would never imagine, menial tasks and duties that are obscure yet necessary. Fortunately, Windows has been honed over the years, and, despite the complexity of the PC, with Windows in charge, your duties as a computer operator aren't really that complex or involved.

Basically, Windows has four duties:

- **Present an interface for you, the human, to use the computer.** This interface is the *desktop,* used to display information and graphically represent things inside the computer.
- **Manage the computer's hardware.** This chore is pretty much automatic, although Windows lets you manipulate certain hardware settings, such as the monitor's resolution or whether your stuff is printed longways or tallways on the printer. But most of the mundane things — keeping the time, fetching information from disk, performing minor maintenance — are done in the background automatically.
- **Manage software.** The applications you install rely on Windows as a bridge between what they do and the hardware inside the PC that makes all that stuff possible. Windows also prevents programs from running amok and, when they do, keeps them contained as best it can so that the system doesn't come crashing down.
- **Manage the files and stuff you create.** Windows helps you store information on your computer so that you can find it again later when you need it. It helps you keep track of files and provides tools to help you organize and order all your stuff.

As the program in charge, Windows is merely the overseer. When you use your computer, you use application software ("programs") to get work done. For example, you use a program such as Microsoft Word to do your word processing, Internet Explorer to surf the Web, or Windows Mail to read your e-mail. You use Windows occasionally to set up or reconfigure your computer's hardware, add new software, or work with the files you create. Beyond that, Windows is simply the program in charge. ***See also*** Part V, which tells you where important things are located in Windows.

The Basics: The Internet

Once upon a time, the Internet was considered a minor part of the PC's existence. Today, PCs and the Internet walk hand in hand. Using the Internet, particularly e-mail, is the number-one reason that most people buy a new PC. Because of this, all new PCs come equipped with all the hardware you need in order to access the Internet. All the software (or most of the important programs) also comes with the operating system, Windows.

The Internet itself isn't a computer. The Internet is not a program or any software you can own. Instead, the Internet is hundreds of thousands of computers all over the world. They're connected together, and they share, store, and swap information.

You can use your PC to access the Internet, where your computer joins the thousands of others already on the Internet. After your PC is connected, you use various software programs to access information on the Internet. These items are the most common programs or things accessed on the Internet:

- **The World Wide Web:** The Web is a convenient way to view information stored on computers all over the world. It displays information the same as you would read text in a newspaper or magazine: very friendly with pictures. The various Web *pages* also contain links to other, related information or similar Web pages. Visiting those pages is as easy as clicking the links.
- **E-mail:** Everyone using the Internet can send or receive messages by using electronic mail, or *e-mail.* Accounts are available all over, and many at no charge. By using e-mail, you can send messages to other Internet users as well as send files, photos, music, videos, and just about any type of information imaginable.
- **File transfer:** The *Internet* is a vast library of stored files and information. You can access those files by transferring them from the Internet into your computer. Some files are free programs you can use to further expand the abilities of your PC.

You use a modem — either a dialup modem or a high-speed cable, DSL, or satellite modem — to gain access to the Internet. You can also get on the Internet through a local-area network, as long as the network is connected to the Internet. (This is how you get on the Internet at large companies or at school.)

Most individuals and home users need to sign up for Internet service with an *ISP,* or *Internet service provider.* These are local or national companies whose purpose is to connect folks to the Internet — like a cable company offers you cable TV. (In fact, most cable TV companies also offer Internet access.) ISPs are listed in the Yellow Pages.

The only other thing you need in order to access the Internet is money; ISPs, like cable companies, require monthly fees. (You can use the Internet for free at a public library, but that's not this book's subject.)

The Basics: Your Stuff

Having a PC is about Windows, the Internet, and software, but all that really boils down to you and the stuff you create or collect. That information is stored on the computer in the form of *files.* Understanding the concept of files is central to getting along well with your computer, *so pay attention!*

Knowing about files

A *file* is an information container. Think of it as an electronic jar, like a Mason jar your grandmother might have used to store jams and jellies, although not as tasty. The type of information the computer file contains is electronic — all those bits and bytes you read about in *Time* magazine or hear in those songs people sing in cybercafés.

Although the contents of a file are digital, the information the file holds can represent a variety of things: text, graphics, music, video, a computer program, a database, or just about any type of information can be stored in a computer file. Indeed, this part of the book is stored as a file on my own computer's hard drive.

All files are born in the computer's memory. That's where they're created. The computer's memory, or RAM, is only temporary storage. RAM is fast and flexible, which is needed to create stuff, but the contents of RAM disappear when the power is off. Therefore, the computer's permanent storage is used to keep files long-term: From memory, files are *saved* to permanent storage — primarily, the PC's hard drive. That's the best location for the safe, long-term storage of computer information.

From the hard drive's permanent storage, files can be *opened* and their contents viewed, modified, printed, or sent over the Internet to another computer for storage or editing. But, all told, it's the file that contains the information, not the computer and especially not the program that created the file.

Working with files in Windows

Obviously, these files are important; they represent the stuff you create or save on your computer. One of the operating system's primary duties is to assist you with maintaining and organizing all the files you collect and create.

Windows Vista helps you keep track of your files in several ways:

Filename: You give a file a name when the file is saved to disk. The name helps you to remember the file's contents as well as to tell the difference between one file and the next.

Icon: Windows gives the file an *icon,* or tiny picture, that helps you remember which type of file you created. Special icons exist for documents, music files, videos, and other types. Each application also uses its own icons so that you can tell the difference between a document created in Microsoft Word and a spreadsheet you made using Microsoft Excel.

Date and time: The date and time the file was saved to disk are also included with the file information.

Size: The amount of disk space the file occupies is tracked.

Windows keeps all this information associated with each file. You can use the information as necessary, but most important is the file's name and its icon, which is your primary clue to the file's contents and purpose (see Figure 1-7).

Figure 1-7

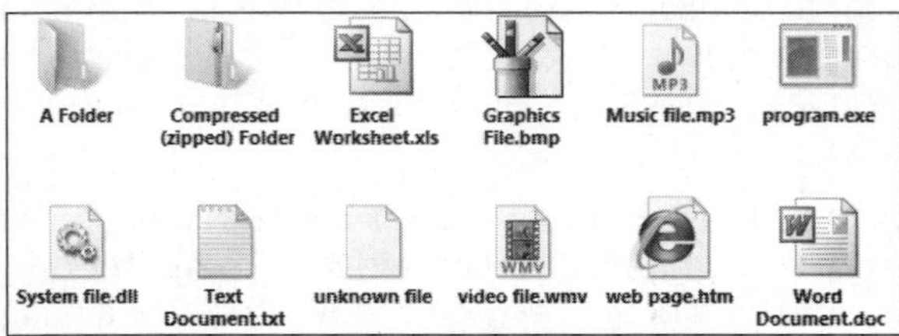

Windows also comes with tools you can use to rename, delete, and duplicate files. You can also send files over the Internet, attach them to e-mail messages, copy them to CD-Rs or DVD-Rs, or share them with other users on a network.

Organizing files in Windows

Files, files everywhere, but who knows which is which?

To help keep files organized, Windows uses special file containers called *folders*. Folders contain files, so files relating to the same project or files of a similar type can be kept together. That way, you can keep all your video files in one place, music in another, and graphics in another folder. Or, you can organize your documents by project. Because folders can be named just like files, you can easily find things by looking in the proper folder. And folder organization helps avoid the ten-thousand-files-all-over-the-place mess that most computer users suffer from. ***See also*** Part VIII.

Part II

Connecting Stuff

Plugging a computer cable into a connector is rather easy — much more so than in days gone by. Unlike connecting a TV or stereo, where the cables are all the same and holes are labeled in Taiwanese, computer cables come in different shapes and colors. If you were good in preschool at putting the red cylinder into the red hole, you'll be an instant expert at connecting things to your PC. This part of the book shows you the ropes, er, cables.

The easiest and most profitable computer consulting job I ever had involved plugging a modem into a phone jack. The customer was watching as I snapped the phone cord into the wall. As a result, he was rather upset to pay my fee. "Any idiot can plug in a cable, so why am I paying you $60?" he asked. I replied, "Because I know which cable is which."

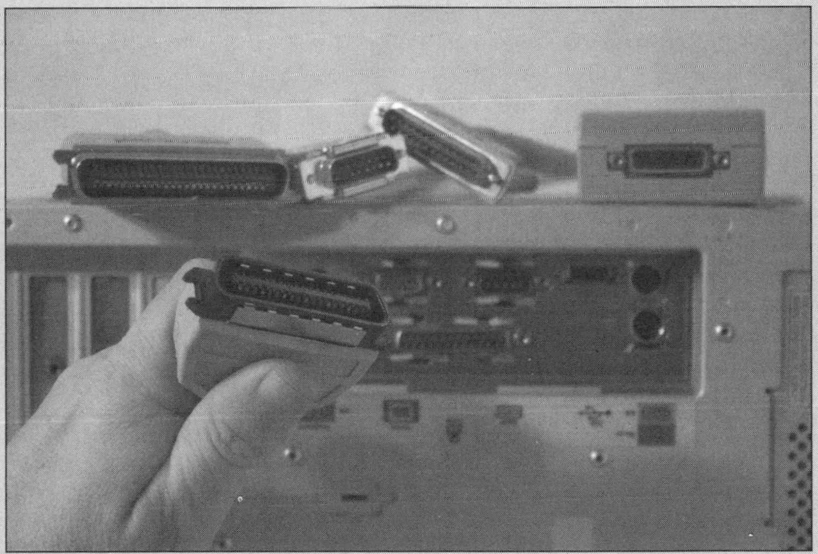

In this part . . .

- Computer cables
- Connecting things
- The USB port
- Wireless gizmos

About Computer Cables

A computer cable is described by which *port* it plugs into and its length.

For example, to connect a printer to the console, you use a printer cable. A USB device connects by using a USB cable. A monitor uses a monitor cable. In each example, (printer, USB, and monitor), the name describes both the type of cable and the port (or hole) it plugs into.

One exception is networking, which uses Cat-5 cable. Even so, you can say "networking cable," and the guy in the computer store won't mock you. The connector on the console is an RJ-45 port, but networking cable isn't "RJ-45 cable." It's Cat-5.

Some cables are permanently attached to their devices: The mouse and keyboard have such cables, for example. Other cables are separate. That just means that you must remember to plug in both ends.

Cable length is measured in feet or meters. USB, IEEE, networking, printer, and serial cables all come in varying lengths.

Good news: Nearly all computer cables are what they call *idiotproof.* That means you can plug them in only one way. You cannot plug in a computer cable backward or incorrectly or in any manner that may damage your computer, the device being plugged in, or the cable itself.

Unless the hardware documentation says otherwise, it's okay to plug in most computer gizmos while the computer is on. There are some exceptions to this rule, so carefully read through the other sections in this part of the book!

Some computer devices plug into the wall *and* into the computer. Some gadgets don't plug into the wall at all. And some devices use a *power brick,* or *transformer,* which is either part of the plug itself or living on the cable between the device and the wall socket.

Audio

PCs have built-in sound, and the console has a teensy, crappy speaker. What you really need are external speakers. Plus, you can use a microphone or headphones or attach an audio cable to any sound-producing device and record that sound on your PC. This is all done thanks to the PC's audio connectors.

All PC audio connectors are of the *mini-DIN* design. That's a common connector-hole combination used on many audio devices. If your audio device doesn't use mini-DIN (for example, standard headphones, which use a much larger connector), you can buy an adapter at any electronics or music store.

- PC speakers connect to the Line Out, speaker, or headphone jack on the console.
- Microphones connect to the microphone connector.
- The Line In connector is used to connect any nonamplified sound source, such as your stereo, VCR, phonograph, mother-in-law, or other device that makes noise.

Yes, the difference between the Line In and microphone jacks is that Line In devices aren't amplified.

Your console may have multiple sets of audio connectors: three on the front, three on the back, or maybe even three on a video expansion card. If so, use the sound connectors on the expansion card first because they're the best. Otherwise, when audio connectors are on the front and back of the PC, the front set is simply a copy or a spare (designed for easy hookup of the mic or headphones).

To record sound, you need software that lets you convert audio input into digital storage inside the computer.

Digital Camera

Your digital camera can connect to the console in one of three ways:

- The USB port
- The mini-IEEE port
- Its own, special cable

The connection used by your camera depends on the camera's manufacturer, not on the PC. Furthermore, to get the pictures from the camera to the computer, you need to run special transfer software, which most likely came with the camera.

Note that you can also use a media card reader on your PC to directly read the camera's digital "film." For example, you can get a CompactFlash memory reader, which you connect to your PC by using the USB port (***see also*** "USB Port"). When you connect the camera's memory card directly to the computer, you can then use Windows itself to copy the picture files from the media card to the PC's hard drive.

See also "Optical Audio" for information on using that specialized connector.

Digital Media Player

Digital media players include gizmos that let you listen to music, such as the popular MP3 players (including the famous iPod), as well as handheld devices that let you view digital photographs or videos — or sometimes all types of media. These popular portable gadgets can connect to your PC in a variety of ways, although the most popular is the USB port.

The digital media player comes with software on a CD or DVD. After installing that software, you connect your media player to the PC by using the provided cable: Plug one end into the media player and the other into the PC's USB port. (Or, when another, specific port is used, plug the cable into that port instead, per the directions.) At that point, the media player's software takes over and synchronizes information between the computer and the media player gizmo.

Some digital media players, such as the iPod, have a special dock or stand in which they snugly sit while the information is transferred. In the case of the iPod, simply plugging the thing into its dock activates software on the PC, and the synchronization program starts by magic!

When the digital media player comes with a media card, you can also use that card to get information between the player and the PC. Use a media card reader attached to the PC to help make that action happen.

IEEE

The IEEE port allows you to use high-speed external devices with your PC. This port isn't as common as the USB port, although the IEEE port behaves in much the same way and connects to a similar variety of devices. The IEEE port is now used primarily for high-speed video transfers.

IEEE devices require an IEEE cable, which may or may not come with the device.

The cable's ends are identical. It matters not which end of the cable goes into the device or which end plugs into the console.

As with USB, it's possible to *daisy-chain* IEEE devices: Plug one IEEE device into the console, plug another IEEE device into the first IEEE device, and then keep on pluggin'. Note that certain IEEE gadgets prefer to be connected to the console directly.

Also similar to USB is the IEEE hub, which allows you to expand the number of IEEE ports beyond what the console offers.

Some devices, particularly digital videocameras, use the mini-IEEE connector. This connector requires a unique cable. (It uses only four wires, whereas the standard IEEE cable has six.)

IEEE is also known as 1394. The two names are often used together, as in IEEE 1394. On Apple computers, the IEEE interface is referred to as *FireWire.* No matter what the name, the standard symbol is shown in the margin.

Most PCs don't come with IEEE ports, although they can be added easily by installing inexpensive expansion cards.

Joystick

An older PC may sport a unique joystick port. It's a 25-pin, D-shell connector (the connector's outline is shaped like the letter *D*), found on the rumps of older-model computers. The joystick port can also be used to connect the MIDI adapter for playing musical instruments with your PC.

Today's joysticks plug into the USB port (***see also*** "USB Port").

The joystick port may also be referred to as the A/D port, where A/D stands for *a*nalog-to-*d*igital.

Keyboard

The PC keyboard plugs into the keyboard port on the back of the console.

Note that the keyboard port looks amazingly similar to the mouse port. Despite their visual similarity, they're two different ports. Your keyboard (or mouse) doesn't work when it's plugged into the wrong port.

A USB keyboard can plug into any USB port. When using a USB keyboard, you don't need to plug anything into the PC's keyboard port.

Some USB keyboards come with lime green adapters, designed to convert the USB ports into keyboard port connectors. Using this type of adapter is optional.

Don't plug the keyboard into the keyboard port while the computer is on. You can plug in a USB keyboard, but don't plug anything into the keyboard port when the computer is on. It can damage the keyboard, the computer, or both.

Microphone

To use a microphone with your PC, plug it into the microphone port. ***See also*** "Audio."

Modem

Thanks to the popularity of broadband Internet, few PCs are now sold with internal modems. When a PC does have a modem, you see a standard phone jack somewhere on the computer's rump. Take a phone cord, plug it into the PC's modem phone jack, and then plug the other end of the phone cord into the telephone company's jack on the wall. The modem is connected.

If the modem has a second phone jack, one designed for a telephone, you can plug a telephone's cord into that jack as well. You can use the phone anytime the computer isn't using the modem to make a call.

External modems also have phone jacks and need to be plugged in the same way as internal modems. Additionally, the external modem needs to plug into the console. This is done by using either a serial cable and plugging the modem into the console's COM port or using a USB cable. External modems must also be plugged into the wall for power.

Don't plug the modem into the network's RJ-45 jack. Although that hole looks the same, it's slightly larger and the phone jack doesn't stay put.

Monitor

The monitor plugs into the VGA, or graphics adapter, jack on the back of the console. It goes in only one way.

If the console has two VGA connectors, you probably want to use the one on an expansion card rather than the one on the console's I/O panel. (***See also*** Part I.)

Mouse

Your computer's mouse plugs into the mouse port on the back of the console. This port looks exactly like the keyboard port, but be sure that you plug the mouse into the right port. The mouse doesn't work otherwise.

USB mice need to connect to the USB port, although many mouse manufacturers also include an adapter that lets you convert the USB connector to a PC mouse port connector. Either way works.

Turn off your computer before you connect or disconnect the mouse to the mouse port.

Network

To connect your PC to a network, or to a network-like device, such as a cable or DSL modem, plug the cable's plastic connector into the console's RJ-45 jack.

The RJ-45 jack looks exactly like a telephone connector, although it's more squat (wider and shorter).

When the network cable is fully inserted, you feel or hear it snap into place.

To remove the network cable, press the tab on the narrow end, and then slide the cable out of the hole — just like you disconnect a phone cord.

Optical Audio

If you're a high-end audio snob, you can use optical audio cables to connect the PC to your high-end optical audio sound equipment. Both devices, input and output, must have optical audio. And, you must obtain special (and not cheap) fiber optic cable to connect the toys.

Optical audio isn't a must.

Be careful not to bang, touch, or taunt the clear glass ends of the optical cable. Better cables come with little protective caps that you can keep on the ends when the cable isn't connected.

Optical Audio Out ports connect to optical Audio In, and vice versa.

Power

Cinchy: The plug goes into the wall socket.

Some power cables are affixed to the devices they power. Others must be plugged in at both ends. Oftentimes, it's that second end disconnecting that's the source of endless computer angst and woe.

You may want to use a power strip or UPS. ***See also*** Part IV for information on turning on your PC.

Printer

The printer plugs into the console's printer port. Nothing could be more "duh."

The standard PC printer cable has two different ends. One is designed to plug into the printer; the other, into the console. It's impossible to confuse the two.

USB printers plug in by using a USB cable. For printers with both printer and USB options, use the USB option.

Printers don't come with cables! You must buy the cable — USB or standard printer cable — separately.

Another name for the printer port is LPT1. Another name for the printer cable is Centronics. Another name for the port is parallel port, with its corresponding parallel cable.

Avoid inexpensive printer cables because they aren't bidirectional. You should ensure that you get a printer cable that talks both ways. That way, you can use all your printer's features.

It's trivial, but printer cables should be no more than about 10 feet long. The signal may degrade over longer distances. Well, and you get tired of walking over to a printer set far away.

Printers can also be connected to computers over the network, in which case you don't need a printer cable but instead must connect the printer to the network directly by using a networking cable.

S-Video

S-Video connectors allow you to send your computer's video output to a standard television set, or to any video gizmo that has S-Video input.

You see higher-quality images with S-Video output than with other types of video output. This type of connector is found only on the rumps of PCs with high-end video adapters.

S-Video is output only. To read video input on your PC, you need a special video adapter that accepts input.

The final thing to remember about S-Video is that it's video only: It doesn't transmit any audio. To get the sound over to your television, you have to string some wires from the Line Out, speaker, or headphone jacks or use the optical audio connections (if your television supports them).

Scanner

Most scanners connect to the console by using the USB port. In fact, they don't even require a power cable; the scanner draws its power from the USB port itself. Amazing.

High-end scanners (used by professionals) connect by using the IEEE port rather than, or in addition to, USB.

Serial

The most common device to plug into the console's serial, or COM, port is now an external dialup modem. You can also plug in serial mice as well as a few serial printers.

At one time, a serial port was the most versatile type of connector on your PC. Now, however, it's kept around mostly for compatibility with older devices.

On consoles with more than one serial port, the ports are named COM1, COM2, and so on.

COM is short for *communications.*

Another term for the serial port is RS-232.

Speakers

Speakers plug into the speaker jack or headphone jack. (***See also*** "Audio.")

Note that speakers can also be a part of the monitor. Even so, a separate cable is required in order to plug the speakers into the speaker jack or headphone jack on the console.

USB Port

USB devices plug into the USB port — any USB port, although some devices specifically want to be connected to the console or to a powered USB port.

Newer USB devices are generally faster and better than the original USB standard. These newer devices are referred to as high-speed or USB 2.0 devices, and they require a USB 2.0 port. Most PCs sold in the past few years come with this port, although older PCs can add the port by adding an internal expansion card.

USB cables have two different ends, dubbed A and B. The A end is flat and exists on the console or the back of any USB hub. The B end is trapezoidal in shape and plugs into the USB device.

USB extension cables are available, but be sure that the extension cable's ends match what you're plugging into: A to A or B to B.

USB hubs allow you to further expand the number of USB devices your computer can use. The hub connects to the console (or to another hub) by using a standard A-B USB cable. The hub itself contains more USB ports, from two to four, up to a dozen or more.

Some hubs must be plugged in to help supply external USB devices with power. These are *powered hubs.*

Many USB devices act as hubs and provide even more USB connectors for even more gizmos.

USB cables come in a variety of lengths, but the cables are never longer than 3 or 4 feet. Any longer and the signal may be compromised.

USB devices can be connected or disconnected whether the power is on or off. If the power is on, the computer instantly recognizes the device and makes it available. But note that some USB devices, particularly external disk drives and other storage devices, cannot be removed unless you first use the PC's operating system to disconnect, or *unmount,* them.

Wireless Gizmos

Yes, even wireless devices require some type of wired connection.

For example, a wireless keyboard and mouse require you to connect the transmitter to the keyboard port and mouse port, respectively, or to a USB connector on the console. Beyond that point, however, the keyboard and mouse aren't tethered to the console by wires.

Wireless networking is generally wire-free. The network card's antenna sticks out of the console's rump. (On a laptop, the antenna may be internal.) Despite the term *wireless,* at some point the system uses wires. For example, a wireless hub needs to connect to the Internet, and you need a wire to do that.

Part III

Installing Hardware and Software

Too many people believe that the computer is in charge. It's not. You control the software, which controls the hardware. And when you feel the need for more power or expanded abilities from your computer, you are the one who adds such things to your PC, by installing new hardware or software.

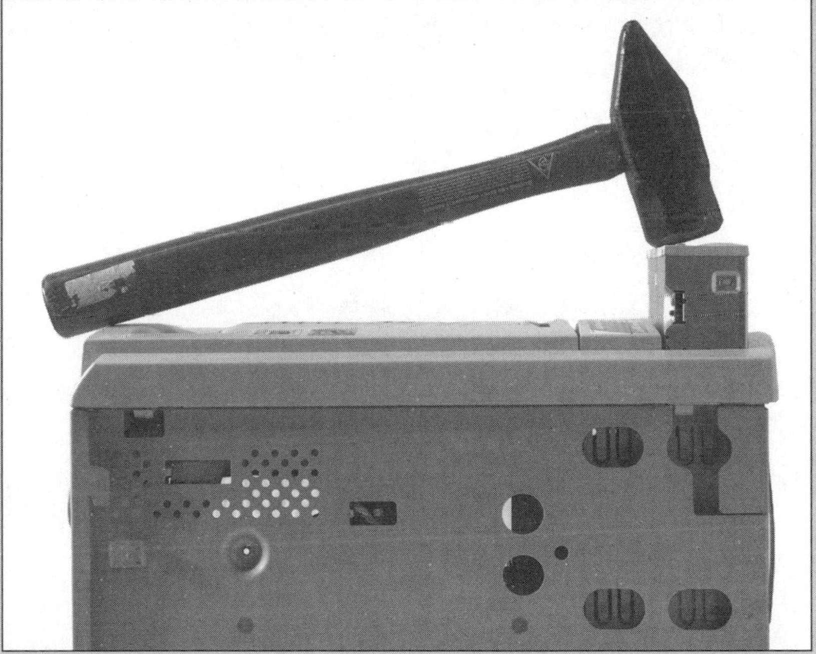

In this part . . .

- Adding new hardware
- Inserting an expansion card
- Installing memory
- Removing USB storage devices
- Installing software

The Add Hardware Icon

During those times that Windows stubbornly refuses to instantly recognize your new hardware, you should visit the Control Panel's Add Hardware icon. To do so, heed these steps:

1. Click the Start button to display its menu.
2. Choose Control Panel from the menu.
3. If Category view is being used, click the text labeled Classic View.

   Classic view displays all the Control Panel icons, which may be confusing, but this view is more useful than Category view. Figure 3-1 shows an example of Classic view.

Figure 3-1

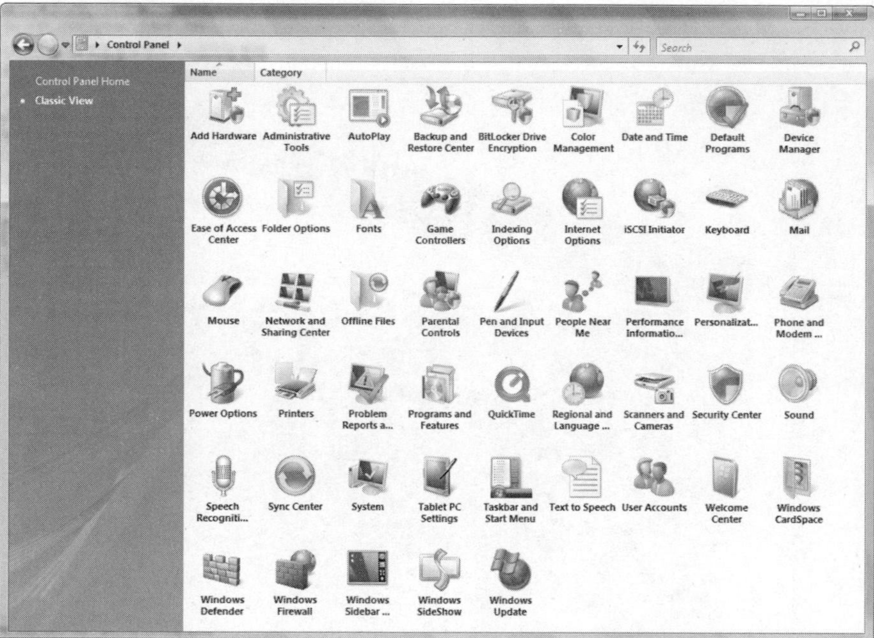

4. Double-click the Add Hardware icon.

   Opening the Add Hardware icon runs the Add Hardware Wizard.

   If you're prompted with a User Account Control dialog box, click the Continue button.

5. Read the wizard's instructions.

   Soak in the tender words of warning. Honestly, here in the 21st century, manually adding hardware is unusual and rare.

6. Click the Next button to continue working through the wizard.

   Heed the instructions that are offered, and make selections and click the Next button as required.

7. Click the Finish button when you're done.

See also "Adding New Hardware."

Adding New Hardware

The best way to add new hardware is to follow the instructions offered with the hardware. The instructions tell you what to do, and in which order, and perhaps offer helpful suggestions, sometimes in English.

Read through the instructions once before installing or adding the new hardware. Then, read through them a second time as you go through the steps.

Windows instantly recognizes most new PC hardware you shove into or attach behind the console. Read the instructions anyway.

When you plug in new USB or IEEE devices, you may hear the computer beep and see a pop-up message where the PC tells you how excited it is about the new device.

Hardware requires software in order to run. In some cases, the software can just be Windows itself, but, many times, additional software is required in order to power the new hardware, and it must be installed. You must follow the software installation instructions properly; sometimes, the new hardware must be installed before the software, and sometimes it works the other way.

Before adding internal components, such as an expansion card or more memory, be sure to turn off *and* unplug the computer's console. Never open the PC's case with the power on!

After adding some new hardware devices, you often must restart Windows. How can you tell? The computer says so.

If Windows fails to recognize the new hardware, use the Add Hardware icon in the Control Panel. (***See also*** "The Add Hardware Icon.")

Adding new hardware may force Windows to require reactivation. Microsoft does this to ensure that all the new hardware is compatible with Windows, and to thwart sneaky software pirates. You must contact Microsoft, either by phone or by using the Internet, to reactivate your copy of Windows. Obey the instructions on the screen, if any.

Adding an external dialup modem

One item that your PC may not instantly recognize, and which the Add Hardware icon in the Control Panel is too dumb to find, is an external dialup modem. To add one to your computer, obey this enumerated procedure:

1. Connect the dialup modem to the PC by connecting a serial cable to the console's serial port as well as to the modem's serial port. (This step may require a special cable or adapter.)
2. Plug the modem into the phone line.
3. Plug the modem into the wall.

4. Open the Control Panel's Phone and Modem Options icon.
5. If this is the first time you've opened the Phone and Modem Options icon, you need to configure your PC's location information before moving on.
6. Click the Modems tab in the Phone and Modem Options dialog box.
7. Use the Add button to help Windows locate your external modem; follow the steps on the screen.

   Ensure that the external modem is on. (External modems have on–off switches.)

Adding a non-USB joystick

Open the Game Controllers icon in the Control Panel to help add a non-USB joystick to your PC. First, connect the joystick. Then open the icon and click the Advanced button. The joystick should be listed in the dialog box. If not, refer to any software that came with the joystick for assistance in setting the thing up.

Inserting an Expansion Card

Anyone who is good with Legos or Tinker Toys can add an expansion card to a PC. Then again, you don't have the threat of electrocution or damaging a $2,000 piece of equipment when you're toying with Legos. But I digress.

You can follow a general way to add an expansion card to a computer. It's rather simple. Specific steps may vary from card to card; therefore, I highly recommend that you follow the directions included with the card. Beyond that, here are the general steps:

1. Turn off and unplug the PC's console.
2. Open the PC's console.

   Use a screwdriver to remove the screws on the back of the console. Note that some consoles don't have screws, and the screws aren't always on the back. Good luck getting that console open!
3. Locate the proper expansion slot (see Figure 3-2).

   The expansion card is an ISA, PCI, or AGP card. You must find the corresponding slot on the motherboard for that card (see Figure 3-3).

Figure 3-2

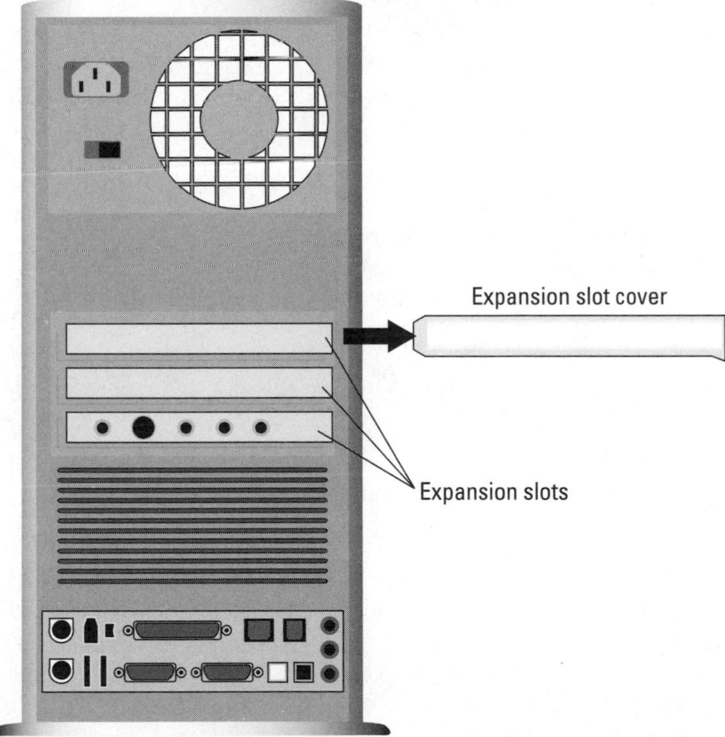

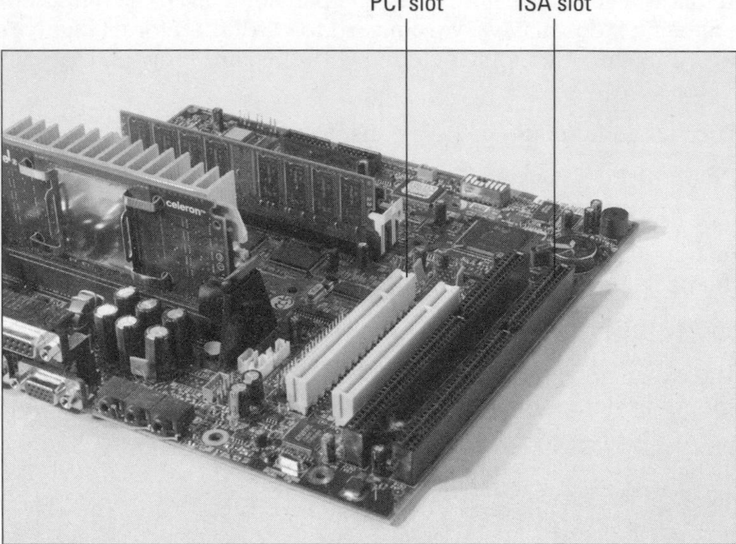

Figure 3-3

Yes, you may have to move some cables out of the way. This is okay, as long as you don't disconnect any of the cables — or as long as you remember to reconnect any that you disconnect.

Some PCI or ISA slots may not be available because other items inside the console are blocking them. Make sure that you choose a slot that has enough room around it to accommodate your expansion card.

4. Remove the ISA/PCI slot's back cover.

   This small, metal cover is just behind the slot. It's where an expansion card's rump is accessible to the world. Remove the slot cover and toss it out — but keep the tiny screw (if a screw is used).

5. Remove the expansion card from its sealed bag.

   Carefully handle the card! Try to touch it only by its edges. Don't touch the components or any metal part of the card.

   It helps if you can keep one hand on the console's metal case while you're handling the expansion card. This precaution zeroes the electrical potential between you, the case, and the card and reduces the chance of that evil static electricity damaging something.

6. Set any options on the card.

   Some cards have tiny switches that must be set in order to preconfigure the card — although this isn't as common as it once was.

7. Insert the card into the slot, as shown in Figure 3-4.

   Be firm but gentle. The card can go in only one way. It also has to seat itself on the back of the computer, where you removed the slot's back cover in Step 4.

Figure 3-4

8. Optionally, connect any cables or wires that the expansion card needs.
9. Screw down the expansion card's back cover.

   Use the screw you took from Step 4. Or, if a clamping or nonscrew system is used, do whatever it takes to firmly secure the card.
10. Double-check everything.

    Are all the cables connected? Everything in snug? No loose items rattling about? No screwdriver left on the motherboard? No flashlight lurking inside the case?
11. Close up the console.
12. Reconnect the power cord.
13. Turn on the console and the computer.

Adding an expansion card can trigger the reactivation of Windows. If so, obey the instructions on the screen to reactivate.

Installing Memory

Adding more memory to your PC is a useful — and inexpensive — way to boost your system's performance. It's simple. Follow these general steps, although if any specific steps come with the memory you purchased, be sure to follow them instead:

1. Turn off and unplug the PC's console.
2. Open the PC's console.

   Remove the screws from the back of the console, or use whatever clever method is required in order to open that sucker.
3. Locate the memory banks.

   You should find a collection of them, usually two or four grouped side by side, as shown in Figure 3-5.

Figure 3-5

4. Remove any old memory, if necessary.

   Hopefully, you just have to add your new memory cards, or DIMMs, into empty slots. But you may have to remove older memory to make room for the new DIMMs. If so, see the following section. Then, come back here to finish installation.

5. Move aside the connectors on the side of the memory slot.

   Figure 3-6 shows the two plastic arms that help hold down the DIMM. Swing them out of the way now.

Figure 3-6

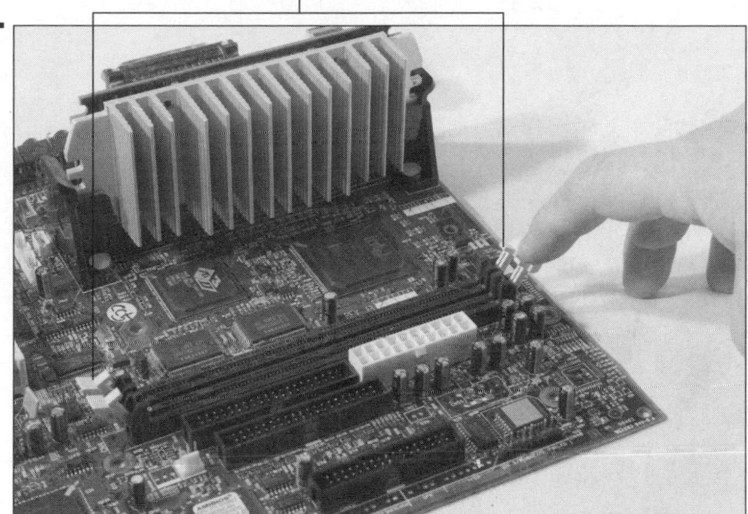

6. Remove the new memory from its sealed bag or tube.

   Be careful with those DIMMs! Touch them only by their edges.

   It helps if you use one hand to hold the DIMM and keep the other hand touching the console's metal case. This precaution zeroes the electrical potential between the memory, the case, and yourself. By doing so, you reduce the chance of generating static electricity and damaging the delicate memory chips.

7. Line up the DIMM with the slot.

   The DIMM and the slot are keyed, as shown in Figure 3-7, so that you can insert the memory only one way. Try to line up the DIMM so that it's properly positioned over the slot.

8. Plug the DIMM into the slot.

   Do it firmly but gently. Do not force! If the thing doesn't "seat" properly, it's most likely oriented improperly. Turn it around and try again.

Figure 3-7

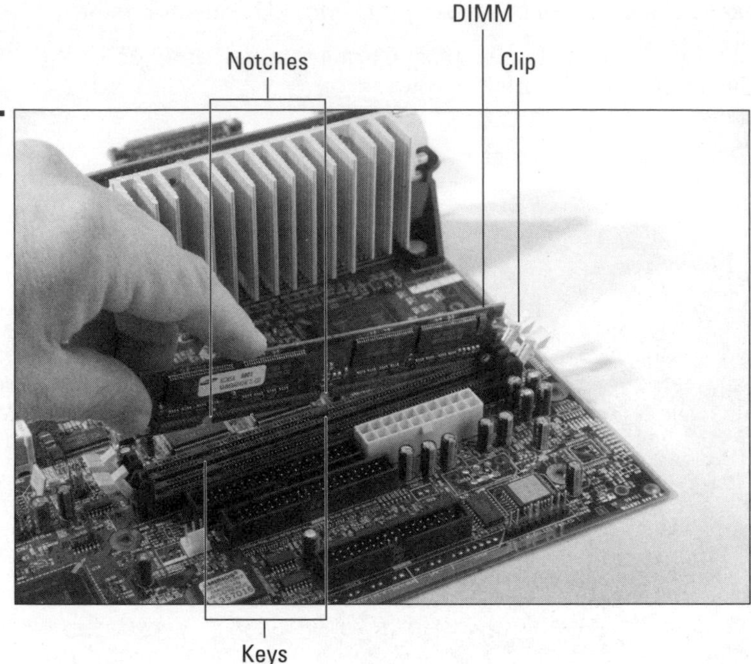

9. Double-check everything.

   Are all the cables connected? Everything in snug? No loose items rattling about? No screwdriver left on the motherboard? No flashlight lurking inside the case? Your fly zipped up?

10. Close up the console.

11. Reconnect the power cord.

12. Turn on the console and the computer.

The computer instantly recognizes new memory when the PC next starts up.

You may see an error message. Relax! This is normal. Follow the on-screen instructions to adjust the PC's BIOS to update the new total amount of memory. Save the changes. Then, restart the computer. (Directions appear on the screen.)

I recommend using the online Web site `www.crucial.com` for buying new memory for your computer. When you know the computer's make and model, you can work the memory-advisor tool on that Web site to figure out exactly how much of what kind of memory your computer needs. It may not be the least expensive memory on the Internet, but the service and support make the price worth it.

Adding more memory may trigger Windows to yearn for reactivation. (***See also*** “Adding New Hardware.”)

Removing Memory

Computer memory should be installed in open or available memory slots. Then again, you probably weren’t thinking about upgrading when you first bought your PC, so all the memory banks are full. To add new memory, you need to remove all or some of the old memory. Here’s how to yank out those memory DIMMs:

1. Turn off and unplug the PC’s console.

   Keep the plug well away from the console, in case it suddenly becomes animated and desires to plug itself in again under its own power.

2. Open the PC’s console.

   Lay aside that can opener: Use a screwdriver to remove screws from the rear of the case. Note that some newer PC cases don’t have screws, and it’s quite easy to open the console.

3. Locate the memory banks.

   They’re on the motherboard in groups of two or four.

4. Push aside the clips on the short ends of the memory card or DIMM.

   The clips keep the DIMM snug in its socket. By pushing them aside, you free up the DIMM. Notice that the DIMM is pushed up a tad out of its socket. Handy.

5. Set the DIMM aside.

6. Proceed with installing any new memory, as covered in the preceding section.

There’s little value in old computer memory. You can try to sell it on eBay, if you like. I don’t recommend throwing it out; instead, keep it in a safe, dry place where it won’t get stepped on or come into contact with any metal or anything that can cause sparks or static electricity.

If you plan on selling the old memory on eBay, repackage it in the container that your new memory came in. That keeps it safe for shipping.

Removing USB Storage Devices

Although you can easily attach and remove USB devices, those USB storage devices must be properly removed, or *ejected,* by Windows. Failure to do so properly may result in missing or damaged files, or it just might make Windows so angry and cross that otherwise happy adults will flee from the computer in terror. Pay attention!

To properly remove the device, locate the Safely Remove Hardware icon in the notification area, as shown in Figure 3-8. Click that icon.

Figure 3-8

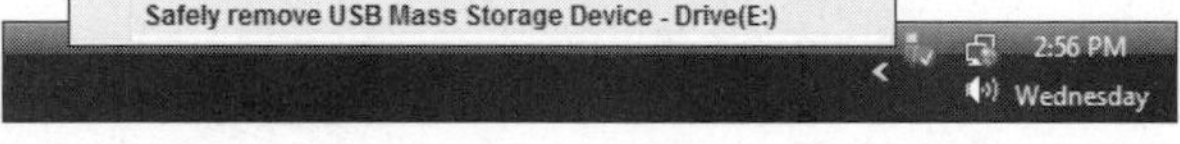

Choose the removable USB device from the pop-up list; click the device name with the mouse.

When the computer tells you that it's okay to remove the disk or device, you can do so; click OK.

If the disk is in use, meaning that open files are on the disk or programs are using the disk, you see a warning dialog box. Click the Cancel button in that case.

Removable USB devices include flash memory drives; media cards; external hard drives and CD-ROM or DVD drives; and any other USB device that is used to store information. You can see the lot listed in the Computer window. (***See also*** Part V.)

Software Installation

Software allows you to get things done on your computer. Windows is just the operating system. Although Windows comes with some small programs, you eventually need to add or install other programs — software — to control your PC and get work done.

You have two ways to install software on a PC. The most common is to install a new program from a CD or DVD. Gaining quickly in popularity is the second method, downloading a program from the Internet. The following sections describe the details.

Installing software from a CD or DVD

Software installation from a disc is cinchy: Simply insert the new software's CD or DVD into the CD drive or DVD drive. Installation should proceed automatically after that; follow the instructions or directions on the computer screen.

When inserting the disk does nothing, try these steps:

1. Click the Start button to display its menu.
2. Choose Computer from the Start menu to display the Computer window.
3. Right-click the CD or DVD's icon in the Computer window.

   A pop-up menu appears.
4. Choose AutoPlay from the menu to start the installation process.

   When this step doesn't work, or you see no AutoPlay option, continue with the next step.
5. Choose Open from the CD or DVD menu.
6. Locate an icon for an INSTALL or SETUP program, and then double-click that icon to run the program and install your software.

   When you don't have an INSTALL or SETUP program, refer to the software's manufacturer for additional help.

Obey the directions on the screen to proceed through the software setup. Generally speaking, the preset options are best unless you know exactly what you're doing.

Installing software you downloaded from the Internet

Programs downloaded from the Internet come in one of two flavors: EXE, or program files that install automatically, or Zip files, which you must decompress and then install.

When you click a link to download a file from the Internet, you see a dialog box prompting you to either save or run (or open) the file. Always choose the Save option. Save the file to the Downloads folder. That way, you always have a copy on your PC's hard drive in case you want to install the program again.

After the file is downloaded, the steps you take are different depending on whether the file is of the EXE or Zip type.

For an EXE file, locate the downloaded file in Windows Explorer. If you heeded my directions, the file is in the Downloads folder. Double-click to open and run the program file. Obey the instructions on the screen.

To install software from a Zip file, you must first remove, or extract, the files from the Zip archive and then run any special Install or Setup program. These steps overview the operation:

1. Locate the downloaded Zip file.

   Zip files appear as compressed folders. The icon is shown in the margin. If you've installed special Zip file-management software, such as WinZip, that Zip file icon is used instead.

2. Open the downloaded Zip file folder.

3. Choose the toolbar button labeled Extract All Files.

   The Extraction Wizard starts. The files are extracted into the folder that's listed, which has the same name as the compressed folder. That's okay.

4. Ensure that a check mark appears by the option Show Extracted Files When Complete.

5. Click the Extract button.

   The files held in the Zip archive are decompressed and saved into a folder that shows up on the screen.

6. Open the installation program, named either Setup or Install.

   At this point, installation should proceed as it would for any program you install in Windows.

When there's no Setup or Install program, you have to see the downloaded program's instructions for further information. Try to find a file named Readme or Readme.doc. Open that file for more instructions.

I recommend keeping the original Zip or EXE file so that you can reinstall the program later, if you desire. You can delete the extra folder that's created by extracting files from the Zip (compressed folder) archive (refer to Step 5).

Uninstalling Software

Although it's not as common as installing software, you can also remove or uninstall programs on your computer. This can be done because the programs aren't used (and to free up the disk space they occupy), because the program is incompatible, or when upgrading to a newer version of the program when uninstalling the previous version is required (although the new program's installation process generally does the uninstalling for you).

You can uninstall software in several ways.

The first thing to try is to look on the All Programs menu for an Uninstall command. That command might be right on the same submenu as the command used to start the program. Start the Uninstall program and heed the directions that are displayed.

The second thing to try is the Programs and Features icon in the Control Panel. Opening that icon displays a window with the title Uninstall or Change a Program, which lists various programs installed on your computer. To uninstall a program, click to select its name and then click the Uninstall/Change button on the toolbar. Follow the directions on the screen. (Each program uninstalls differently.)

Finally, the worst thing to do is to manually delete the program from your computer. Although that rids you of the program's main file, it doesn't completely uninstall the program. Remnants and pieces of the program continue to lurk on your computer's hard drive and eventually cause you much woe. Because of that, I don't recommend manually deleting programs.

Deleting a program doesn't delete the files you created with that program. For example, removing Microsoft Word doesn't also cause all your document files to be deleted. Likewise, deleting a drawing program doesn't remove all your artwork from the computer. Removing a game may not delete any saved games or high score files from the computer. You can manually delete such files (***see also*** Part VII), but I don't recommend that unless you desperately need the hard drive space for something vital.

Part IV

The On–Off Thing

Traditionally, general reference computer books began with a chapter describing how a computer is turned on. The reason wasn't that you had to have a university degree to throw a switch, no. What the authors did was to describe what happens inside the computer after that switch is thrown. (This book spares you those details.) Of course, what those early titles missed was how to turn the PC off — and specifically, when it was appropriate to do so. A computer-on, computer-off chapter is necessary in this book because, unlike the blender or a table lamp, your PC lacks a true On–Off switch; it has a *power button.* And therein lies the rub: The power button does more than just turn the sucker on.

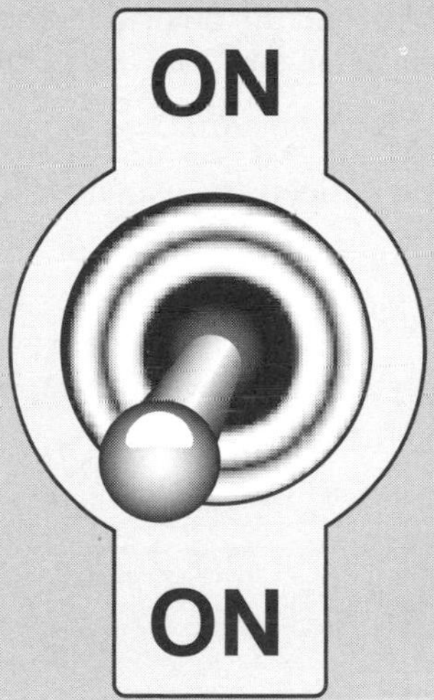

In this part . . .

- Changing the power button's function
- Changing the Start menu's power button function
- Logging on and off
- Sleep (Stand By) mode
- Turning the computer system off

Changing the Power Button's Function

Modern PCs lack an on–off switch. In its place is a power button. The power button most definitely turns on the PC. After it's on, however, the power button's function can be changed, so it doesn't necessarily turn the computer off.

To change the power button's function, obey these steps:

1. Open the Control Panel.

   You can get there from the Start button's menu; choose the Control Panel item.

2. Open the Power Options icon.
3. Click the task on the left labeled Choose What the Power Buttons Do.

   A new window appears, listing available power buttons for your PC: the main power button, a sleep button (if available), and the lid on a laptop. (See Figure 4-1.) Each button can do four things, chosen from a drop-down list:

   - **Do nothing.** Pressing the button doesn't do squat.
   - **Sleep.** The computer enters Stand By (sleep or suspended) mode.
   - **Hibernate.** The computer enters Hibernation mode.
   - **Shut down.** The computer shuts down.

4. Select an option from the list to indicate what you want the specific power button to do.
5. Click the Save Changes button.

Figure 4-1

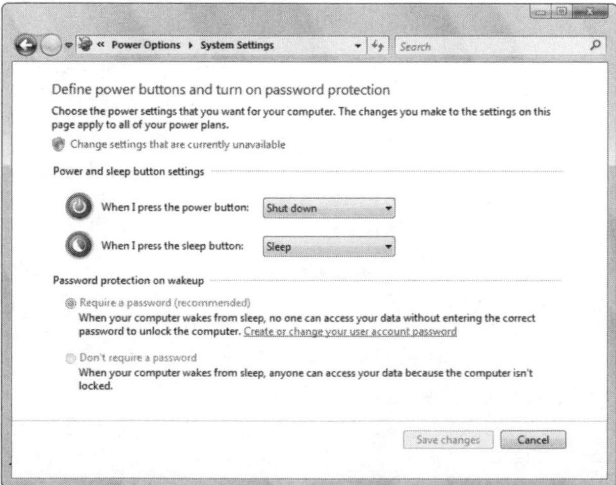

Regardless of which function you assign to the power button, you can shut down your computer by choosing the Shut Down command from the Start menu. ***See also*** "Turning the Computer System Off."

Changing the Start Menu's Power Button Function

The Windows Vista Start menu sports a virtual power button, as shown in the margin. As with the PC's physical power button, you can assign a function to the virtual power button and then use it to turn off the computer, put the computer to sleep, hibernate, or what-have-you. Here's the secret process:

1. Open the Control Panel's Power Options icon.
2. Click the link that says Change Plan Settings.

   It doesn't matter which of the three links you click.
3. On the next screen, locate and click the link labeled Change Advanced Power Settings.

   The Power Options dialog box appears.
4. In the scrolling list, click the plus sign (+) next to the option labeled Power Buttons and Lid.
5. Click the + next to the Start Menu Power Button option.

   Next to the word *Setting,* you see a word in blue, such as *sleep.*
6. Click that word in blue to display a pop-up list of options.
7. Choose an option for the Start menu power button.
8. Click OK to confirm your choice and close the dialog box.

   Optionally, close any other windows as well.

The Start menu's power button now serves whichever purpose you chose. ***See also*** "Changing the Power Button's Function," for an explanation of the power button's options.

Forcing the Computer Off

After you abandon all hope of properly shutting down your PC, you can try this simple trick to turn the thing off: Press and hold the power button. Keep holding it for about five seconds or so. Eventually, the console turns off.

Well, you can also try unplugging the thing or turning off the UPS. Nothing wrong with that — as long as the computer *is* locked up and you have tried to properly shut down.

Hibernation

An alternative to turning your computer off is the Hibernation option. It saves the PC's current state: the open files, information in memory, and all that stuff. Then the computer is turned off, like a bear sleeping out the winter in a cave. The next time you turn the computer on, it starts up and loads everything back into memory, and you're ready to go — often faster than had you shut it down and started it up normally.

The PC can be hibernated by either pressing the power button on the console or using the virtual power button on the Start menu. The button must be configured to hibernate, as covered elsewhere in this chapter.

To unhibernate, just turn the computer on as you normally would. The system revives from Hibernation mode and returns to the way it was before you hibernated, with open programs and everything.

Not every computer has the Hibernation option.

Logging On and Off

Windows requires you to identify yourself properly before you can use the PC. This is true for all modern computer operating systems. It's done for security reasons, to ensure that you are who you say you are. That way, you, and only you, can access your own files. Also, the computer can remember any personal settings or foofoo you set up inside Windows.

Log, or *logging,* is an ugly term, but it's the most accurate. The term *log* goes back years. It helps to think of a ship's log, where the captain would write down information about the vessel and its travels. For a computer, a user must log in to identify himself to the system.

Log in and *log on* mean the same thing: to identify yourself to the computer system.

The term *log off* is used when you're done with the computer and sign out for the day, but the computer is left on so that someone else can log in and use it.

A *login* is the name you use to identify yourself to the computer system. This unique name identifies you and your account on that PC.

Log on is a verb that means to log on or log in to a computer system.

Logging on and off are necessary for security, but are useful only when more than one person is using the same computer.

Logging in

To log in to Windows:

1. Click the picture or name associated with your account.
2. Type your password.
3. Press the Enter key or click the right-arrow button.

After a few moments, Windows completes its startup, and you can begin using the computer.

Logging off

To log off Windows, obey these steps:

1. Click the Start button.
2. Click the right-pointing triangle in the lower-right corner of the Start menu (next to the padlock icon).
3. Choose Log Off from the pop-up menu. (See Figure 4-2.)

Figure 4-2

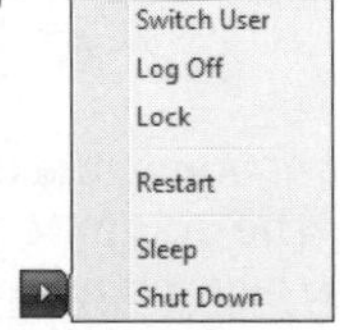

Windows proceeds just as it would for shutting down the computer, but rather than complete the job, it merely pauses and redisplays the logon screen while it waits for someone else to use the computer.

When you choose the Switch User option (in Step 3), Windows doesn't bother to shut down your programs. Instead, those programs and windows stay open, and Windows merely allows another user to log in at that point. The user who logs in can work on the PC, but Windows still remembers what the first user was doing.

By switching users, you can have one person quickly use the computer while the other waits. This saves time over logging out all the way or turning the computer off and then on again.

You don't need to log off the computer if you're done for the day. Instead, simply shut down Windows or hibernate the computer.

Locking the Computer

You don't need a key to lock up your computer; all you need is the Lock command. What it does is quickly batten down the PC's hatches, by hiding the Windows desktop and displaying your account's password-entry dialog box. At that point, the computer is *locked:* You cannot see what a person is doing or even use the computer unless you type in a password or switch to another user's account.

- To quickly lock the computer, press Win+L, where Win is the Windows key on the PC keyboard.
- You can also click the padlock icon on the Start menu to lock the PC.
- Finally, the Lock command is on the Start menu's Shutdown menu, along with Switch User, Log Off, and other shutdown options.

When you need to step away from your computer for a short time, consider using the Lock command.

Quitting Windows

When you're done using Windows, you need to quit, or *shut down,* the operating system. Because Windows is the same program that runs the computer, quitting Windows is the same thing as turning the computer off. In fact, on modern PCs, quitting Windows also turns off the console. (It doesn't turn off the rest of the computer system, though; ***see also*** "Turning the Computer System Off.")

To quit Windows, pursue these steps:

1. Save your stuff! Close open programs!

   Windows prompts you to save if you forget, but I recommend starting out the shutdown procedure by saving and closing first.

2. Click the Start button.
3. From the Start menu, click the right-pointing triangle in the lower-right corner to display a menu of shutdown options.
4. Choose Shut Down.

   The computer shuts itself down.

For turning off other hardware attached to the console, see "Turning the Computer System Off," later in this part.

If the computer immediately restarts, you have a problem — typically, a hardware problem. Refer to my book *Troubleshooting Your PC For Dummies* (Wiley) for more information.

Restarting Windows

Sometimes, it's necessary to start over again with a clean slate. For example, after installing some new hardware or new software or performing a Windows update, you have to restart Windows. It also helps to cure common ills and quirks, such as a wacko mouse. Here's how to restart Windows:

1. Click the Start button.
2. From the Start menu, click the right-pointing triangle in the lower-right corner to display a menu of shutdown options.
3. Choose Restart from the menu.

   Windows begins shutting down, and then the computer restarts.

If any unsaved documents are open, you're prompted to save them before the computer restarts.

Restarting Windows is just like turning the computer off and then on again, although you don't need to use the power button. The computer shuts down and closes all programs and, eventually, Windows itself. Then the computer immediately restarts, just as though it were turned on.

Restarting Windows can also be referred to as *resetting* the computer.

Old-timers refer to restarting Windows as a *warm boot.*

If your console sports a Reset button, don't use it to restart Windows. Follow the instructions in this section instead.

Sleep (Stand By) Mode

All modern PCs are equipped with energy-saving hardware and software. One energy-saving feature gives the computer the ability to go to sleep, also known as using *Stand By,* or *suspended,* mode, where the computer is still on but consumes less power.

You can configure your PC to enter Stand By mode after a given period of inactivity, immediately, or never, depending on your whim and how much you enjoy saving energy.

Putting your PC to sleep

To manually sleep the computer, follow these steps:

1. Click the Start button.
2. From the Start menu, click the right-pointing triangle in the lower-right corner to display a menu of shutdown options.
3. Choose Sleep from the menu.

   The computer enters its power-saving mode.

The screen goes dark, and you may hear the hard drive warble down to a stop. The computer is asleep. Shhhh!

The computer isn't really totally turned off (unlike in Hibernation mode). Some functions are still working. But most of the power-draining tasks that the computer does are halted.

You can program the power button, as well as the Start menu's virtual power button, to put the PC to sleep; see "Changing the Power Button's Function" and "Changing the Start Menu's Power Button Function," earlier in this part.

Automatically going into sleep mode

You can configure the PC to automatically enter Stand By mode after a period of inactivity, such as an hour or so after any key on the keyboard was pressed or the mouse was moved. The Power Options icon in the Control Panel is where you need to go:

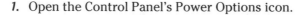

1. Open the Control Panel's Power Options icon.
2. Click the task on the left that says Change When the Computer Sleeps.

   A window is displayed, as shown in Figure 4-3, listing various items in the computer that can be put to sleep and when (if ever) they will be put to sleep.
3. Set a timeout value for each item.

   Click the button next to the item to display a menu full of timeout options. Choose Never to disable sleep for that item, or choose a minute or hour interval.
4. Click the Save Changes button to lock in your settings and, optionally, close the window.

Figure 4-3

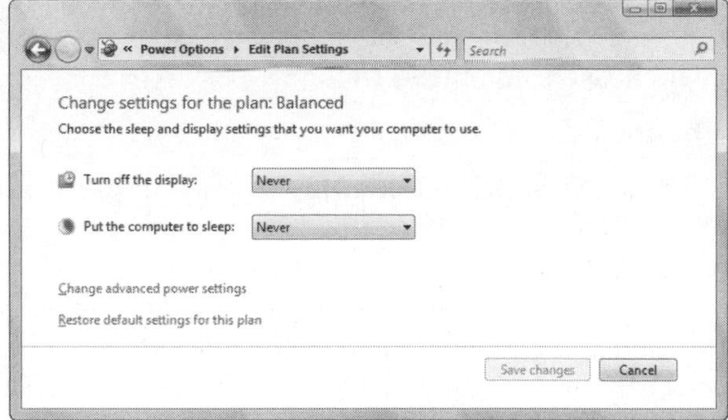

I don't recommend setting a timeout for your computer's hard drives. Doing so makes the computer act sluggish because it takes a while for the hard drives to spin back up to speed.

If you're using a screen saver, note that the timeout value for the monitor in sleep mode overrides the screen saver's timeout setting. For example, if the screen saver comes on after 45 minutes but the monitor goes to sleep after 30 minutes, you never see your screen saver.

Waking the computer

To rouse the computer from its slumber, press any key on the keyboard or jiggle the mouse. The computer wakes up after a moment.

The best "any key" to press is the Ctrl key on the keyboard. That key generally doesn't interact with any program, so nothing should change when the computer comes to life.

If the PC doesn't wake up, it may have gone comatose. This happens sometimes; PCs can crash in their sleep. ***See also*** "Forcing the Computer Off," earlier in this part. ***See also*** *Troubleshooting Your PC For Dummies,* which I wrote (Wiley).

Switching Users

Windows Vista offers you the option to set up several user accounts on the same PC. Each person can then customize Windows and have their own e-mail accounts, favorite Web pages, and other information, separate and secure from other users.

When you're using a multiperson PC, you should switch users when you're done for the day or when another user desperately desires to use the computer. Simply hoist up the Switch Users command thusly:

1. Click the Start button.
2. From the Start menu, click the right-pointing triangle in the lower-right corner to display a menu of shutdown options.
3. Choose Switch User from the menu.

The screen goes dark, almost as though you shut down Windows or logged off. But you didn't! Instead, Windows displays the Welcome screen again, allowing you or any other user to log in and use the computer.

Note that unlike the initial Welcome screen you see when you start Windows, your account is listed as Logged On. In fact, if other users try to shut down the PC, they're warned that your account is being used (and that programs may potentially be running).

Turning the Computer System Off

If you want to be good to your PC, and have your computer system last a good long time, pay attention to shutting it down properly. Too many people ignore this good advice, and their PCs suffer for it. Don't be one of them. Instead, turn off your computer system like this:

1. Quit Windows.

   See also "Quitting Windows," earlier in this part.
2. Turn off the console if it doesn't turn itself off automatically.
3. Turn off the monitor and any other peripherals attached to the PC.

You're done. Walk away.

The key is to turn off the console first and then turn off other devices connected to the console: the monitor, printer, scanner, and external disk drives.

Not every external device has a power switch; some external disk drives and scanners have no on–off switch. Just let them be.

If everything is plugged into a power strip, you can turn off everything by turning off the power strip. When the power strip is lying on the floor and you have a hole in your sock, you can turn off the computer power by using your toe.

When computer hardware is plugged into a UPS, you can turn it off by turning off the UPS. You can even do so with your toe. (But don't unplug the UPS because that could run down the battery.)

The worst thing to do is simply unplug the computer to turn it off. Sometimes, that's necessary in instances of dire need. But don't make it a habit.

Turning the Computer System On

The best way to turn on your computer system is in this order:

1. Turn on the computer's peripherals: monitor, printer, external disk drives, and scanner, for example.
2. Turn on the console.

This order is more traditional than official or necessary. The original reason for turning on the console last is that it's in charge. When all the peripherals are on, toasty, and up to speed, the console can easily and quickly recognize those devices. That's no longer the case, yet if you stew over which things to turn on first, follow the steps just listed.

If you're using a power strip or UPS, the procedure works the same: peripherals first and then the console, although it really doesn't matter if everything is turned on all at once.

After the computer comes to life, you need to log in to Windows. ***See also*** "Logging On and Off," earlier in this part.

The Uninterruptible Power Supply

One of the best things you can buy for your PC is a UPS, or *u*ninterruptible *p*ower *s*upply. That gizmo is essentially a large battery inside a power strip. The battery supplies power so that no gizmos plugged into the UPS suffer instant death after a power outage.

Many UPSs are also equipped with special electronic filters and noise protection that further insulate your delicate electronic equipment from various electrical evils.

Connect only the console and the monitor to the UPS. Specifically, connect them to the battery-backed-up sockets on the UPS. You can connect your other peripherals to the non-battery-backed-up sockets or to a regular power strip. (See Figure 4-4.)

Figure 4-4

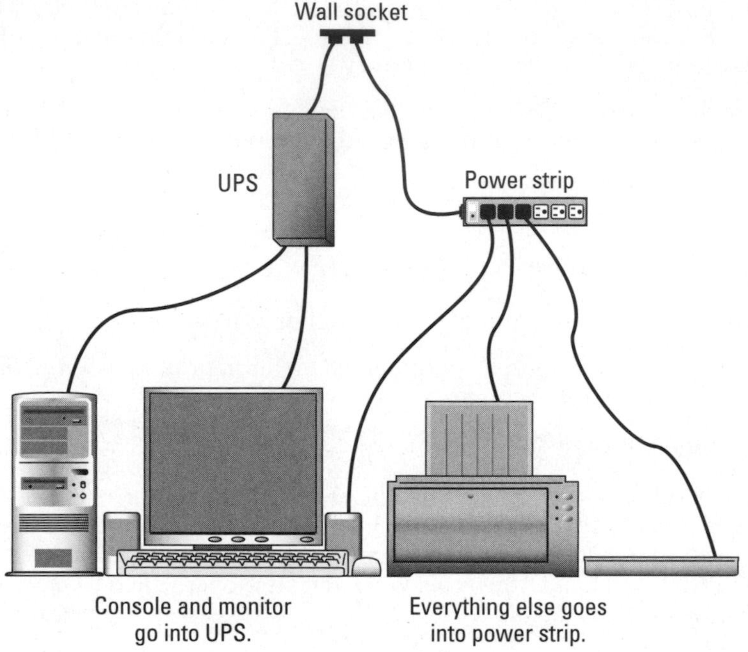
Wall socket
UPS
Power strip
Console and monitor go into UPS.
Everything else goes into power strip.

The idea here is to keep the console and monitor active during a power emergency. That way, you can save your stuff and properly shut down. Printing, scanning, and using the Internet can wait until the power comes back on.

You can get a UPS at any office supply or computer store. They're rated by how long they can keep things powered after a power outage, and also by how many sockets they have, how many are battery-powered, and other features.

Note that having a UPS isn't your ticket to computing in the dark. When the power goes out, you should immediately save your stuff and shut down the computer safely and properly.

The UPS beeps when a power disruption occurs, or it beeps constantly when the power is out. That's your signal to save your stuff, close Windows, and shut down the PC.

The time rating on a UPS is for comparison purposes only. In my experience, most UPS batteries give up only a few minutes after the power goes out — even though the UPS may be rated for 30 or 45 minutes. Be safe: Save your stuff, power down, turn off. Wait for the power to come back on. (Go read a book . . . by candlelight!)

Part V

Popular Places in Windows

A computer system is composed of both hardware and software. Most folks believe the hardware to be more important. It's not. Software rules the computer's roost because it tells the hardware what to do. And the main piece of software on your PC is the operating system: Microsoft Windows Vista. It not only tells the hardware what to do, but also coordinates all the programs in your PC, plus it gives you the necessary knobs and levers to control the whole thing. Windows is a mighty big enchilada! Although this book isn't about Windows, this part of the book shows you the popular places in Windows where you can help keep your PC healthy, happy, and alive.

In this part . . .

- Account folder
- All Programs menu
- Control Panel
- Notification area
- Start menu
- Taskbar

Account Folder

Windows Vista creates a central location for you to store your files — the things you create and stuff you download from the Internet or collect from anywhere. It's your own, personal folder. Its official name is the User Profile folder, but I like to call it your *account folder.*

The actual folder name is the same as the name of the account you use to log in to Windows. For example, my account is named *Dan,* so the account folder is named *Dan.* The folder can be your name on your computer, or an assigned name, such as User.

To view the contents of the account folder, open the account folder icon on the desktop. The folder is also accessible from the Start menu, in the upper-right corner.

The account folder, shown in Figure 5-1, is the home of all the documents, files, and whatnot you create on your computer. The folder is divided into some specific subfolders for further organization, and you can create your own, specific folders within the account folder or in any of its subfolders.

Figure 5-1

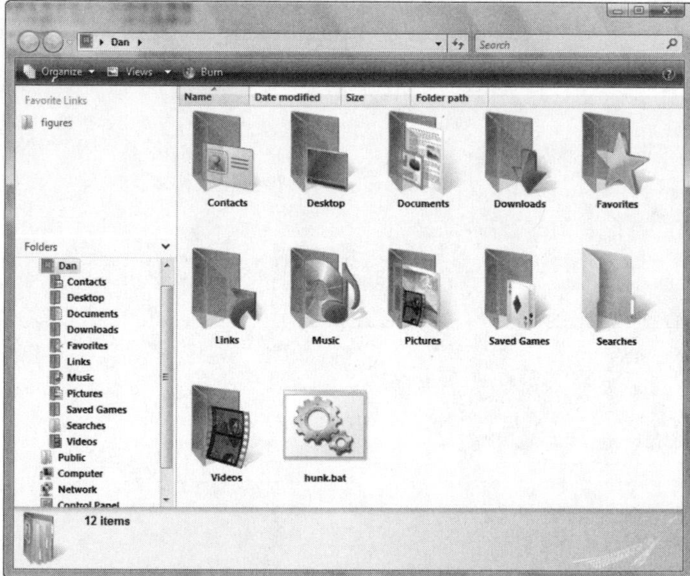

Common folders found in your account folder are listed in the following table. Many Windows applications are preset to use these folders. For example, Windows Media Player uses the Music and Video folders; Microsoft Office applications use the Documents folder; and graphics programs use the Pictures folder. Any other folders you find in your account window were created by some software you installed, or you added them yourself. Regardless, the whole notion behind all these folders is to help keep your stuff organized. (***See also*** Part VIII.)

Common Account Subfolders

Icon	Folder Name	Contents
	Contacts	E-mail address book, contacts from Windows Mail
	Desktop	Icons on the desktop
	Documents	Documents, reports, general stuff
	Downloads	Files downloaded from the Internet
	Favorites	Web page favorites and bookmarks
	Links	Favorite links to folders and such for Windows Explorer
	Music	Audio files and music collected and organized by Windows Media Player
	Pictures	Graphics and images
	Saved Games	Information from various games, saved games
	Searches	Preset and saved searches for information on your computer
	Videos	Video and similar media files

Each user on the PC has his own, separate User Profile folder. What you see in your account folder window is unique to your account. When another user logs on to Windows, he has his own account folder and doesn't see or have access to the files in your User Profile folder.

All Programs Menu

Every program installed on your computer, as well as the programs that come with Windows, can be found in one spot: the All Programs menu. To visit this important spot, heed these steps:

1. Click the Start button to pop up the Start menu.
2. Choose All Programs.

The left side of the Start menu changes to display the All Programs menu, similar to what you see in Figure 5-2. You see a list of top-level programs and then a list of folders that contain more programs, or perhaps more folders with even more programs inside.

Figure 5-2

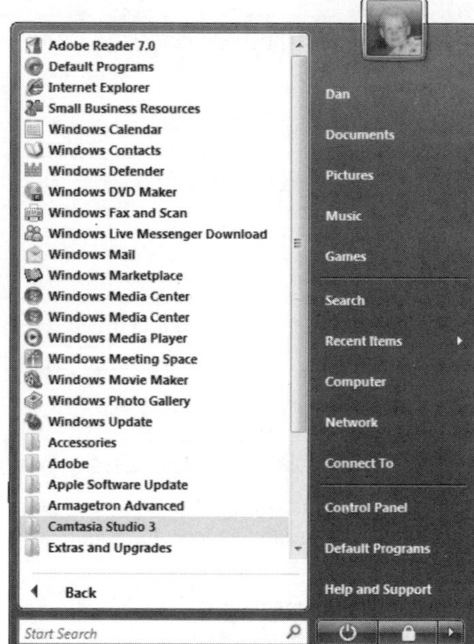

From the menu, you can choose a program to run. That's the idea: Click to choose a program; it runs.

You need to click things only once on the All Programs menu.

Selecting a submenu displays that submenu's contents, from which you can choose a program or select another submenu to peruse.

New programs may appear highlighted on the menu. This is helpful when looking for a program you just installed, because the All Programs menu can get rather cluttered.

To back out of the All Programs menu, choose Back from the bottom, below the list.

The program itself isn't placed on the All Programs menu. Instead, a program *shortcut* is used. The real program is installed elsewhere on the computer's hard drive.

Not all programs are listed on the All Programs menu. Some of the more obscure Windows utilities aren't listed. Some programs you download from the Internet aren't listed either.

Starting a program

You use the All Programs menu to start a program. For example, to start the Notepad text editor, follow these steps:

1. Click the Start button to display the Start menu.
2. Choose All Programs.
3. Choose Accessories.
4. Choose Notepad.

   The Notepad program starts and opens its window.

These instructions can also be written this way:

1. Click the Start button to display the Start menu.
2. Choose All Programs➪Accessories➪Notepad.

   The Notepad program starts and opens its window.

You can close Notepad: Choose File➪Exit from its menu.

Popular menus on the All Programs menu

Windows preconfigures a few submenus (places you may find yourself visiting from time to time) on the All Programs menu. Here are a few of the more popular All Programs submenus and what you may find there:

- **Games:** This is where the Windows games are! Note, though, that other games are installed on their own, separate submenus (usually named after the game developer or distributor).
- **Accessories:** Many of the smaller Windows assistant programs appear on the Accessories menu: Calculator, Command Prompt, Notepad, Paint, Windows Explorer, and WordPad are among the more popular.

- **Accessories⇨System Tools:** This sub-submenu contains lots of handy Windows utilities and programs, including Backup, Disk Cleanup, Disk Defragmenter, and System Restore.

The Startup submenu

A special menu on the All Programs menu is named Startup. Any program shortcuts placed on this submenu start automatically when Windows starts.

Some applications automatically put their programs on the Startup submenu when they're installed.

To prevent a program from starting, move it from the Startup submenu to another submenu. Just drag the item with the mouse or, better, edit the menu. (***See also*** "Organizing the All Programs menu.")

Creating a desktop shortcut to a program

Navigating the menus and submenus of the All Programs menu can be tricky. For programs you use often, consider creating a desktop shortcut icon to the program rather than having to use the All Programs menu.

To copy a program from the All Programs menu to a shortcut icon on the desktop, follow these steps:

1. Click the Start button to display the Start menu.
2. Choose All Programs and find your program on the menu.

   For example, choose Accessories and then locate WordPad.
3. Right-click the program's icon.

   So, rather than left-click the command, which would start the program, you right-click. This step displays a pop-up menu.
4. Choose Send To⇨Desktop (Create Shortcut).

   The program's icon appears on the desktop as a shortcut file.
5. Press the Esc key on the keyboard to back out of the submenus and hide any other menus that are displayed.

The shortcut icon on the desktop can be double-clicked to run the program. Many PC users find this technique easier than wading through the All Programs menu. But do this trick for only those programs you use most often, lest the desktop get cluttered.

See also Part VI for information on shortcut icons.

Putting a program on the Quick Launch bar

A great place to put the four or five programs that you use most often is on the Quick Launch bar, typically found nestled betwixt the Start button and the taskbar on the bottom of the screen. To add a program as a button to the Quick Launch bar, heed these steps:

1. Click the Start button to display the Start menu.
2. Choose All Programs and find your program on the menu.
3. Right-click the program's icon.
4. Choose Add to Quick Launch.

   The program's icon is added to the Quick Launch bar, although you may not be able to see it right away.
5. Press the Esc key on the keyboard to back out of the menus that are displayed.

See also "Quick Launch bar," later in this part, for more information, including directions for making the Quick Launch bar wider so that you can see all the icons.

Pinning a program to the Start menu

Before the All Programs menu covers it up, the left side of the Start menu displays a list of recently used programs. Atop that list are programs permanently attached, or *pinned,* to the Start menu. To add one or two of your favorite programs to that pin-on list, obey these steps:

1. Click the Start button to display the Start menu.
2. Choose All Programs and find your program on the menu.
3. Right-click the program's icon.
4. Choose Pin to Start Menu.

   The program's icon now appears at the top of the Start menu.
5. Press the Esc key on the keyboard to back out of the menus that are displayed.

I recommend putting only a few programs at the top of the Start menu, because it's a tiny, limited space. Any more than three program icons make the Start menu look junky.

Organizing the All Programs menu

Just about any new program you install desires to create its own submenu on the All Programs menu. This leads to a messy situation after a while. I've seen some All Programs menus that are just folder after folder, which takes forever to scroll through. Plus, it's not organized.

You can organize programs and menus on the All Programs menu easily. The idea is to create main folders and then organize the programs and submenus into those folders.

As an example, here are some ideas for the main folders on the All Programs menu:

- Internet
- Utilities
- Games
- Microsoft Office
- Accessories
- Misc

There's no definitive list; you can create and use whichever folders you believe will best keep you organized.

To do the organization, you need to move around the various existing menus and commands. Right-click the Start button and choose Open from the pop-up menu. Creating and arranging the items is done in a manner similar to managing folders. ***See also*** Part VIII. (Remember that folders are submenus and that shortcut icons are commands.)

Computer

Computer is the name of an icon and a window where you can find information about your computer and its storage devices. It was named *My Computer* in earlier versions of Windows.

To access the Computer window, open the Computer icon on the desktop or choose Computer from the Start menu. The Computer window, shown in Figure 5-3, lists the storage devices inside your computer — primarily, the disk drives but also any digital cameras or scanners attached to your computer.

The Computer window is often used as a starting place when navigating through various disk drives and when file hunting. ***See also*** Part VI.

Figure 5-3

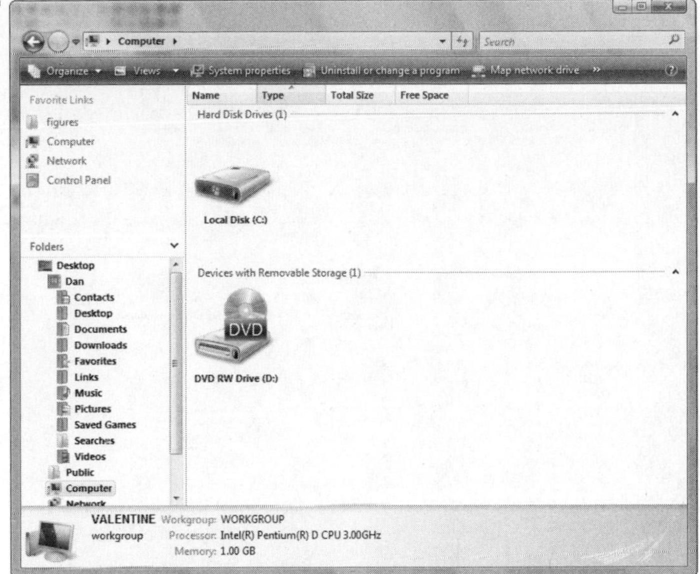

Control Panel

Windows uses the Control Panel to help you manage many aspects of your computer. The *Control Panel* is a window populated with icons, each of which controls some specific aspect of Windows, your hardware or software, or a combination of each.

To display the Control Panel, click the Start button and choose Control Panel from the menu.

You can also see the Control Panel from any Windows Explorer window: Click the first right-pointing arrow on the Address bar and select Control Panel from the drop-down list.

The Control Panel has two visual modes: Classic and Category. Classic view displays all the icons in one window, as shown in Figure 5-4.

Category view displays only the most popular icons and tasks, as shown in Figure 5-5. Other icons are accessed in subcategories.

You can change views by choosing the proper link on the left side of the Control Panel window. I prefer Classic view because it's easier to get to any icon. This book assumes that you're using Classic view for that reason.

Figure 5-4

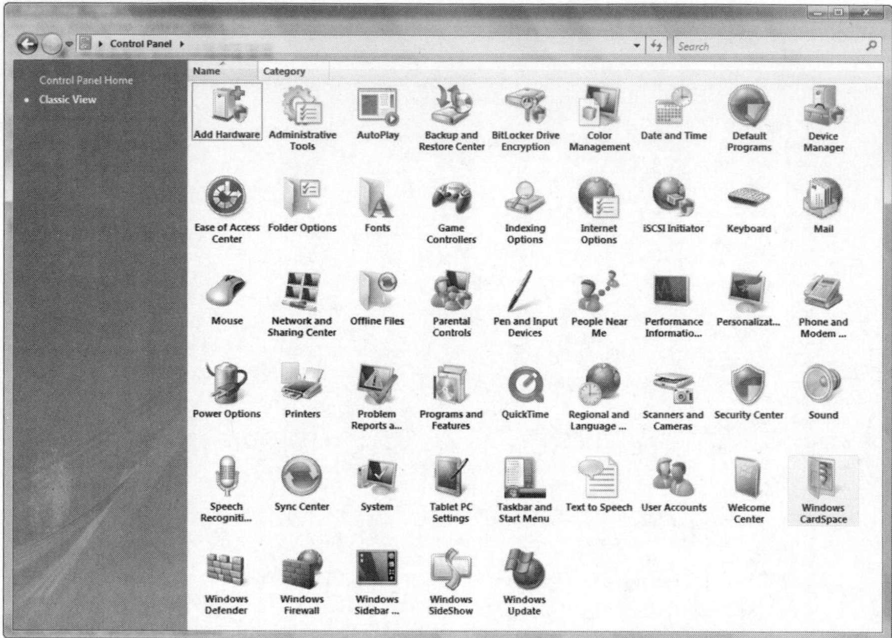

Figure 5-5

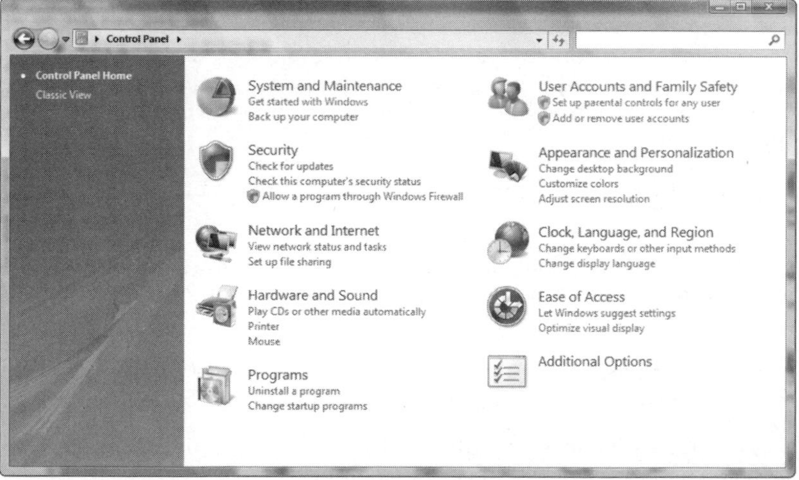

When the Control Panel isn't available as an item on the Start menu, follow these steps to make it so:

1. Right-click the Start button.
2. Choose Properties from the pop-up menu.
3. In the Taskbar and Start Menu Properties dialog box, click the Customize button.

   The Customize Start Menu dialog box appears.
4. Locate Control Panel on the scrolling list.
5. Choose the option below Control Panel that reads Display As a Link.
6. Click OK to close the various open dialog boxes.

The Control Panel now appears as a command on the main Start menu.

To make the Control Panel appear as a menu, with its icons showing up as submenu commands, choose the option Display As a Menu in Step 5.

Desktop

The *desktop* is the main interface that Windows provides, similar to the one shown in Figure 5-6. It's what you see when you first start Windows — home plate, as it were.

The desktop is where various program windows appear as you use Windows.

The desktop is also home to numerous icons. The icons are considered to be "on the desktop." That keeps them handy.

The desktop can have a background, or *wallpaper,* image, or it can be a solid color. Use the Control Panel's Personalization icon to customize the background. That icon is also used to set the desktop dimensions (referred to as the *resolution*).

The taskbar appears on the desktop, although it's not a part of the desktop. (***See also*** "Taskbar," at the end of this part.)

The desktop may also be home to the Windows sidebar.

The term *desktop* has little to do with the thing today. In older, original graphical operating systems, the desktop appeared as a metaphorical representation of a desktop, complete with a pad of paper, a calendar, a glue pot, scissors, and other items commonly found on a real desktop.

Figure 5-6

Network

Windows provides the Network icon to access various locations on the local network, a wireless network, or the Internet. The icon is found on the desktop or the Start menu, or you can access it from the Address bar in the Windows Explorer window. This icon was named My Network Places or the Network Neighborhood in earlier Windows versions.

Opening the Network icon reveals a window, shown in Figure 5-7, that lists available resources on the local network — if any. The resources are shown as icons representing various network devices or computers. Opening those icons lists any resources, such as folders or printers, available for sharing.

Figure 5-7

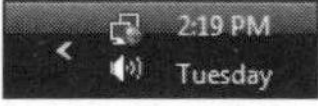

Notification Area

The notification area sits on the opposite end of the taskbar from the Start menu, as shown in Figure 5-8. When the taskbar rests on the bottom of the screen, the notification area is on the right side of the taskbar. The notification area is also referred to as the *system tray.*

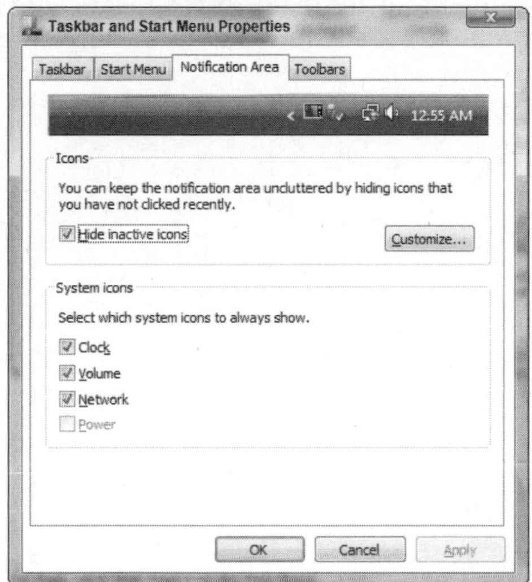

Figure 5-8

The notification area contains information, usually in the form of tiny icons that control or allow access to parts of windows or certain programs or utilities running in the computer. For example, the volume control in the notification area is used to adjust the sound volume in Windows, or even to mute sound. An antivirus program may show its icon in the notification area.

The notification area normally displays the time of day in addition to the day of the week.

Some icons in the notification area may occasionally pop up information balloons offering helpful information or alerting you to something important or to certain changing conditions in the computer.

Use the mouse to control the icons in the notification area. Clicking, double-clicking, or right-clicking the icons controls their behavior, making them pop up a menu, display a window, or do something else (although some icons don't do anything). Sometimes, merely pointing the mouse at an icon does the job. What the icon does, of course, depends on which program the icon represents.

You can eliminate many of the items displayed on the system tray, but you cannot fully eliminate the system tray from the taskbar.

Controlling the notification area

The notification area has its own dialog box, in which you can customize its look and control some of the icons displayed. Here's how to get at that dialog box:

1. Right-click the time display on the notification area.
2. Choose Properties from the pop-up menu.

   The Taskbar and Start Menu Properties dialog box appears with the Notification Area tab up front and ready for your input, similar to what's shown in Figure 5-9.

Figure 5-9

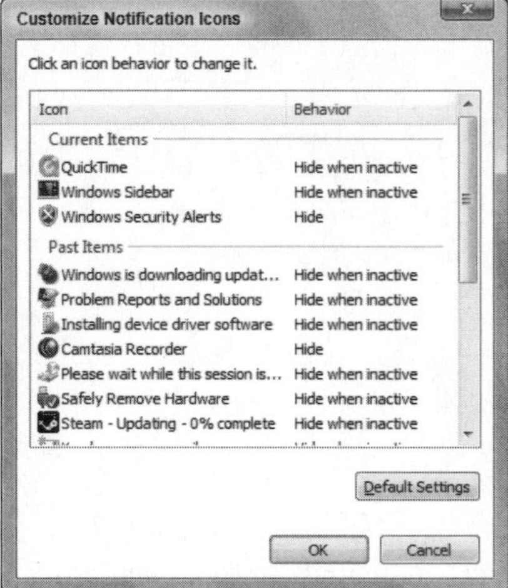

3. Make any necessary changes.
4. Click OK.

In Step 3, you can immediately adjust whether the notification area displays the day and time (Clock), the volume control (Volume), the little networking dudes (Network), or the battery meter on a laptop (Power) by adding or removing check marks next to those items.

Controlling the visibility of the notification area icons

The notification area can quickly become crowded with numerous and meaningless icons. To help combat the bloat, the notification area automatically hides seldom-used icons and can be customized to show or hide any or all icons — although remember that you cannot totally remove the notification area.

To show all icons in the notification area, click the left-pointing chevron. For a few seconds, all the notification icons are shown, and the chevron points to the right. But then things return as they were.

For more control over the icons, you can use the Customize Notification Icons dialog box, as shown in Figure 5-10. Summon that dialog box by following the steps in the preceding section to display the Taskbar and Start Menu Properties dialog box. In that dialog box. Click the Customize button to display the Customize Notification Icons dialog box.

Figure 5-10

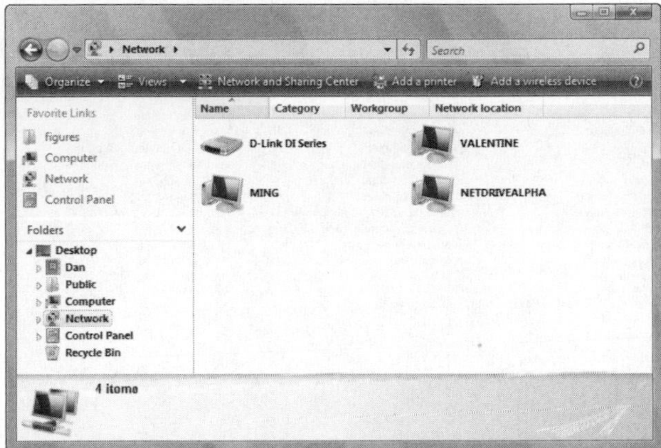

The Customize Notification Icons dialog box lists all potential icons that can show up in the notification area. To determine which ones show up, click next to a particular icon in the Behavior column. The behavior listed then becomes a pull-down menu from which you can choose one of three options:

- **Hide when inactive:** The icon shows up when its program is being used or when the icon thinks that it's active.
- **Hide:** The icon is always hidden.
- **Always show:** The icon is always shown.

Note that changing how individual icons show up may or may not work for all the teensy icons on the system tray.

Recycle Bin

The Recycle Bin is file heaven; it's the place where deleted files go to rest. It's the place from which those deleted files can be undeleted, although a file may expire anyway if it stays in the Recycle Bin long enough.

The Recycle Bin may appear as an icon on the desktop. Its contents can also be displayed by using the Address bar in any Windows Explorer window.

Opening the Recycle Bin icon displays the contents of the Recycle Bin folder, a collection of all files you deleted on your computer, as shown in Figure 5-11.

Figure 5-11

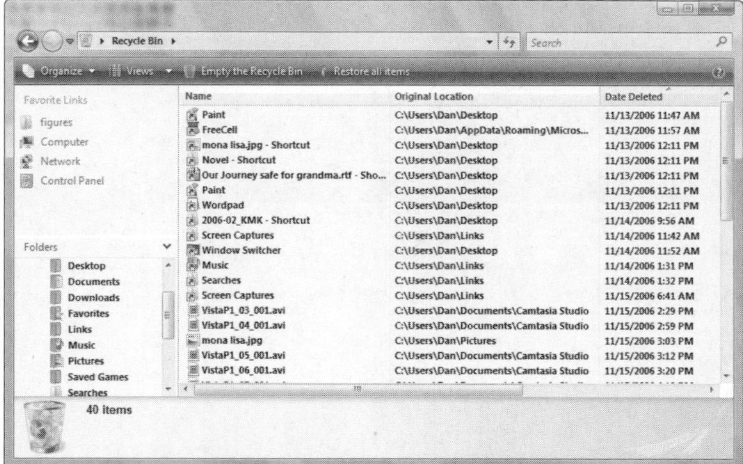

To see the most recently deleted files listed first, choose View⇨Arrange Icons By⇨Date Deleted from the menu.

Files stay in the Recycle Bin until they're removed. Files are removed automatically over time as the Recycle Bin is being used. You can also manually remove or empty the Recycle Bin.

Removing files from the Recycle Bin helps improve the amount of disk storage space available. But, sadly, removing files from the Recycle Bin means that there's no way to recover them if you need them again.

Start Menu

Indeed, the Start button is pretty special, but it's merely the gatekeeper. The real action takes place on the Start menu, which appears whenever you click the Start button or press the Windows key on the computer keyboard. The Start menu is the key you turn to start just about anything in Windows: programs, activities, adjustments, fine-tuning — even stopping the computer. It's all done from the Start menu.

The Start button lives on one end of the taskbar. Normally, the taskbar sits on the bottom of the screen (although it can be moved), and the Start button dwells in the screen's lower-left corner.

Activating the Start button pops up the Start menu, as shown in Figure 5-12. You can activate the Start button by clicking it with the mouse. Or, you can press the Win key on the keyboard, which also pops up the Start button's menu.

Figure 5-12

If your keyboard lacks a Win key, pressing the Ctrl+Esc key combination pops up the Start button's menu.

The Start button's menu contains many shortcuts for getting to other places in Windows, as well as accessing commonly used programs and the powerful All Programs menu.

The top of the menu lists your user ID and picture. (Windows refers to the logon ID, or login ID, as a *user ID*.)

You can change the picture by clicking it with the mouse. That opens the User Accounts icon from the Control Panel, where user accounts are messed with.

The left side of the Start menu lists popular programs. The upper-left area of the menu is the *pin-on* area, where certain popular programs can be placed. The bottom left side lists recently used programs.

The right side of the Start menu contains popular places and folders to visit in Windows.

Press the Esc key or the Win key to make the Start button's menu go away. You can also click the mouse on the desktop to banish the Start menu.

Changing the Start menu's look

You can view the Start menu in Windows in two ways: the new way and the boring, classic way. To choose one or the other, follow these steps:

1. Right-click the Start button.
2. Choose Properties from the pop-up menu.

   The Taskbar and Start Menu Properties dialog box appears, with the Start Menu tab forward.
3. Choose Classic Start Menu.

   The classic Start menu is reminiscent of the old Windows 98/Me/2000 Start menu. Boring.
4. Click OK to change the Start menu, or click the Cancel button to keep it as is.

Configuring the Start button's menu

The Start button's menu is customizable. You can change just about any aspect of the menu, from what appears and how it appears to where specific things go. To wield such might, mind these steps:

1. Right-click the Start button.
2. Choose Properties from the pop-up menu.
3. Click the Customize button.

   The Customize Start Menu dialog box, shown in Figure 5-13, lets you control what does or doesn't show up on the Start button's menu.

   The scrolling list shows items that you can place on the Start menu. Removing a check mark removes the item from the Start menu.

   Some items have three options: Show the item as a link, show it as a submenu, or don't show it.
4. Click the OK button after making your choices.

   Close any other open dialog boxes or windows.

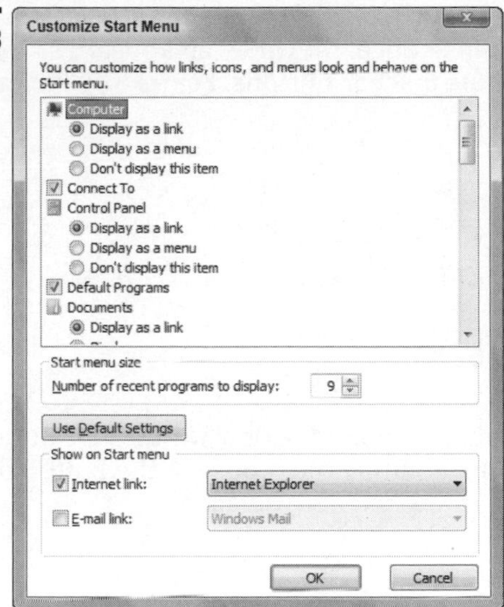

Figure 5-13

I call the upper-left part of the Start button's menu the *pin-on* area. You can attach any program icon to this area by right-clicking that icon and choosing the Pin to Start Menu command.

Icons can be removed from the pin-on area by right-clicking them and choosing the Unpin from Start Menu command from the pop-up menu.

Taskbar

The taskbar, shown in Figure 5-14, exists as a strip, usually found along the bottom of the desktop (although it can move). On the left end of the taskbar is the Start button. The right end of the taskbar is the notification area.

Figure 5-14

In the middle, the taskbar displays buttons, one for each running program or open window on the desktop.

Clicking a button on the taskbar instantly switches attention to that button's window and brings the window up front and ready for action. Other windows, if any, are shuffled behind the open window. The open window is then said to be "on top."

Multiple buttons may be stacked on the taskbar; for example, when several Internet Explorer windows are open at once, they may all appear as a pop-up menu button rather than as separate taskbar buttons. Figure 5-15 illustrates this concept in a beautiful way.

Figure 5-15

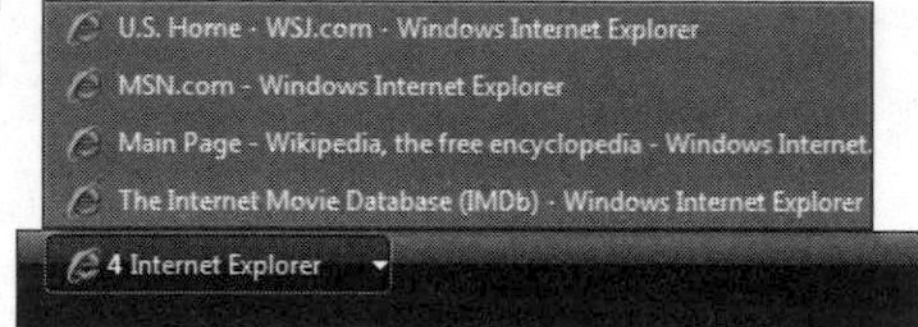

Your computer may show a pop-up thumbnail preview window for buttons on the taskbar, as shown in Figure 5-16. Pointing the mouse at the button displays the thumbnail. (This option may not be available on all PCs.)

Figure 5-16

The taskbar is also host to various toolbars, which appear on the taskbar between the Start button and system tray. One of the most popular toolbars is the Quick Launch bar, often found just to the right of the Start button. Yes, the taskbar can be a very crowded place.

Locking and unlocking the taskbar

You can lock the taskbar. This prevents it from being relocated, resized, or changed against your will. But it's good to know how to unlock it in case you want to adjust things, add another toolbar, or just mess around. Here's how:

1. Right-click the time in the notification area.
2. Choose Lock the Taskbar from the pop-up menu.

   This step either locks or unlocks the taskbar. When there's a check mark by Lock the Taskbar, choosing that command removes the check mark and unlocks the taskbar. Otherwise, you're locking the taskbar.

A locked taskbar has a slightly different look to it. It appears narrower; the top "lip" is missing. And the handles, used to move toolbars on the taskbar, disappear.

Moving the taskbar

The taskbar can be relocated to any edge of the screen: top, bottom, right, or left. Here's how to move the taskbar:

1. Unlock the taskbar.
2. Point the mouse at a blank part of the taskbar.

   Find a spot in the middle, away from other buttons or graphical whatnot.
3. Drag the mouse to another edge of the screen.

   The taskbar doesn't move as much as it "snaps" into position when you have the mouse pointer in the proper location.
4. Release the mouse button to drop the taskbar into its new position.
5. Lock the taskbar.

Be aware that most documentation assumes that the taskbar is at the *bottom* of the screen. That affects the position of the Start button and the notification area.

You can use these instructions to move a wayward taskbar back to the bottom of the screen if it goes AWOL.

Resizing the taskbar

The taskbar can be made fatter to accommodate more buttons, or made so thin as to be only a small line on the edge of the screen.

To resize the taskbar:

1. Unlock the taskbar.
2. Position the mouse on the taskbar's outer edge, between the taskbar and the desktop.

   ↕ When you find the sweet spot, the mouse pointer changes to a this-way-that-way arrow (as shown in the margin).
3. Drag the mouse inward, toward the desktop, to make it thicker, looking somewhat like Figure 5-17.

Figure 5-17

   Or, drag the mouse outside, toward the edge of the screen, to make it thinner.

4. Release the mouse.

   The taskbar assumes the new size.

5. Lock the taskbar.

Setting taskbar options

A clutch of interesting taskbar options can be set in the Taskbar and Start Menu Properties dialog box, on the Taskbar tab. To see this dialog box, right-click a blank part of the taskbar and choose Properties from the pop-up menu. The dialog box is shown in Figure 5-18.

Figure 5-18

You can elect to have the taskbar automatically shy away, to provide more room for windows on the desktop. This feature, known as Auto-hide, is activated by putting a check mark by the item labeled Auto-Hide the Taskbar.

Likewise, if you prefer to have more screen space, remove the check mark by the item Keep the Taskbar on Top of Other Windows.

The item Group Similar Taskbar Buttons allows windows from the same program to be stacked, as shown earlier.

The item Show Window Previews (Thumbnails) directs Windows to display a tiny preview window for any button you point the mouse at. This item is available only when your PC has a beefy graphics system.

After making the proper choices, click the OK button to lock them in.

Other toolbars

The taskbar is also home to other toolbars. In fact, you can stack the taskbar with an endless number of toolbars, which seems impractical, although it's possible.

Add a toolbar like this:

1. Right-click a blank part of the taskbar.

   Don't click a button or icon.

2. Choose a new toolbar from the Toolbars submenu.

   The number and variety of toolbars that appear depend on which features and applications you have installed in Windows.

After you choose a toolbar, the menu goes away and the new toolbar appears on the taskbar.

For example, adding the Address toolbar provides the taskbar with an Address text box, shown in Figure 5-19, just like a Windows Explorer or Internet Explorer window.

Figure 5-19

You can type the name of a Web page to visit, or you can type the name of a program to run — all from the taskbar's Address toolbar.

Yes, adding toolbars can make the taskbar a busy place. ***See also*** "Moving a toolbar," later in this part.

When a toolbar is cut off and buttons or options are hidden, the toolbar grows a Show More button on its right end. Clicking this button (see the margin) displays the hidden toolbar options as a pop-up menu.

Quick Launch bar

A special toolbar, the *Quick Launch* bar, appears automatically when Windows Vista is first installed or run on a new PC. The Quick Launch bar contains buttons showing icons that represent popular programs. To run a program, click the button. That's how the toolbar gets its name — clicking a button quickly launches that program.

To display the Quick Launch bar, follow these steps:

1. Right-click the time display in the system tray area of the taskbar.
2. Choose Properties from the pop-up menu.

3. Click to put a check mark by the item labeled Show Quick Launch.
4. Click OK.

To add a new icon to the Quick Launch bar, locate the program on the All Programs menu. Right-click the icon and choose Add to Quick Launch from the pop-up menu. (Adding an icon may require that the Quick Launch bar be made wider; ***see also*** "Moving a toolbar," later in this part.)

To remove an icon from the Quick Launch bar, right-click the icon and choose Delete from the pop-up menu. Answer Yes if you're confronted with a confirmation dialog box.

If you want to see smaller or larger icons on the Quick Launch bar, right-click the left end of the Quick Launch bar (on the dimple bar) and choose View⇨Large Icons or View⇨Small Icons from the pop-up menu.

Moving a toolbar

Toolbars can be moved or rearranged, although it's not the easiest thing in the world to do.

First, the taskbar must *not* be locked.

Second, you must grab the toolbar by its left edge, or *handle.* The handle appears as a dimpled part of the unlocked taskbar, as shown in the margin. Just point the mouse at the handle. The mouse pointer changes to a multidirectional arrow when you find the sweet spot.

When you have the mouse properly pointed at a toolbar's handle, you can slide the handle left or right to change the toolbar's width. You can drag the toolbar up or down to move it and even stack toolbars one atop the other.

Finally, when you have the toolbar positioned just right, let go of the mouse! The toolbar should stick where you left it. You can optionally lock the taskbar at this point.

Note that it's very easy to accidentally move toolbars on the taskbar. You can also remove the toolbar from the taskbar, in which case the toolbar becomes a *floating palette window.* Don't let that distress you! Instead, merely drag the window back down to the toolbar, where it automatically reattaches itself.

Removing a toolbar

The easiest way to zap a toolbar from the taskbar is to right-click the taskbar and choose Toolbars from the pop-up menu. From the Toolbars submenu, choose the toolbar you want to banish.

Part VI

Disk Storage

The thing that makes a computer different from a calculator, and far more useful than the ancient typewriter or abacus, is that it can store information. The computer remembers! It's like an electronic closet. And just as with closets in real life, you'll spend a lot of your time on the computer creating and finding things to store in the computer's digital closet. Of course, it isn't really a closet. The thing used for long-term storage in a PC is the disk drive.

In this part . . .

- About disk storage
- CD-ROM and DVD drives
- Drive letters
- Ejecting a removable disk
- The floppy drive
- Inserting a removable disk

About Disk Storage

Computers have always had storage. They need it. The stuff the computer works on or creates must be held in storage. But for years that storage was temporary: When the power went off, all the stuff in storage went away as well.

As computers evolved, it became obvious to computer users and scientists that people didn't enjoy re-creating everything on a computer each time they turned the thing on. Yet, re-creating stuff was necessary because computers of the day had no long-term storage.

Now, things are different. Now, computers have long-term storage.

Long-term and short-term storage

Inside a computer, there is storage found in the microprocessor, RAM, and disk drives.

The microprocessor itself has some storage, but only a small amount, hardly enough to do anything more than basic math.

Computer memory, or *RAM,* provides storage to supplement what the microprocessor has. That storage is actively used by the microprocessor, and it's where programs run, where you create things, and where information is stored as you're using it. But just like those computers of old, computer memory is temporary.

Long-term storage in a computer system is provided by disk drives. Information can be written to a disk drive for later retrieval. Unlike computer memory, the stuff stored on a computer disk stays there until it's erased (or the disk is damaged).

Disks and media

As technology marches forward, the traditional notion of a computer disk drive is rapidly being replaced by the more general term *storage media.* That's because not all the long-term storage in a PC is really a disk drive any more.

The hard drives are disks, literal spinning disks inside the computer. The D in CD and the second D in DVD refers to a disc (the British spelling for *disk*), which is still a spinning disk inside the computer. But the newer forms of long-term storage don't use disks, discs, or anything that spins. Therefore, the more generic term *media* applies to them.

Storage media include USB flash drives as well as the media cards used to store images in digital cameras and other devices. The flash drives and media cards provide long-term storage, just like their spinning disk cousins do. But no matter what the format or how the device attaches to the computer, it's still storage media.

Saving and loading

To transfer information from memory to disk, you *save* that information. Indeed, the information is saved from the certain peril of short-term memory to the long-term safety of a disk drive.

To transfer information from a disk drive to memory, you *open* that information. (*Open* is the common term used in Windows, although some documentation uses the term *load* instead.)

AutoPlay

Windows sports a handy ability named *AutoPlay.* When you insert a removable disc or storage media, Windows may automatically run a program, play its music, install software, or do a number of interesting things, depending on how AutoPlay is configured.

At the simplest level, AutoPlay displays a dialog box asking you what to do with the newly mounted media, as shown in Figure 6-1. Windows examines the media's contents and then displays a list of options in a dialog box. Choose one, or choose to merely open the media to view the files (the last choice).

Figure 6-1

To disable AutoPlay, press and hold the Shift key while inserting a removable disc or storage media.

AutoPlay doesn't work with floppy disks.

Use the AutoPlay icon in the Control Panel to configure or change AutoPlay's behavior. Opening the icon displays the AutoPlay window, as shown in Figure 6-2. On the left side of the window appears a list of media. The list may also indicate the primary content for media, such as *Pictures* to describe a media card from a digital camera. On the right side appears the action associated with that media, the thing that Windows does when a disc matching the media type is inserted.

Figure 6-2

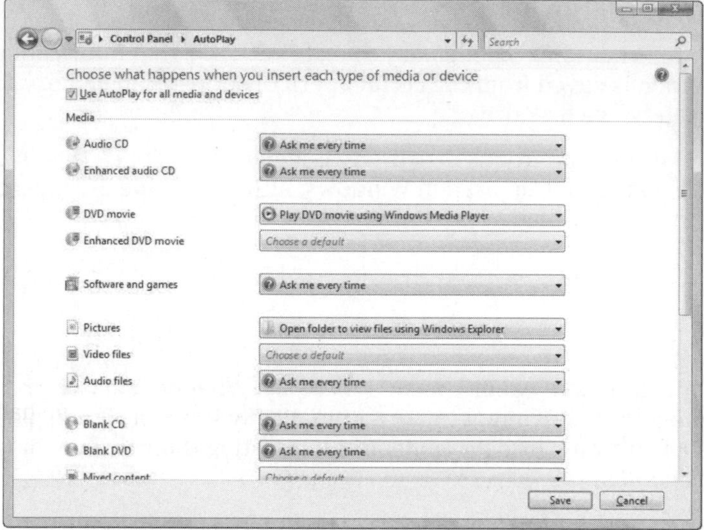

You can choose a new action from the list button, depending on the media. By doing so, you direct Windows not to display the AutoPlay dialog box, but, rather, to merely carry out whichever action is selected. Or, to see the AutoPlay dialog box, choose the option labeled Ask Me Every Time.

Click the Save button to confirm your choices and leave the AutoPlay window.

Bits and Bytes

Computer storage is measured by the byte, just as distances are measured in miles or kilometers — or inches or centimeters — and weight is measured by the ounce or gram. In computers, it's the byte.

A *byte* is a single character of information. The letter *A* can be stored in a byte, as can any letter, number, or symbol. For many bytes, common abbreviations are used, as described in this table:

Name	Abbreviation	Characters (appx.)
Byte	B	1
Kilobyte	K	1,000
Megabyte	MB	1 million
Gigabyte	GB	1 billion
Terabyte	TB	1 trillion

To give you a mental picture of these quantities, consider a kilobyte of information equal to about a page full of text.

Lincoln's Gettysburg Address is 1,477 bytes long, about 1.5K in size.

A typical picture on a Web page occupies anywhere from 30 to 80 kilobytes of storage.

The size of the document file used to store this chapter's text is approximately 74 kilobytes.

A high-resolution picture taken with a digital camera is about 5 megabytes.

You can store all of Shakespeare's works in about 3 megabytes of space.

One minute of music can be stored in a 1-megabyte file.

A ten-minute movie can be stored in 500 megabytes of space, or one-half gigabyte.

CD-ROM and DVD Drives

For *high-capacity* (meaning "lots of room") removable storage, your PC uses a CD-ROM or DVD drive. Some PCs have one of each, but most modern PCs have a single DVD drive. (All DVD drives can read CDs.) That DVD drive may also be able to record CDs and DVDs.

The DVD drive eats DVDs and CDs, those 5-inch plastic, shiny discs. The discs can contain computer data, music, video, new software to install, reference material, photographs, or just about anything.

CD-ROM stands for Compact Disc, Read-Only Memory. Some PCs may come with only a CD-ROM drive, in which case DVDs cannot be read.

The ROM in CD-ROM means that the disk cannot be written to; you cannot save information to a CD-ROM as you can to other disk drives. But the computer can read CD-ROM discs (hence, the *read-only* part of the acronym).

DVD stands for Digital Versatile Disc, or sometimes the V means Video. (The standards people called an early lunch before the exact acronym was agreed on.) The drives read DVD-ROM discs, similar in appearance to CDs, but can store much more information. Otherwise, beyond the disc's capacity, a DVD drive is very similar to a CD drive on a computer.

It's often hard to tell which drive is a CD or DVD drive. Generally speaking, CD drives have a CD logo on them, and DVD drives sport the DVD logo, as shown in Figures 6-3 and 6-4.

CD-ROM or DVD discs may be referred to as CDs, DVDs, disks, or discs. Physically, all the discs look alike. Some discs may be labeled as CDs or DVDs, or you may see *CD* or *DVD* specified in the tiny text around the disc's center hole.

Figure 6-3

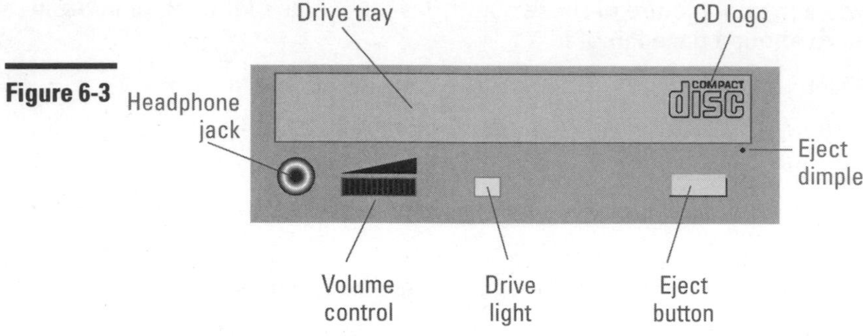

Figure 6-4

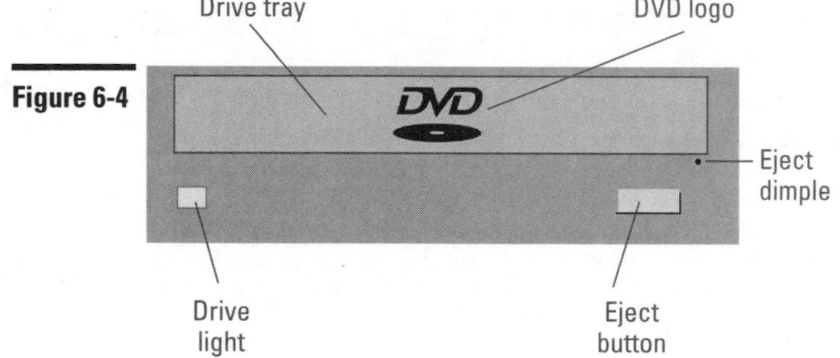

A typical computer CD stores anywhere from 650MB of data up to about 720MB.

A typical computer DVD stores up to 4.7GB of information.

See also "Ejecting a Removable Disk" and "Inserting a Removable Disk," later in this part.

Types of shiny discs

There exists a variety of CDs and DVDs. Originally, there were just CD-ROMs and DVD-ROMs. (Often, the *ROM* part isn't used when describing the disc.) Beyond those two read-only formats are CDs and DVDs that can be written to, by saving information similar to other disk drives in your computer system.

To use recordable CDs and DVDs, your PC must be equipped with the proper CD or DVD drive, one that can record information as well as read it from the disc. The type of drive you have determines which type of disc you can record to.

Here are the currently popular types of recordable CDs and DVDs:

CD-R: This type of CD can be written to, but only once. After the CD is *burned,* it can be used in any computer and read just like any CD. Data and music CDs can be created by using CD-Rs. Note that some CD-Rs are specifically manufactured for music, and others are made for data. The label on the CD-R package tells you which is which.

CD-RW: This type of CD can be written to just like a CD-R. Unlike a CD-R, however, this disc can be completely erased and used again, if needed. These discs are slightly more expensive than regular CD-Rs and can be played only on CD-RW-compatible CD players.

DVD-R: The most compatible format, DVD-Rs can be played on most computer DVD players as well as on video DVD players. If you want to make "home movie" DVDs, this format is the one you want.

DVD-RW: This format is the same as DVD-R, although the discs can be completely erased and used again.

DVD+R: This write-once version of the DVD+RW format is more efficient than the DVD-R format, although it's not widely supported.

DVD+RW: In this DVD-writing format, the disc can be erased and used over again. This format is very efficient, but it's not fully compatible with all DVD drives.

DVD-RAM: The oldest writeable DVD format is completely incompatible with all other DVD formats and is rarely used any more.

Some DVD drives allow recording on both sides of the disc. These double-sided discs sport a capacity of 9.4GB, which is simply double the 4.7GB you get on the single side of a DVD. Make sure you get a double-sided DVD if you plan to use such a drive.

See also Part XI, which covers creating your own data CDs and DVDs and musical CDs.

Playing a music CD or movie DVD

To play a musical CD or movie on a DVD, simply insert the disc into your computer's CD or DVD drive. The music or movie should play automatically. ***See also*** "AutoPlay," earlier in this part.

Drive Icons

Windows assigns unique icons to different types of disk drives. You can see these in the Computer window and in other locations in Windows where disk drives are referenced:

If your computer has a retro floppy drive, its icon appears in the Computer window, as shown in the margin.

The primary hard drive, the one that contains the Windows operating system, is flagged with a Windows logo. Additional hard drives don't sport the Windows logo.

An empty DVD drive sports its own icon. A CD drive is similar, although "CD-ROM" replaces the "DVD" text.

Inserting a DVD movie or data disc into a DVD drive results in a new icon, such as the one shown in the margin. Some movies and data discs have a unique icon, such as a logo or tiny picture.

The music CD icon replaces the standard CD or DVD icon whenever a musical CD is inserted into the drive.

Inserting a CD-R/RW or recordable DVD results in an icon appearing, indicating the type of disc inserted, such as the DVD+R disc icon shown in the margin.

All removable drives, such as flash memory drives, share this icon.

Any drive on the network that has been mapped to your PC appears with "network plumbing" beneath its icon.

Any disk drive or folder on your PC that is shared for networking appears with a special "sharing buddies" icon in the lower-left corner.

Some special media may show other icons. For example, Zip disks appear with their own, unique icon — unless the Zip software isn't running, in which case the generic "removable media" icon appears instead.

Drive Letters

Disk drives in your PC are assigned famous letters of the alphabet, starting with A and moving on from there. This historical thing with PCs dates back to the first PC, which lacked a hard drive. That explains why the drive letter assignment isn't exactly logical.

Disk drives A-B-C

The first three drive letters are the same for all PCs:

- **Drive A:** Drive A is reserved for the PC's floppy drive, even if your PC doesn't have a floppy drive.
- **Drive B:** Drive B isn't used on modern PCs. Originally, it was assigned to the PC's second floppy drive.
- **Drive C:** Drive C is the first hard drive. This is the PC's main hard drive, the one on which the operating system (Windows) is usually found.

Drive D and beyond

Beyond drive C, there are no rules regarding which drive is given which letter. This situation causes some confusion in that many users mistakenly believe that drive D is always the CD-ROM drive. That's not true.

The PC's startup program assigns drive letters D and up to any disk storage devices found beyond the first hard drive. Priority is given to any additional hard drives. So, if your PC has two hard drives, the second one is drive D.

After hard drives, the next priority is given to internal disk drives, such as CD-ROMs or perhaps a Zip drive. Those drives receive the next letter in the alphabet after the hard drives are assigned letters.

Finally, removable disk drives are given drive letters in the order in which the computer finds those drives.

Network drives can be manually added to your computer system at any time. When the drive is added, you're allowed to choose a drive letter based on whatever letters are left. ***See also*** Part X, about adding a network drive to your PC.

Drive Z

The highest letter allowed for any disk drive on your PC is drive letter Z.

Changing drive letters

For many weird and unexplained reasons, removable drives may not always be assigned the same drive letter when they're attached to your PC. Even so, you can change the letter for any non–hard drive in your computer's disk system. Obey these steps:

1. Open the Control Panel.
2. Open the Administrative Tools icon.
3. In the Administrative Tools window, open the Computer Management icon.

   Click the Continue button if you see a User Account Control security warning.
4. In the Computer Management window (it's a "console"), select Disk Management from the list on the left.

   Wait a moment while the console is populated with information about your PC's disk system.
5. Right-click the disk drive volume you want to change.

   For example, right-click the CD-ROM drive or a removable USB drive.
6. Choose the command Change Drive Letter and Paths from the pop-up shortcut menu.
7. Click the Change button.

8. In the Change Drive Letter or Path dialog box, shown in Figure 6-5, choose a new drive letter from the pop-up menu.

Figure 6-5

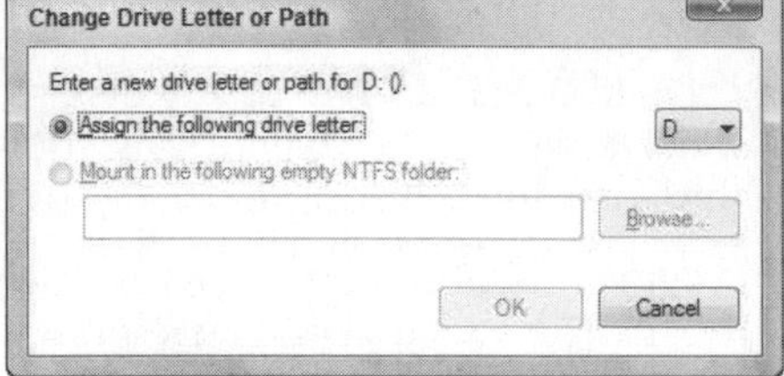

9. Click OK to confirm the change.
10. Click Yes after reading the warning message.

    This warning is true, especially with regard to CD/DVD drives from which you've installed software. Those installation programs assume that the same drive letter is used every time they're run. Changing the drive letter may confuse them and lead to much anguish and woe in the future.

    Regardless, the drive letter is changed.
11. Close the AutoPlay window, if it rears its ugly head.
12. Close any other open windows or dialog boxes.

Windows remembers the drive change; the next time you start Windows or insert a removable drive, the new letter is used and can be seen in the Computer window.

Ejecting a Removable Disk

When you use a drive that has removable media, such as a floppy drive, CD/DVD drive, or even a media card reader that connects to a USB port, you must properly eject the disk or media when you're done with it. The worst thing to do is to yank the media out of the drive. That's bad! Instead, heed the ejecting words of wisdom in the following sections.

Ejecting a floppy disk

Don't eject any floppy disk you're still using. Be certain that all the files you opened are saved and closed. Be certain that any open window displaying the floppy disk's contents is closed.

To eject the disk, push the floppy drive's disk ejection button. This pushes the disk out of the drive just a tiny bit. Pinch the disk with your fingers and remove it the rest of the way.

Ejecting a CD or DVD

When you're done with a DVD or CD, eject it as follows:

1. Open the Computer window.
2. Click to select the CD-ROM or DVD drive icon.
3. Click the Eject button on the toolbar.

If the disc is still in use, Windows lets you know by displaying an error message. Heed that message to fix things (such as to quit a program or close an open program window). Then try again.

Put the disc back into its protective envelope or container, and store it in a proper place.

Don't leave discs lying about, where they can be scratched and damaged permanently.

For tray-type drives, press the drive's Eject button to retract the tray after the computer ejects the disc.

When the disc is stuck or the power is off and you need to eject the disc, use the dimple, or small hole, near the tray or insertion hole. Sticking a straightened paper clip into the hole and pushing gently pops the disc out of the drive.

Ejecting other media

When you're done using a USB flash drive, media card, or other media, properly eject that card by following these steps:

1. Open the My Computer window.
2. Click to select the media card's icon.
3. Click the Eject button on the toolbar.
4. Remove the media.

When you're using a media card reader, do not just yank it out! The eject command is only for the media. To remove the media reader, you must follow other steps. ***See also*** "Working with Removable USB Drives," later in this part.

The Floppy Drive

The former king of removable disk storage is the floppy drive and its floppy disk. Today, it's rare to find a floppy drive on a new PC, yet that drive letter A (and B) is reserved for the fallen crown. And the floppy drive still has many fanatic followers.

The PC's one and only floppy drive is labeled Drive A. This is consistent with all PCs.

The floppy drive consumes a standard PC floppy disk. The floppy disk is contained inside a hard-plastic, 3½-inch shell. The shell has a sliding door to protect the disk.

Floppy disks can be purchased at any computer or office-supply store. Buy the disks labeled IBM PC-compatible. To save time, buy floppy disks that are preformatted.

Formatting floppies

A floppy disk must be formatted before you can use it. This *formatting* is merely a technical process that prepares the disk for use, for storing information.

Formatting can also be done to completely erase a disk and start over afresh. In this case, it's also referred to as *reformatting.*

Here's how you format or reformat a floppy disk:

1. Insert the floppy disk into Drive A.

   Any information already on the disk is erased by formatting. Do not format any disk that you don't want to fully erase.

2. Open the Computer icon on the desktop.
3. Right-click Drive A, the floppy drive.
4. Choose Format from the pop-up menu.

   There's no need to mess with any of the settings in the Format dialog box, shown in Figure 6-6. If you're merely reformatting a disk, however, you can click the Quick Format option, which saves some time.

5. Click the Start button.
6. If a warning dialog box appears, click the OK button to continue with the format operation.
7. Wait. (Formatting takes some time.)

   If the disk fails to format, you can try again: Eject the bum floppy disk and throw it away. Insert a new floppy disk and start over with Step 3.

8. Click OK to confirm that formatting is complete.

   You can optionally remove the disk here, insert another floppy disk, and click the Start button to format the disk.

9. When you're done, click the Close button to dismiss the Format dialog box.
10. Use your floppy disk.

Figure 6-6

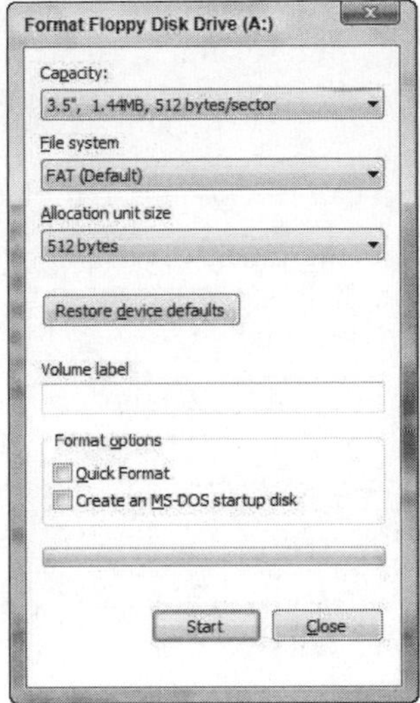

Copying a file to Drive A

A floppy disk is used just like any other disk in your computer system. You merely choose that disk from a window or from the Address bar's drop-down list. Then, you can start using the files stored on a floppy disk.

To copy a file to Drive A, regard these steps:

1. Ensure that a formatted floppy disk is in Drive A.
2. Select the file or group of files.
3. Choose File⇨Send To⇨Floppy Disk Drive (A:) from the menu.

Remember to remove the floppy disk from Drive A when you're done with it.

See also Part VII for more information on working with files.

Floppy do's and don'ts

Don't save information directly to a floppy disk. Save to the hard drive first; use the floppy disk only for *copies* of information.

Don't download information from the Internet directly to a floppy disk. Someone somewhere offered this as a tip once, but it's not a tip. It's a gross mistake because the floppy disk cannot handle most downloads. Download to the hard drive, which is why your PC has a hard drive.

Remember to remove the floppy disk when you're done with it. If you forget, the PC may try to start itself from the floppy disk, which results in an error message. (Remove the disk in that case, and then press the Enter key to continue starting the PC.)

Don't touch the floppy disk itself, although you can freely handle the outer shell.

Don't try to eject or remove a floppy disk when the floppy drive's light is on. The light indicates that the computer is reading the disk. It's a bad thing to remove a floppy disk while the computer is reading from that disk.

Floppy disks come with labels. Use them! Peel and stick the label on the disk and give the disk a descriptive name.

Don't use a sticky note as a floppy disk's label. Those notes can peel off and get stuck inside the drive.

Don't insert a floppy disk into a Zip disk or CD-ROM drive. Likewise, don't try to wedge a floppy disk into one of the PC's cooling vents.

Don't remove a floppy disk from the drive until you're done with it. That means that any open window referring to the floppy disk is closed and that any files you've opened from the floppy disk are saved and closed.

Avoid getting a floppy disk wet.

Don't leave a floppy disk in direct sunlight because it will warp and damage the disk.

Don't leave the floppy disk around magnets, which erases the disk's contents. Magnets can be found in speakers, so don't leave a floppy disk on or near your PC's speakers.

Avoid the temptation to use a floppy disk as a drink coaster.

Floppy disks go bad over time. That's because the disk itself is being rubbed by the drive as information is written to and read from the disk. Therefore, don't keep any valuable information only on the floppy disk.

Hard Disks and Drives

This is the skinny on the hard disk/hard drive puzzle: The *hard drive* is the physical unit. It's the whole enchilada. A hard disk lives inside the hard drive. So, unlike a DVD drive, where the disc can be removed from the drive, the hard disk inside the hard drive isn't going anywhere.

Technically, you should use the term hard drive to refer to the main source of long-term storage inside your PC: Drive C, Drive D, and so on.

Another term for a hard drive is *fixed disk* because the disk cannot be removed. It's "fixed" inside the hard drive. (In this sense, fixed means immobile, not repaired.)

All PCs have at least one hard drive, which is called Drive C.

Your PC can have additional hard drives, given letters D and higher.

External hard drives can also be added to the system.

It's possible for one physical hard drive to be split up into separate or logical hard drives. For example, a 100GB hard drive can be *partitioned* into two 50GB hard drives. This partitioning is usually done at the factory or when the disk is first installed. The partitions show up in the Computer window as separate hard drives. So, one physical hard drive inside your PC may appear as *logical* hard drives C, D and E.

Inserting a Removable Disk

Disk drives with removable disks, such as floppy drives, CD/DVD drives, and others, allow you to both insert and remove media. Of the two, inserting is the easier task. Ejecting a disk is trickier in that the computer might still be using the disk. For inserting a disk, though, there's no timing issue or question of when the computer is ready. Most of the time, you just stick in the disk and go.

See also the "AutoPlay" section, earlier in this part, for information on what happens after you insert a disk in your computer system.

Inserting a floppy disk

Floppy disks must be inserted into the floppy drive in order for them to be useful. Stick the disk into the drive with the label side up and the metal cover in first.

After you push in the disk almost all the way, the drive mechanism grabs the disk and quickly pulls it in the rest of the way. This makes a pleasing "thunk" sound.

Unlike other media, floppy disks aren't automatically detected by the computer system; AutoPlay never comes up. You must manually access the floppy disk to read its contents, by either opening the disk's icon in the Computer window or accessing the disk from an Open or Save As dialog box.

Inserting a CD or DVD

Inserting a CD or DVD is done differently, depending on the design of the drive. There are two types: slot and tray.

- **Slot:** The drive has a narrow slot into which you insert the disc. About one-third to halfway in, the drive's mechanism grabs the disc and pulls it in the rest of the way.
- **Tray:** The disc sits in a tray that slides in and out of the drive. To extend the tray, press a button on the front of the drive. When the tray is fully extended, drop the disc into the round holding area atop the tray. When the disc is centered, push the button again to retract the tray.

The button to extend or retract the tray is often labeled with the universal symbol for *eject,* as shown in the margin.

You can also retract the tray by gently pushing it back into the drive. Gently!

Discs are inserted label side up.

If the disc lacks a label, it may be double-sided. In any case, nothing bad happens when you insert the disc upside down. Just eject the disc, flip it over, and try again.

Inserting media into a card reader

Four common types of digital media are used in today's PCs. Each of them has a label side and a business end. The label side goes up, and the business end, which is either an edge full of tiny holes or metal teeth, goes in first.

Press firmly! Do not force. When the media seems to be stuck, it's probably in the wrong orientation. Try again.

See also "Working with Removable USB Drives," later in this part.

Putting a Drive's Shortcut Icon on the Desktop

One way to make a disk drive handy is to put a shortcut to that drive on the desktop. Here are those all-important steps:

1. Open the Computer window.
2. Right-click the drive icon that you want to place on the desktop.
3. From the shortcut menu, choose Create Shortcut.
4. Close the Computer window.

The drive's icon now appears as a shortcut on the desktop for handy access.

You can rename the icon by using the standard file-renaming command (***see also*** Part VII).

You can also put shortcuts to folders on the desktop (***see also*** Part VII).

It's okay to delete a shortcut icon, even a shortcut icon for a disk drive. This doesn't erase the drive or remove the drive from your system; you can always access the drive from the Computer window.

Types of Storage

Many types of media are used as permanent storage in a computer. In fact, this part's title, "Disk Storage," will most likely be anachronistic in a few years, when PCs no longer have true spinning disks in them. (My guess is that long-term computer storage will be solid state in the future.) But that's just picking nits.

A modern PC can have many types of long-term storage media. The most popular two are

- **Hard drive:** Primary storage. Pluses: Fast, cheap, high capacity. Minus: Not removable.
- **DVD/CD recordable drive:** Massive storage and distribution of new software. Pluses: Removable, widely used, reliable. Minuses: Slower than a hard drive.

These types of permanent storage media are also popular:

- **Flash memory:** Another handy form of removable storage. Pluses: Inexpensive, common, easy to use. Minuses: Relatively low capacity, slow.
- **Media cards:** Essentially the same thing as flash memory, though designed for use with various gizmos, such as digital cameras, MP3 players, handheld gaming devices, cellphones, and the like. A media card reader is required in order to access the card's information on the PC. Sometimes this reader is built in, although more often it's an extra device to add. Pluses: Popular and cheap. Minuses: Slow and low capacity.
- **Zip disk:** A great floppy disk replacement. Pluses: Easy to use, high-capacity compared to floppies, good support. Minuses: Not universally used, disks are expensive, slow.
- **Floppy drive:** Once the only form of storage on a PC, then the primary form of secondary storage. Pluses: Very few any more. Minuses: Rapidly vanishing, unreliable, low capacity.

Even more forms of permanent storage exist. At one time or another, you could have attached a vast variety of disk drives to a PC: WORM drive, MO drive, Bernoulli drive, tape drive, DAT drive, Super Floppy drive, Jaz drive, or another of various and sundry removable hard drives. Some of these more esoteric drives may still be available for specific purposes. Other drives were temporary solutions to problems long since solved in the technical arena.

Working with Removable USB Drives

Windows instantly recognizes any USB drive you attach to your PC. The drive is examined first; you may see a pop-up bubble from the notification area. The bubble may claim that Windows is looking for drivers for the device. After a while, the drive is added to the list of storage media in the Computer window, and the drive is ready for use. (The AutoPlay window may appear, prompting you for what to do next.)

Any USB drive added to your system can be used just like any other disk drive. Whether it's a USB hard drive, CD/DVD, or a flash memory drive, it all works the same: Insert or attach the drive. Use the drive.

Unlike with other drives, however, when you're done with the USB drive, you can remove it from the system. You must do it properly, or else you can damage the drive or lose information. So pay attention!

To properly remove a USB drive — whatever the type of drive — heed these steps:

1. Open the Computer window.
2. Right-click the drive icon.
3. From the shortcut menu, choose the item Safely Remove.

   Do not choose Eject! The eject command is used to remove media from the drive, such as a CD from a USB CD-ROM drive. When you want to remove the entire drive, you choose Safely Remove.
4. Remove the drive.

   Disconnect its USB cable or turn off the drive's power.

The drive may be busy; a warning message alerts you to the fact that the drive is still being used. If so, close any programs you were using that accessed the drive and try again. If that doesn't work, keep closing windows. If that doesn't work, restart Windows. That always works.

Part VII

The Stuff You Create

It's no longer a question of what a computer can do. The list of things that a computer *cannot* do is a short one. As computers have grown in power and storage, the list of things that they can manipulate and create is practically endless. Add in stuff that you'll collect from the Internet and you'll have a computer full o' stuff in no time! The consequence to all that is that you need to be deft at storing things in your computer — the stuff you create. The key to understanding the stuff you create is to know the *file*. Knowing about files and how to manipulate them is perhaps the best thing you can do to make your PC experience a happy and productive one.

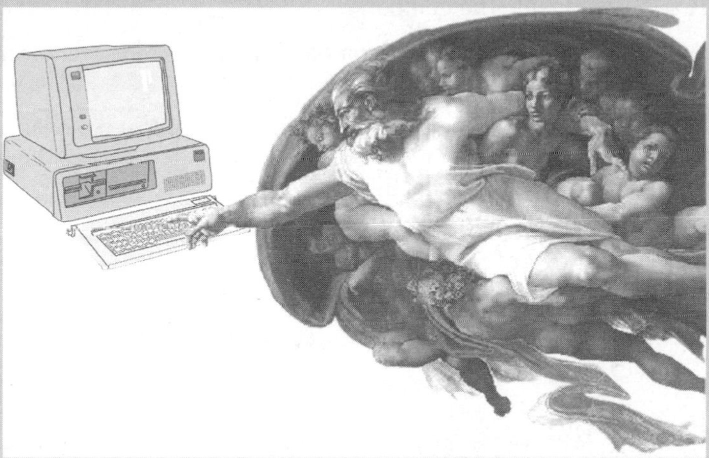

In this part . . .

- About a file
- Finding lost files
- Managing files
- Naming and renaming files
- Saving files
- Selecting icons

About a File

Aunt Trudy stores her preserves in jars. Uncle Marvin puts his coin collection into a safe. Joyce's recipes are in an index card box. Your neighborhood mad scientist stores his genetic mutations in plastic tubs. And your computer puts everything you create into a digital container called a file.

The file itself is a collection of stuff on disk. The contents can be anything, thanks to the versatility of the computer. Even so, the contents are the most important part about the file, just as the contents of a container are more important than the container itself.

The file is merely a bunch of binary digits — raw computer information. In fact, the file really doesn't know what its contents are. Other things tell the operating system about what's in a file, but on a basic level, all files are merely digital information stored inside the computer.

The information in a file is created in memory. Only when that information is stored on disk does it become a file.

The file is the basic storage unit in a computer. A graphical image is stored in a file. Text is stored in a file. Music is stored in a file. Video is stored in a file. Programs are stored in files. Everything is a file!

On the PC, files are stored on the permanent storage media. The primary storage for files is on the hard drive. But files can also be stored on removable disks, network drives, flash memory drives, and other media.

Another term for the stuff inside a file is data. *Data* is just the fancy computer term for "stuff" or "information."

Describing a file

A *file* is nothing more than a collection of bits, separate and unique from other files on the disk. The way that the computer — and you, the computer operator — knows about a file is by observing a number of clues. Those clues are file *attributes,* or ways to describe the file. Specifically, a file has these attributes:

- **Filename:** The name used to identify the file. The name is given when the file is first saved to disk. Hopefully, the name is descriptive and not too long.
- **Filename extension:** The last part of the filename, in which a one- to four-character code gives a hint about the file's contents or the type of file, or at least a clue to which program created the file.
- **File type:** A term related to the filename extension. It gives a clue to the file's contents or the program that created it.

- **Icon:** In the Windows graphical environment, the tiny pictures given to files to represent their presence. The icon that appears depends on the file type, which the computer knows by reading in the filename extension.
- **File size:** The number of bytes, or characters, that the file occupies.
- **File creation date:** The date that the file was first created and saved to disk.
- **File modified date:** The date the file was last written to, changed, or modified.
- **Attributes:** Determines whether the file is hidden (invisible), compressed, or read-only; has been backed up; is a system file; or has a number of other interesting effects or conditions.

Even more tidbits of information are available about a file, but those are too technical to bother with here.

Common file icons

There are zillions of icons for the zillions of types of files that exist. Even so, certain files are common and identified by common icons. Here's a small sampling:

Icon	*Extension*	*File Type*
	BMP	Windows Paint graphics; bitmap image
	EXE	Generic program file, although most program files have their own, unique icons
	(Varies)	Generic file, no specific type, because all files must have an icon
	HTM or HTML	Web page or HTML document
	DLL, SYS	System file, used by Windows
	MP3	Music file
	WMV	Video file
	PDF	Adobe Acrobat Reader document
	TXT or TEXT	Plain text

Many icons in Windows Vista show tiny previews of their contents, especially when larger versions of the icons are viewed.

Viewing file details in Windows Explorer

The best way to get more information about a file is to view it, to locate that file by using the Windows Explorer program (***see also*** Part VIII) and look at the file, as shown in Figure 7-1.

Figure 7-1

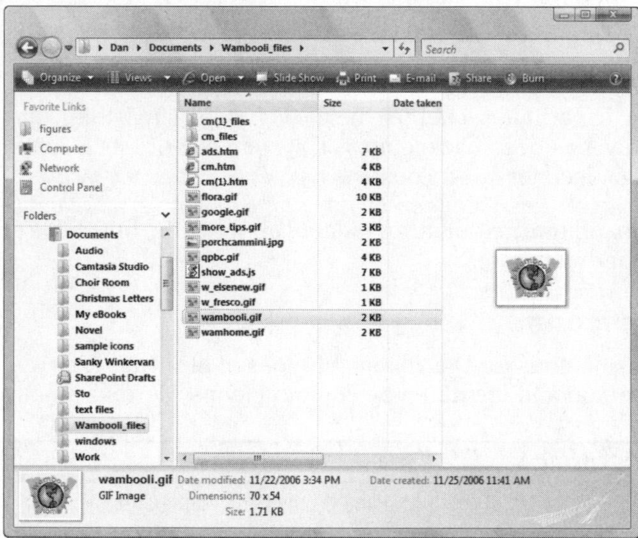

Immediately, the file's icon tells you a bit about the file, especially if you can recognize the file's icon. Otherwise, to see more information, you have many options in Windows Explorer.

First, use the Details pane at the bottom of the window. This area displays brief file details about any individual icon that's selected. If the details aren't visible, click the Organize toolbar button and, from its menu, choose Layout⇨Details Pane.

Second, you can use the Preview pane in Windows Explorer to preview the contents of most files. The Preview pane offers a sneak peek at graphics files and at other common file types. But the Preview pane doesn't preview all file types. To view the Preview pane, choose Layout⇨Preview Pane from the Organize toolbar button's menu.

Third, you can view the icons large or extra large. When you choose Large Icons or Extra Large Icons from the View button's menu on the toolbar, Windows Explorer offers a preview into the file's contents by displaying a thumbnail view on the file's icon.

Finally, you can view a host of file details by displaying the files in the Windows Explorer Details view: Click the Views button on the toolbar and choose Details from the menu.

In Details view, file information is shown in a table. Each row starts with the icon and filename. Columns of information march across the screen, displaying more information about each file.

You can adjust the columns, and the window's display, in many ways:

- The list of files can be sorted simply by clicking the column header. Click the same column header again to sort the list in reverse order.
- The column used to sort the list has a triangle in the top center. The triangle points up or down, depending on how the column is sorted (in ascending or descending order).
- Columns can easily be rearranged. Use the mouse to drag a column heading left or right. For example, to put the Type column before the Size column, drag the Type column heading to the left of the Size column.
- Column width can be resized by dragging the right edge of the column's heading left or right. Double-clicking the right edge resizes the column's width to match the widest item in that column.

You can add or remove columns from the Windows Explorer windows, in Details view: Right-click the mouse on any header to display a shortcut menu full of optional headers. Selected headers have check marks by them. When you choose the More option from the header shortcut menu, a Choose Details dialog box appears, as shown in Figure 7-2, listing dozens of potential headers and file description attributes.

Not every potential column applies to every file. Most columns describe attributes of music files.

A file's Properties dialog box

Discover information about any file by viewing the file's Properties dialog box. To see it, right-click the file's icon and choose the Properties command from the pop-up menu.

A file's Properties dialog box has two or more tabs, shown in Figure 7-3. The first one is the General tab, which offers lots of descriptive information about the file.

Figure 7-2

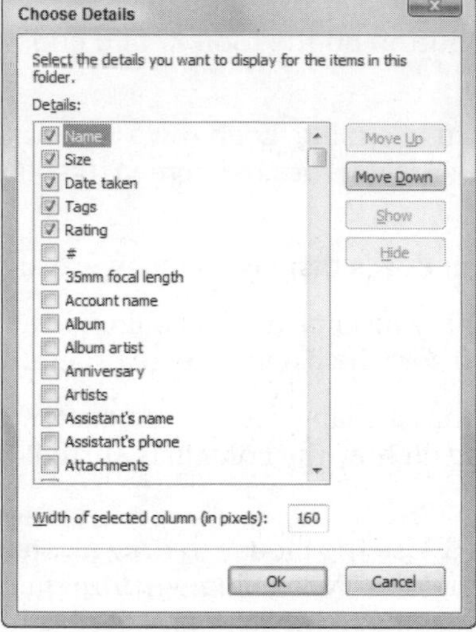

Figure 7-3

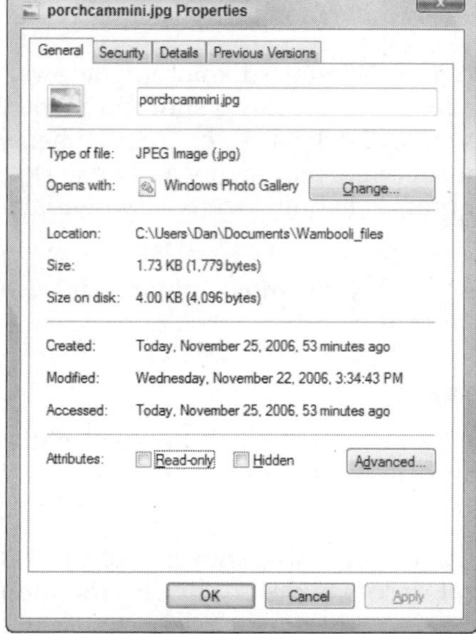

The other tabs offer further descriptive information about the file or, depending on the type of file, can be used to modify settings or control certain specifics of the file.

Creating Files

The breath of life inflates files into existence in one of three ways:

- You use software on your computer to create something and save that stuff to disk as a file.
- You copy a file from another computer, either over a network or from a removable disk.
- You download a file from the Internet, which is really the same point as in the previous bullet, but most people don't think in such a nerdy way.

The bottom line is that all files are created on some computer somewhere. The file starts out as amorphous bits hovering in RAM. Those bits are created and crafted by some program into meaningful information. That information is then saved to a disk somewhere as a file. From there, the file can go anywhere, to other computers across a network or to the Internet or a removable disk or to another computer.

All Windows programs use the Save As command to initially save a file to disk. ***See also*** "Saving Files," later in this part.

Finding Lost Files

Files get lost all the time. They're misplaced as they're copied, or often a file is quickly saved into the wrong folder, or you may just forget whatever crazy names you assigned to them. Lost files happen to beginners and experienced users alike. Even when you take pains to organize your information with folders and subfolders, you find yourself losing files.

Searching from the Start menu

The easiest place to start your file search is the Start menu. Near the bottom of that menu is a Search input box. Type a word or two as a starting point for your search, and Windows quickly fills the left side of the Start menu with items matching your search: You see matching filenames, files with the words you typed in their contents, e-mail messages, and all sorts of things to sift through, similar to what's shown in Figure 7-4.

Similar search text boxes are found in the upper-right part of any Windows Explorer window. For real searching power, though, use the Search window instead.

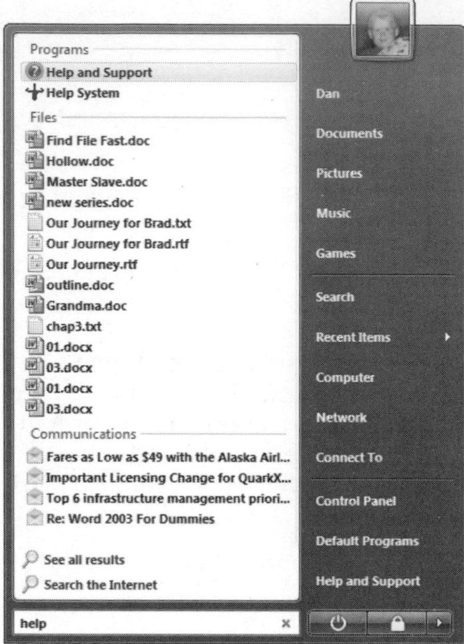

Figure 7-4

Summoning the Search window

Windows has a special Search window, specifically geared to meet your file-finding efforts. To use the Search window, choose the Search command from the right side of the Start menu.

The Search window, shown in Figure 7-5, appears when you press the F3 key when viewing the desktop. It also appears whenever search text is typed into the search box in the upper-right part of any Windows Explorer window.

The main advantage of the Search window is that it gives you access to the Advanced Search panel: Click the Advanced Search button to see that panel. The controls in the Advanced Search panel help you refine the search and search places outside the normal realm of Windows searches (such as the system folder or various program folders).

The Search Only buttons are used to refine what is being searched, specifically limiting the search to e-mail, documents, pictures, music, or the "other" category, which is just any other type of file.

Figure 7-5

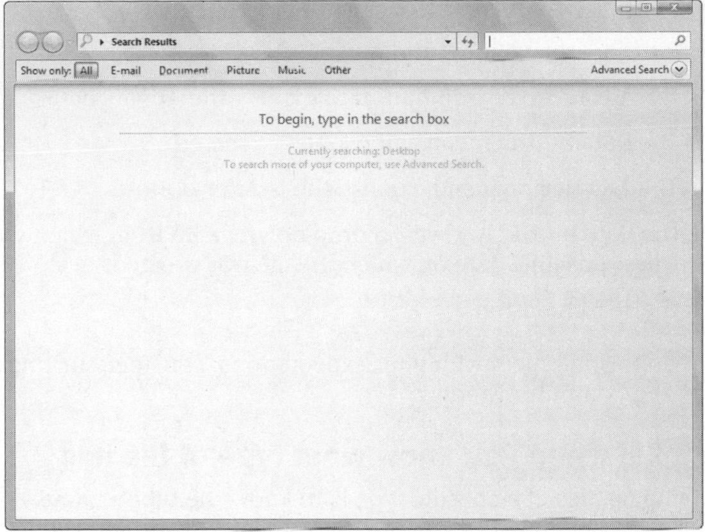

After a search is complete, the results appear in the Search window. Files are listed in Details view. To open a file, double-click its icon. To open the folder containing the file, right-click the file's icon and choose Open File Location from the shortcut menu.

Occasionally, the search results window is empty; no matching files could be found. This could mean that, indeed, there are no matching files, but most likely you're simply searching in the wrong place. Double-check the Address bar to confirm that the search starts in the proper folder, such as your account folder. When the proper folder isn't set, the search results may be misleading.

Finding a file when you know its name

If you named a file property and know its name, follow these steps to locate that file on your computer:

1. Open the Computer window.
2. Type the filename into the Search text box, found in the upper-right part of the window.

   You can type part of the name, all of the name, or even something remotely close to the name.
3. Press the Enter key.

To limit the search to just your account, open your account folder's window in Step 1.

Finding a file when you just created it recently

Beckon forth the Search window and pursue these steps:

1. Click the Advanced Search button to display the Advanced Search panel.
2. From the Date button menu, choose Date Created.
3. From the Any Button menu, choose the Is After option.
4. Click the Date button to reveal a drop-down menu from which you choose the earliest possible date on which the file was created.
5. Click the Search button.

When the results don't meet with your expectations, consider starting the search from the Computer window.

Finding a file when you know what type of file it is

The key to finding files of a specific type is to know the type's name. For example, music files can end in MP3, AIX, AU, or WAV. As long as you know the file type's filename extension, you can search for that file type, and Windows displays the full list of matching files.

When you don't know the type, simply search for all files: Specify an * (asterisk) in the Search text box. Then use the Type column heading to sort the list of found files by type, and scroll through the list to find what you want.

Searching for * (all files) creates a huge list!

Finding a file when you know that it contains a specific word

The Search command automatically scans through files to search for the word you type. So, to look for a file that contains the word *mountebank,* just type **mountebank** into the Search text box.

Managing Files

To help keep your files organized, Windows supplies you with a host of file-manipulating tools. You can copy, move, delete, and undelete files.

See also "Selecting Icons," later in this part, to work with groups of files at a time.

Copying files

When you copy a file, you create a duplicate — an exact copy — of that file in another folder or on another disk drive. In Windows, you have many ways to copy a file or group of selected files:

Copy and paste: Select the files to be copied. Press Ctrl+C to copy the file. Open the folder in which you want to place the copy, and then press Ctrl+V to "paste" the file.

You can also choose the Copy and Paste commands from the Organize button's menu: Click the Organize button on the toolbar to see the menu and access the Copy and Paste commands.

Dragging to copy: You need to have two windows open and visible on the desktop: the folder containing the original file and the folder to which you want to copy the file. Press and hold the Ctrl key on the keyboard, and then use the mouse to drag the file from one window to the other. (Pressing the Ctrl key ensures that the file is copied and not moved.)

Whenever you drag a file from one disk to another, the file is automatically copied.

Copy to folder: Select the files to be copied. Press Alt+E to access the hidden Edit menu. Choose Edit⇨Copy to Folder from the menu. Use the Copy to Folder window to locate the disk drive or folder for the file copies. Click to select that folder, and then click the Copy button.

Duplicating files

A file *duplicate* is merely a copy of a file made in the same folder. After following any of the directions from the preceding section, choose the same folder as the location for the file copy. The file is then duplicated, with the addition of the text *Copy* appended to the filename. The duplicate has the same contents, is the same size, and is the same type of file as the original.

See also "Making file shortcuts," a little later in this part.

Moving files

When you move a file, you create a duplicate of that file — just like a file copy — but the original is then destroyed. Windows has many commands for moving a file or group of selected files, and these are the most popular:

Cut and paste: Select the files you want to move. Press Ctrl+X to "cut" those files, preparing them for the move. (Nothing is moved yet; the files haven't been deleted.) Open the folder to which you want the files moved. Press Ctrl+V to paste the files, placing them in the new folder and removing them from the original folder.

You can also choose the Cut and Paste commands from the Optimize button's menu: On the toolbar, click the Optimize button, from which you can access the Cut and Paste commands.

Dragging to move: Open two folder windows on the desktop. The first window contains the file to be moved. The second window is the folder or disk drive to where you want the file moved. Use the mouse to drag the file from the first window to the second. If you're dragging the file to another disk drive, press and hold the Shift key while you drag the mouse. By holding down the Shift key, you ensure that the file is moved and not copied.

Whenever you drag a file from one folder to another folder on the same disk drive, the file is automatically moved.

Move to folder: Select the files you want to move. Press Alt+E to activate the Edit command on the (hidden) menu bar. Choose Edit⇨Copy to Folder. In the Move to Folder window, choose the disk drive or folder where you want to move the file. Select that folder, and then click the Move button.

Making file shortcuts

A *shortcut* is the same thing as a file copy, but without all the bulk of making a file copy. In a way, the shortcut is simply a placeholder icon. Internally, the icon references the original file so that when you open the shortcut, the original file opens instead.

Creating a shortcut works just like copying a file with Copy/Paste. The difference is that rather than use the regular Paste command, you make the shortcut by using Paste Shortcut instead.

Access the Paste Shortcut command by right-clicking in the folder in which you want the shortcut: After right-clicking, choose the Paste Shortcut command from the pop-up menu. You can also press Alt+E to summon the hidden Edit menu, and then choose Paste Shortcut from there.

A shortcut icon is flagged by a tiny arrow in its lower-left corner.

You can move, copy, rename, or delete a shortcut icon. Doing so doesn't affect the original file.

Moving, renaming, or deleting the original icon doesn't update the shortcut icon. In this case, the shortcut may get "lost." When you try to open the shortcut, Windows attempts to locate the original for you.

A file shortcut works only on your computer. You cannot e-mail a file shortcut to another computer and have it work. If you need to send a copy of a file to another computer, send a copy of the original; don't create a shortcut.

Deleting files

To delete a file, click to select the file's icon and choose the Delete command from the Organize button's menu on the toolbar. You can also use the Delete key on the computer's keyboard as a shortcut.

A warning may appear when you delete a file, to confirm that you really want to delete it. Click the Yes button to delete the file.

Permanently deleting files

If you want to delete a file permanently, with no possibility of recovery, select the file's icon and press Shift+Delete on the keyboard.

Files removed with Shift+Delete cannot be recovered from the Recycle Bin. They don't even go to the Recycle Bin! Some third-party utilities may be able to recover the file, but my point here is that you should be careful with Shift+Delete. Don't use it lightly.

Undeleting files

Deleted files are sent to the Recycle Bin. The deleted files aren't gone for good, though: You can recover deleted files from the Recycle Bin. Here's what to do:

1. Open the Recycle Bin icon on the desktop.
2. Choose Details from the View button's menu.

   In Details view, it's easier to sift and sort through the deleted files to find exactly what you're looking for.
3. If you know the filename, click the Name column heading to sort the deleted files alphabetically by name; if you know the date that the file was deleted, click the Date Deleted column heading.
4. Click to select the files you want to undelete.
5. Click the Restore This Item button or the Restore the Selected Items button on the toolbar.

   The file is returned to the folder from which it was deleted.
6. Close the Recycle Bin window.

You cannot preview or open files stored in the Recycle Bin.

Files can be restored to only the folder on the disk drive from which the file was originally deleted. To restore a file to another folder, first restore it to the original folder, and then move it to another folder.

There's a time limit on how long a file sits and waits in Recycle Bin purgatory. The limit depends on how many files occupy the Recycle Bin, so files can be in there quite a long time, or they may disappear after a few weeks. Either way, don't rely for too long on files dwelling in the Recycle Bin. If you need to restore a file, do so soon after it's deleted, or else it may be gone forever.

Recovering the previous version of a file

Files that you update, by saving a new version over the old version, as well as old files that are overwritten when you create a new file with the same name as an existing file, cannot be recovered from the Recycle Bin. After all, those files weren't deleted — they were replaced. But Windows Vista allows you to recover these replaced files by using the Previous Versions feature.

For example, if you change or accidentally overwrite a file, or if you merely need to recover an earlier version of a file that has been hopelessly modified, heed these steps:

1. Locate the file you want to recover, by opening its folder window.
2. Right-click the file's icon.
3. From the shortcut menu, choose Properties.
4. In the file's Properties dialog box, click the Previous Versions tab.

   The Previous Versions tab lists older editions of the file, including all recent updates and saves, as shown in Figure 7-6.

Figure 7-6

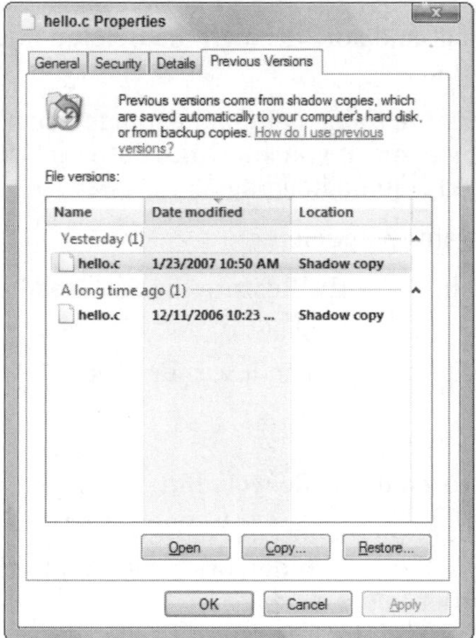

5. Select the previous version of the file you want to recover.
6. Click the Restore button.
7. Click the Restore button in the confirmation dialog box.
8. Click OK, and then close the file's Properties dialog box.

The previous version of the file is restored.

Naming and Renaming Files

All files stored in the computer need to be given a name. Here are the official rules:

- Filenames can contain letters, numbers, spaces, and most of the symbols you find on the computer keyboard.
- A filename must be at least one character long.
- A filename can be over 200 characters in length.
- Filenames cannot contain these specific characters:

  `" * / : ? \ | < >`

- Contrary to popular myth, you can start a filename with a number or punctuation symbol.
- Two files in the same folder cannot have the same name.

Short, descriptive filenames are best. (As filenames get longer, it's more difficult to see their full names displayed in a folder window.)

Windows isn't case sensitive when it comes to filenames. You can use upper- or lowercase letters in a filename. Note that other operating systems, as well as many Web page addresses, are case sensitive.

Although spaces are allowed in a filename, most folks opt to use underlines instead; for example:

```
Special_Finance_Report
```

The filename extension

A very special and important part of a filename is its *extension.* This last part of a filename begins with a period and is followed by up to four characters. Those characters are used in Windows to identify the file type.

Windows may or may not show you the filename extension. Often, it's hidden, especially for common file types. To show or hide the filename extension, heed these steps:

1. Open the Folder Options icon in the Control Panel.
2. Click the View tab.
3. Add or remove a check mark next to the option Hide Extensions for Known File Types.

   Adding the check mark hides all extensions. Removing the check mark directs Windows to display all filename extensions.
4. Click OK to dismiss the dialog box; close the Control Panel window.

See also "Common file icons," earlier in this part, for a sample list of filename extensions.

Renaming a file

You can change the name of a file by using the Rename command. Here's the easiest way to do that:

1. Select a file to rename.
2. Press the F2 key on the keyboard.

   The filename becomes selected. Note that the filename extension is *not* selected. You should not rename a file's extension.
3. Type the new name.
4. Press Enter to confirm the name.

I find that the F2 key works best because you're using the keyboard to rename the file anyway. Otherwise, you can choose the Rename command to access the Organize button's menu on the toolbar.

If Windows doesn't let you rename a file, you're probably using a forbidden character in the name or trying to use the name of a file that's already in the folder. Try again.

You can use the standard Windows editing keys when you rename a file. You can move the cursor left or right, select text, delete or insert text, and do just about anything else that you can do with regular text when you rename a file.

To rename a group of files all at one time, simply select the group and then use the Rename command on one of the files. The files are all given the same name, but with a numbered suffix from `(2)` up to however many files were selected.

You can use the Undo command to restore the original name. Undo must be used as the very next file command, though, or else it doesn't work.

Filename wildcards

Windows uses two characters, * and ?, as wildcards when specifying filenames. These wildcards can be used when you're searching for files, to help narrow or expand the search when you may not know all of a file's name.

The ? character is used to represent any single character in a filename.

The * character is used to represent a group of characters in a filename. Or, the * can be used by itself to represent all files.

Two other wildcards exist: . (dot) and .. (dot-dot). The single dot represents the current folder, or all the files in the current folder. The double dot represents the parent folder. ***See also*** Part VIII for more information on folders and parent folders.

Opening Files

To work on a file — a document, graphical image, music file, or anything you have created or collected — you need to open that file, to transfer it from permanent storage on disk into temporary storage in RAM. That's the only way you can work on the file; files must be in memory for the microprocessor to access and manipulate the data in the file.

There are many ways to open a file in Windows:

- Locate the file's icon in a folder window. Double-click the icon to open it, which either starts the program that created the file or runs a program to view the file's information.
- Locate a shortcut icon to the file. Opening the shortcut opens the original file itself.
- In an application, choose File➪Open from the menu or click the Open button on a toolbar to access the Open dialog box. Use the Open dialog box to locate the file. The keyboard shortcut for the Open command is Ctrl+O.
- From the Start button's menu, locate the Recent Documents submenu and choose the file from there. (Only recently opened files appear on the list.)

Opening a file opens the application that created that file — unless another application has priority. For example, opening a Paint document (graphical image) in Windows displays the image in the Windows Photo Gallery program, not in Paint.

When Windows cannot locate a program to open a file, it displays a dialog box asking you what to do or how to open the file. The best thing to do in this case is click the Cancel button. Windows cannot open the program, or the application that created the program isn't available.

To open a file in a specific program, right-click the file's icon and choose Open With from the pop-up menu. Then, you can select a specific program from the Open With submenu, and that program opens the file.

Pathnames

A pathname is a file's full address. Just like your house address, the pathname describes where a file is located: on which disk drive and in which series of folders the file can be found.

Pathnames are used on the Internet to open specific Web pages. The Web page address

```
http://www.microsoft.com/windowsvista/default.aspx
```

is a pathname, indicating the specific location of a file on a computer on the Internet.

On your PC, a pathname describes the location of a file. The pathname is composed of several parts:

- **Drive letter:** The drive letter is always followed by a colon.
- **Folders:** Starting with the root folder, represented by a single backslash, the pathname lists each folder and subfolder up to the file's location. Folder names are separated by the backslash character.
- **Filename:** After the last backslash comes an optional filename, complete with extension.

A *full pathname* contains all these elements. It starts with a drive letter and colon, and then it lists folders down to a filename; for example:

```
C:\Users\Dan\Documents\address.txt
```

The full pathname starts with a drive letter, a colon, and folders separated by backslashes, and then ends with a filename. To get to that file, you follow its path: Open drive C; open the Users folder; open the Dan folder; open the Documents folder; and then locate the `address.txt` file.

A full pathname can be used to run or open any program or file. The full pathname is merely a specific name telling the computer exactly where to find a file.

A partial pathname can be used to give the location for some files. For example, you may tell a co-worker to find the graphics files on this path on your computer:

```
Documents\Projects\2005\Summer\2341\Images
```

Using the path, the co-worker knows to start in the Documents folder and then open the following folders: Projects, 2005, Summer, 2341, and, finally, the Images folder.

The drive letter can be replaced by the name of another computer on the network. In this case, the pathname becomes a *network path;* for example:

```
\\MING\Public\current
```

The two backslashes at the start of the path identify a network pathname. The network computer is named MING. The folder being shared by MING is named Public. The subfolder named `current` is the location the network pathname refers to.

The Windows Explorer Address bar can be used to display pathnames: Simply click the icon on the far left side of the Address bar, and the pathname to the current folder appears.

Saving Files

Files are created by saving your stuff to disk. You work in a program. You make something. To keep it, you save it to disk: The file's contents are copied from memory to the disk drive.

Saving is simple: The computer does all the hard work. But the idea is important: You must save your stuff to disk so that you can have it later, just to keep, modify, print, or do whatever you will. But, to do all that stuff, you have to save your stuff in the first place.

Saving for the first time

Saving is a common task, so it has a universal command: File⇨Save. From the keyboard, the shortcut is Ctrl+S. This is consistent for just about every program in Windows.

When you save something for the first time, a special Save As dialog box appears. It allows you to do up to four things:

- Assign a descriptive name to the file.
- Choose a location for the file.
- Create a new folder for the file (if necessary).
- Save the file as a special type (if necessary).

You don't have to type the filename extension when you're saving a file. The application automatically adds the proper extension for the type of file being saved.

Saving after the first time

After the file is saved for the first time, it's associated with the filename and location you specified in the Save As dialog box. To save the file again, choose File⇨Save or use the Ctrl+S keyboard shortcut. This updates the existing file previously saved to disk.

Save often. The more you work, the more you save. Save before you print. Save when you get up to take a break. Save after doing something brilliant. Save before you quit.

Closing a document

The last thing you do with a document is close it. When you're done working on the document, or when you're done with the program, you can choose File⇨Close from the menu. If the document needs to be saved, you're asked to save it one last time. Then the document is closed, safely saved on disk.

The keyboard shortcut for the Close command is Ctrl+W. This is common to most, but not all, programs.

If you just plan on quitting a program (you're done for the day), you can use the File➪Exit command to both close the document (saving it to disk) and quit the program. The keyboard shortcut for closing a program is Alt+F4.

Selecting Icons

Windows lets you work with multiple files at a time. The key is to *select* the gang of files. After they're selected, the files can be manipulated as a group, which saves time over repeatedly issuing the same command on individual files.

The standard file-manipulation commands — Cut, Copy, Delete, Rename — affect all selected files.

Files can be selected in only one folder at a time. When you need to work with files in multiple folders, you must do so one folder window at a time.

The following sections discuss the many techniques for selecting a group of files.

Selecting a single icon

To select a single icon, click it with the mouse. The icon is then highlighted, indicating that it has been selected for action.

Selecting all icons in a window

To select all icons in a folder window, choose the Select All command from the Organize button's menu on the toolbar. The keyboard shortcut for the Select All command is Ctrl+A.

Selecting more than one icon

The Ctrl key is the secret to selecting more than one icon in a window. Press and hold the Ctrl key, and then click each individual icon with the mouse. By holding down the Ctrl key, you direct Windows to remember the files you clicked, keeping them all selected.

An icon stays selected even when you scroll around the window to search for new icons. As long as you Ctrl+click an icon, the rest of the selected icons in a window stay selected.

If you click the mouse (no Ctrl key) anywhere in the window, all selected files become deselected and you have to start over again.

Lassoing a group of icons

To select a group of icons, drag the mouse over them. Drag the mouse down and to the right to "lasso" the icons, selecting a rectangle of icons at once. (This technique doesn't work well in List view and Details view.)

Selecting all but a few icons

Select all the icons in the window first. Then press and hold the Ctrl key to click the icons you don't want selected. As you Ctrl+click icons, they're unselected.

Grabbing a range of icons

When you choose List or Details or Small Icons from the toolbar's View button menu, you can select a swath of icons by following these steps:

1. Click to select the first icon in the list.
2. Press and hold the Shift key, and then click to select the last icon in the list.

   The icons between the first and second click are all selected.
3. Release the Shift key.

Selecting two ranges of icons

To select multiple ranges of icons, follow the instructions in the preceding section. To select the second range, press and hold the Ctrl key. Keep the Ctrl key down and click the first icon in the range. Release the Ctrl key. Press and hold Ctrl+Shift and click the last icon in the second range. Release Ctrl+Shift.

Deselecting an icon from a group

Pressing and holding the Ctrl key while you click a selected icon deselects that icon. Release the Ctrl key when you're done deselecting.

Part VIII

Organizing Your Stuff

The topic of organizing files is directly related to the concept of folders. Folders contain files. Folders can also contain other folders, or subfolders, and thus begins the organization adventure: By grouping similar files into folders, or by organizing files into folders by project, you begin to organize your stuff.

In this part . . .

- About folders
- About Windows Explorer
- Compressed (Zip) folders
- Directories
- Folder options
- Folders for your stuff
- Managing folders
- The root folder
- Subfolders

About Folders

Folders are containers for files — just like in the real world. In fact, the file cabinet metaphor has been used for dozens of years to describe a PC's hard drive.

In a computer, a folder can hold a huge (virtually unlimited) number of files. Of course, you don't want to pack zillions of files into a single folder. That would defeat the purpose. Instead, folders are used to keep like files together.

A folder in Windows is flagged with a folder icon. The icon shown in the margin represents a generic folder. Folder icons can be customized and changed; ***see also*** "Changing a folder icon," later in this part.

When a folder contains files, it shows a thumbnail preview of those files, which is best seen when viewing icons in the Large view or Extra Large view in the Windows Explorer window.

Opening the folder icon displays its contents in a Windows Explorer window. The window lists the files that live inside the folder.

Folders can also contain other folders — folders within folders — just to keep things organized.

About Windows Explorer

Windows uses a program named Windows Explorer to display the contents of folders and to list files (icons). It's a Windows Explorer window you see whenever you open a folder.

To start Windows Explorer, you simply find a folder and open it.

To manually start Windows Explorer, from the Start button's menu, choose All Programs⇨Accessories⇨Windows Explorer.

The keyboard shortcut for Windows Explorer is Win+E, where Win is the Windows key.

Around the Windows Explorer window

The Windows Explorer window, delightfully illustrated in Figure 8-1, is extremely customizable. At minimum, it displays a list of files, but even that list can be shown in several different views.

At the top of the Explorer window is the *Address bar.* It indicates which folder is being shown, but can also be used to navigate through the folders, as shown elsewhere in this part.

Figure 8-1

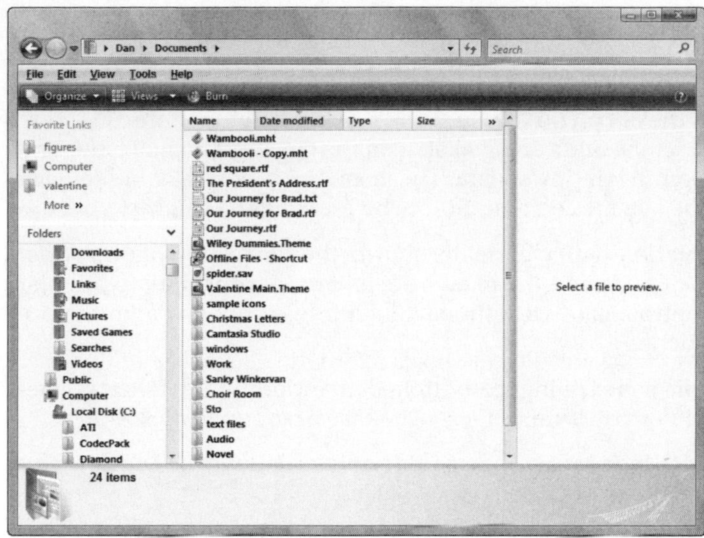

In the middle of the window are the icons or contents of the folder. The icons can be shown in several different ways, depending on which option you choose from the Views button's menu on the toolbar:

- **Extra Large Icons:** Files and folders are shown in the largest size, with many icons previewing the file or folder contents.
- **Large Icons:** Files and folders are shown using large icons with previews, but not as huge as with the Extra Large Icons option.
- **Medium Icons:** When you select this "Goldilocks" option, files are shown neither too large nor too small, but *just right.* Various icons to preview the file and folder contents are available.
- **Small Icons:** Icons are shown in a small format, without any preview.
- **List:** Icons are the same size as with Small Icons, but appear in a multi-columned list.
- **Details:** The icon size is small, but each icon appears as a row in a grid with various informative columns displaying additional file information.
- **Tiles:** Icons are shown in the same size as Medium Icons, but next to each icon appears additional information, such as the file type and size.

Around the list of files, the Windows Explorer window optionally displays up to four different items:

- **Menu bar:** A throwback to Windows XP, the menu bar is only for those who miss the old menu-driven version of Windows Explorer. Most of the useful menu commands are available on the Organize menu or by right-clicking in a folder in Windows Vista. The menu bar is normally hidden, although it can be summoned temporarily by pressing the F10 key.
- **Navigation pane:** Normally shown, the Navigation pane consists of two parts: On top is a list of favorite folders — shortcuts to popular places. On the bottom is the traditional folder tree, although I admit that it's rather scrunched.
- **Details pane:** Along the bottom of the window, the Details pane offers specific information about a selected file or group of files.
- **Preview pane:** On the right side of the window, the Preview pane can show the contents of certain types of files.

To show any of these items, or to hide one, choose the item's command from the Organize button's menu: Click the Organize button on the toolbar, choose Layout, and then choose the proper item from the Layout submenu.

The size of each pane can be adjusted to be wider or narrower. To make the adjustment, point the mouse at the border between the pane and the list of files. When you find the sweet spot, the mouse pointer changes to a two-way arrow. You can then drag the mouse in or out to resize the pane.

You can hide the folder list in the Navigation pane by clicking the downward-pointing arrow to the right of the word *Folders.* To redisplay the folder list, click the upward-pointing arrow next to Folders when it appears at the bottom of the Navigation pane.

See also Part VII for information on the Search text box, which appears in every Windows Explorer window.

The Address bar

In the Windows Vista version of Windows Explorer, the Address bar becomes quite powerful, by gaining new navigation abilities not previously seen in Windows.

At its most basic level, the Address bar shows which folder is being viewed, as shown in Figure 8-2. The *pathname* to the folder is shown, starting with either the account folder name or the top-level disk drive or network folder name.

Figure 8-2

A downward-pointing triangle on the far right end of the Address bar can be clicked to display a drop-down menu full of previous pathnames and locations. This menu comes in handy when revisiting certain locations.

Use the Refresh button to update the folder contents displayed in the window. This update is necessary for removable disks or network drives where the content may change (new files are added or old files are removed). Clicking the Refresh button directs Windows to update the folder's contents.

The Back and Forward buttons can also be used to help move from one folder to another. The tiny Recent Pages triangle can also be used to hop to and from folders recently displayed in the Windows Explorer window.

Each folder shown on the Address bar is separated by a triangle. Clicking the far-left triangle displays the top-level storage areas in your computer, as shown in Figure 8-3. Clicking any other triangle displays a menu of folders available at the same level as the folder that's listed. I believe that you'll find using the triangles on the Address bar a more efficient way to navigate through the PC's storage system than using the tree structure found in the Navigation pane.

Figure 8-3

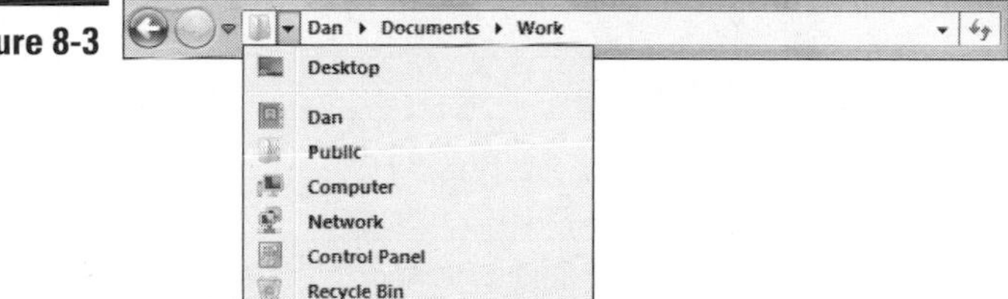

Managing your favorite folders

The top part of the Navigation pane contains a list of *favorite* folders, or links to folders you may find that you visit most often. For example, the list of links may contain shortcuts to the Computer folder, the Network folder, the Control Panel, your account folder, or a number of popular folders or locations. You can even add other folders, such as project folders or places you visit most often.

To add a folder to the list of favorites, simply drag it from the main part of the window into the favorites list.

To remove a folder from the list of favorites, right-click the folder's icon. Choose Remove Link from the pop-up menu, and the folder's link is gone. I highly recommend removing any preassigned links; the Favorite Links area is yours, and you should customize it to your needs.

Items in the Favorite Links area appear as shortcut icons in your account's Links folder. Even so, adding and removing links as just described is easier than messing with shortcuts directly in the Links folder.

The tree structure

Holding over from the earliest days of Windows is the *tree structure,* a visual representation of your computer's storage system that can be found in the bottom part of the Navigation pane, on the left side of the Windows Explorer window.

The tree structure lists storage devices on, and available to, your computer, beginning with the desktop and then going "down" from there. The purpose of the tree structure is to help you navigate through disk drives, and the folders on those drives, to help find the location you want. It's a shortcut.

Items in the tree structure that contain subfolders have a triangle to their left. The triangle points to the right and appears hollow when the folder is closed. Clicking that icon opens the folder to display any subfolders.

Open folders have a dark triangle next to them, pointing down and to the right.

You can also use the keyboard to navigate through the tree structure, if you clicked a folder to select it:

Key	*Action*
Up	Move up
Down	Move down
Left	Move left or open a closed branch
Right	Move right or close an open branch
+	Open a branch (without moving)
–	Close a branch (without moving)
*	Open all branches

The toolbar

Windows Explorer may have banished the menu bar, but replacing it is a handy, multifunction toolbar. The toolbar comes with two standard buttons, Organize and Views, both of which display menus with common file and folder commands.

Beyond the standard buttons, the toolbar displays contextual buttons, depending on which items are selected (or not) in the window. Here's a smattering of buttons you may find:

Burn: The selected files or folders are marked for immediate burning to a DVD or CD. When a recordable disc isn't in the drive, Windows prompts you to enter a disc so that it can be immediately written to.

Email: The Email button loads up any selected files in the window and attaches them to a new e-mail message.

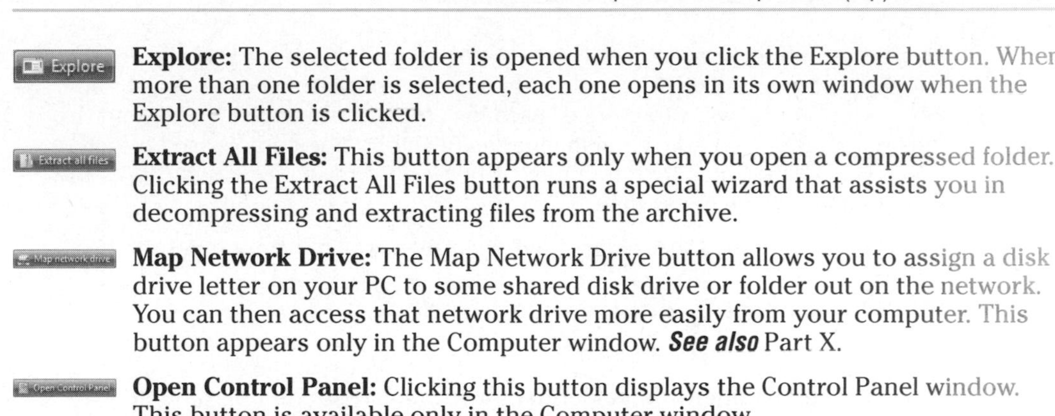

Explore: The selected folder is opened when you click the Explore button. When more than one folder is selected, each one opens in its own window when the Explore button is clicked.

Extract All Files: This button appears only when you open a compressed folder. Clicking the Extract All Files button runs a special wizard that assists you in decompressing and extracting files from the archive.

Map Network Drive: The Map Network Drive button allows you to assign a disk drive letter on your PC to some shared disk drive or folder out on the network. You can then access that network drive more easily from your computer. This button appears only in the Computer window. ***See also*** Part X.

Open Control Panel: Clicking this button displays the Control Panel window. This button is available only in the Computer window.

Open: Clicking the Open button opens whatever files are selected. For individual files, the Open button displays a menu full of programs that can be used to open that file.

Print: The Print button is used to print the selected file or files. The files are opened by the program that created them (or by whichever program is assigned to open the file), where the file is then printed. The program then closes.

Share: The selected files are flagged for sharing by other users on the same computer when you click the Share button. This option involves a bit more setup than most others; I recommend that you use instead the Public folder on your PC to share files; ***see also*** Part X.

System Properties: This button appears only in the Computer window; clicking the System Properties button displays the System Properties dialog box, normally accessed from the Control Panel.

Uninstall or Change a Program: Clicking this button opens the Programs and Features icon from the Control Panel, allowing you to remove or change an installed program. This button appears only in the Computer window.

Note that some buttons are available only in some windows. Also, when more buttons are available than can appear on the toolbar, a Show More chevron appears on the right end of the toolbar. Click that chevron or button to display the remaining toolbar buttons.

Compressed (Zip) Folders

A special type of folder in Windows is the compressed folder, also known as a *Zip* file. This folder holds other files (and folders), just like any other folder in Windows. But the files inside it are digitally compressed and take up less disk space.

Compressed folders aren't really used like regular folders for storing files. Instead, they work like shipping containers: You put into a compressed folder any stuff that you want to store or perhaps ship via e-mail elsewhere, and the files are stored in as efficient a manner as possible. The compressed folder keeps the various files together; plus, it takes up less space, which makes the file-sending task take less time.

In Windows, compressed folders have their own, special zipper icon.

Making an empty compressed folder

To create a compressed folder, abide by these steps:

1. Open the folder in which you want to create the compressed folder.

   Or, you can create the compressed folder on the desktop, although I don't recommend using the desktop for creating new files.

2. Right-click in the folder window.
3. From the pop-up menu, choose New⇨Compressed (Zipped) Folder.

   The new folder appears with the name `New Compressed (zipped) Folder.zip`.

4. Type a new name for the folder; press Enter to lock in the name.

Compressed folders are named just like files. Ensure that you don't rename the `.zip` filename extension when renaming a compressed folder.

Adding files to a compressed folder

Adding files to a compressed folder works just like adding files to any other folder: You can copy and paste, drag and drop onto the compressed folder's icon, or open the compressed folder window and then drag and drop.

You cannot use either the Move This File or Copy This File command to place files into a compressed folder, nor can you use the Save As dialog box to save a file to a compressed folder. Remember that compressed folders aren't real folders.

Making a compressed folder from one or more files

When you know which files you want to place into a compressed folder, you can easily create the folder and put the files into that folder all at once. The secret is to select the files you want to compress first. Then right-click one of the selected files and choose Send To⇨Compressed (Zipped) Folder from the pop-up menu. The files are packed into the compressed folder and given the name of the first file that's selected (but with the .zip file extension). You can then rename the file, or press Enter to accept the given name.

Extracting files

Files inside a compressed folder exist in a compacted state. You can view their names, and some types of files can be previewed. But to truly make use of the file, such as to open a document for editing or to run a program file, that file must be *extracted* from the compressed folder and placed into a real folder.

To *extract,* or decompress, files from a compressed folder, heed these steps:

1. Open the compressed folder.

2. Click the Extract All Files button on the toolbar.

   A special file-extraction wizard window appears, assisting you in the file-extraction operation.

3. Choose a folder as a destination for the extracted files.

   Windows assumes that you want the files in a folder with the same name as the compressed folder. This assumption is okay most of the time, although you can use the Browse button to choose another folder.

   I recommend keeping a check mark next to the option Show Extracted Files When Complete.

4. Click the Extract button.

   The files are all pulled from the compressed folder and placed into the folder you specified, which is then opened and displayed in a window.

After extracting the files, feel free to delete the compressed folder. An exception to this recommendation is when you're downloading a program from the Internet. In that case, I recommend keeping the original compressed folder in the Downloads folder for possible later use.

You can also extract files from the archive by using any of the standard file-copying or -moving techniques. For example, you can cut or copy a file from the compressed folder window and paste the file elsewhere, or you can drag files from a compressed folder window into another folder window.

Directories

The old, original term for a file folder was *directory.* This term, which hearkens back to the early 1970s, was used widely. Remember that way back when, computers were mostly text devices. A directory of files was like a directory of tenants in a building, a simple list of contents.

Folder is merely a newer term for *directory.*

A subfolder is the same thing as a *subdirectory.*

The root folder can also be called the *root directory.*

Although Microsoft shuns the term *directory,* occasionally you still see it used in documentation and bandied about by old-timers who refuse to change with the times.

Folder Options

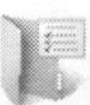

The way folders look and how they behave in Windows is controlled via the Folder Options icon in the Control Panel. Opening that icon displays the Folder Options dialog box. Two tabs in the Folder Options dialog box control how a folder behaves: General and View.

On the General tab, you can control how folder windows work. You choose whether opening new folders happens in the same window or in a new window. You can also select whether one or two clicks are required to open files. (Note that this book and other documentation assume that two clicks are required to open files and folders.)

On the View tab, you can control various details about what shows up and what doesn't show up in a folder window. One item worth noting is the display of *hidden* files. If you want hidden files to appear in a window, put a check mark by the item labeled Show Hidden Files and Folders. Note that this option is really needed as much in Windows Vista as it was in previous versions of Windows.

You can also elect to show all filename extensions, by removing the check mark by the item labeled Hide Extensions to Known File Types.

Choosing a folder template

If you know that a specific folder will be used to hold a specific type of file — music, graphics, text — you can customize that folder with a template, which makes Windows really shine and offers you the best way to view certain types of files.

To modify a folder with a template, follow these steps:

1. Right-click the folder.

   Do not open the folder; just right-click its icon.

2. Choose Properties from the shortcut menu.

3. In the folder's Properties dialog box, click the Customize tab.

   What you see should look similar to Figure 8-4.

Figure 8-4

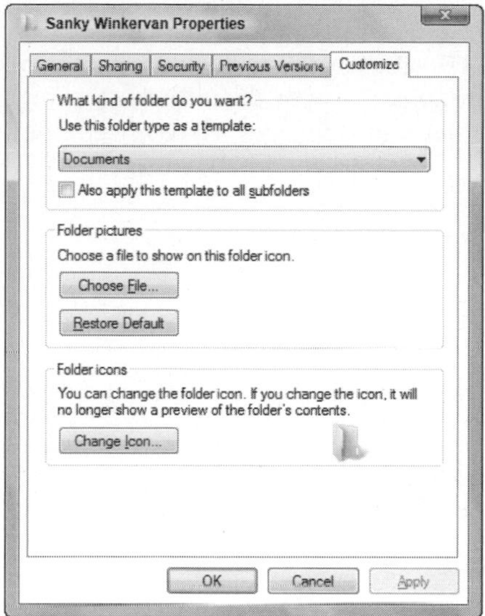

4. Select a template from the drop-down list.

   You can find different templates for pictures, music, and videos.

5. Click the OK button.

Adding a picture to a folder's icon

You can shove a picture into a folder's icon just like you stick an 8-x-10-inch glossy photograph into a folder in the real world. Here's how:

1. Right-click the folder you want to modify.
2. Choose Properties from the pop-up menu.
3. In the folder's Properties dialog box, click the Customize tab.
4. Click the Choose File button.
5. Use the Browse dialog box to locate a graphical image for the folder's face.
6. Click the Open button after you find and select an image.
7. Click the OK button.

Note that you can click the Restore Default button to remove the picture, in case you tire of it later.

Changing a folder icon

Windows lets you use any icon to represent a folder. So, when you tire of the generic manila folder icon, you can replace it with something else, although that something else needs to be another icon in Windows. Here are the details:

1. Right-click the folder you want to change.
2. From the pop-up menu, choose Properties.
3. Click the Customize tab.
4. Click the Change Icon button.
5. Browse in the Change Icon dialog box for a new icon.

   You can also use the Browse button in the Change Icon dialog box to locate another icon file on the hard drive, or an icon file you may have created yourself by using a graphics program.
6. Click OK after you find a better icon.
7. Click the OK button to close the Properties dialog box.

Folders for Your Stuff

Folders are your key to organizing all that stuff you collect and create on your computer. Windows helps you along by doing a bit of folder organization for you: In your account folder are a series of pre-created folders. Each folder sits ready for you to use, to place specific types of files into the proper folder.

Or, you can toss the whole thing aside and create your own series of uniquely named folders to help keep your stuff organized (although many Windows programs are tuned to using the specific folders that are pre-created for you).

Here's the list of the folders you may find already created in your account:

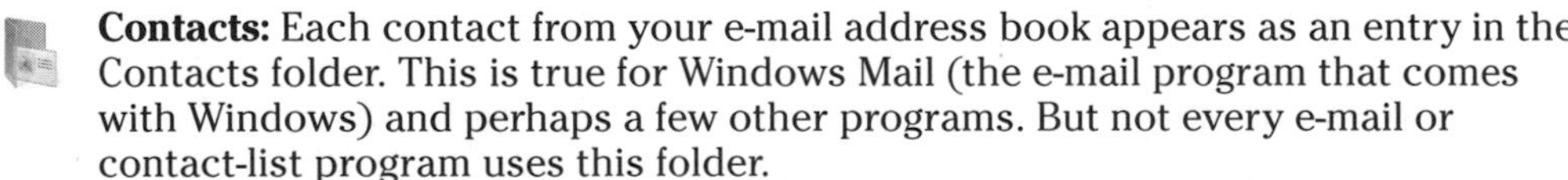

Contacts: Each contact from your e-mail address book appears as an entry in the Contacts folder. This is true for Windows Mail (the e-mail program that comes with Windows) and perhaps a few other programs. But not every e-mail or contact-list program uses this folder.

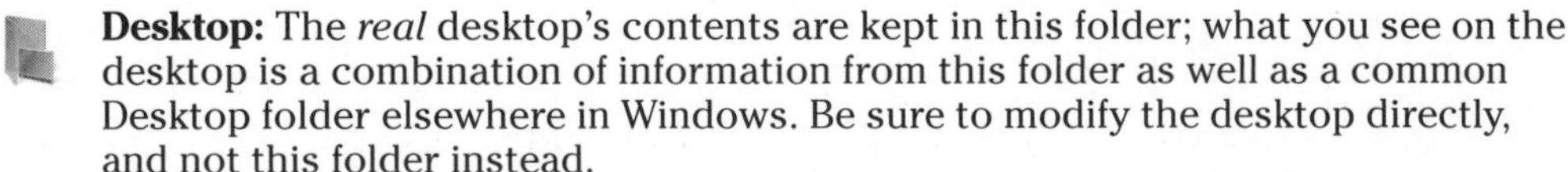

Desktop: The *real* desktop's contents are kept in this folder; what you see on the desktop is a combination of information from this folder as well as a common Desktop folder elsewhere in Windows. Be sure to modify the desktop directly, and not this folder instead.

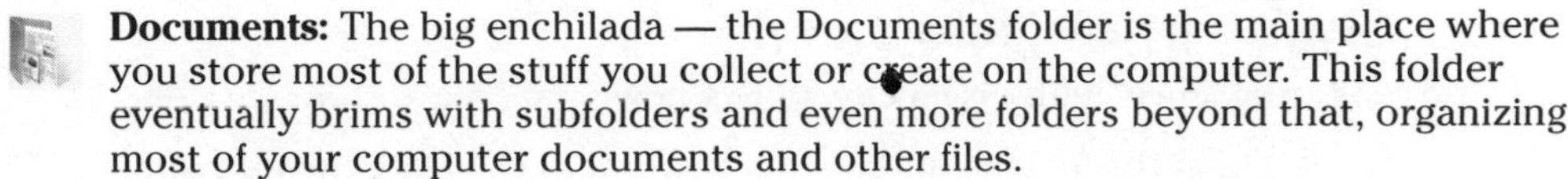

Documents: The big enchilada — the Documents folder is the main place where you store most of the stuff you collect or create on the computer. This folder eventually brims with subfolders and even more folders beyond that, organizing most of your computer documents and other files.

Downloads: Files copied from the Internet are automatically saved in the Downloads folder.

Favorites: This folder is where Web page bookmarks are stored and organized. The bookmarks are referred to as *favorites* in Internet Explorer. Information held in the Favorites folder is best manipulated from within Internet Explorer itself.

Links: This folder contains the folder shortcuts that appear in the Favorite Links part of the Windows Explorer Navigation pane. I recommend using the Favorite Links pane, as described elsewhere in this part, over manipulating files in the Links folder directly.

Music: Anything audio or musical is stored in the Music folder. This folder is where the Windows Media Player stores and manages the many music and audio files you collect and save on your PC.

Pictures: All graphics images, photos, drawings, doodles, and diagrams can be saved in the Pictures folder. This folder is where many graphics programs look to first for opening or saving images. As with the Documents folder, the Pictures folder can be further organized into subfolders. Programs such as the Windows Photo Gallery use this folder to organize images.

Saved Games: Many computer games, including all of Windows's own games, use this folder to store saved games, favorite settings, and other game-related information.

Searches: This folder contains some predefined searches you can use again and again. Or, when you choose to save a file search, this folder is the one in which they're saved.

Videos: Computer videos are stored here. Many videos are managed by Windows Media Player, which may also create its own folders here to keep its stuff organized.

You can create more folders, if the mood hits you. Or, simply use the Documents folder to store other folders for things random and specific that you create on your computer.

Managing Folders

Folders can be tossed about, battered, and bruised, just like any file. Yet it's important to remember that a folder isn't just a file; it's a location for other files. So, when you mess with a folder, you also mess with the folder's contents. *Beware!*

Making a new folder

Creating a new folder is cinchy. Here's how:

1. Open the folder window where you want to create the new folder.

   For example, to create a new folder in the Documents folder, open the Documents window.

2. Choose New Folder from the Organize button's menu.

   The new folder appears in the window, given the name `New Folder`, but the name is selected so that you can immediately type a new name for the folder.

3. Give the folder a new, short, descriptive name.

   The folder name should reflect its contents.

See also Part VII for file-naming rules, which also apply to folders (although folders don't need to have filename extensions).

Renaming, copying, moving folders

Folders can be manipulated just like files; the same rules apply. You can rename a folder, copy and paste it, and cut and paste it. You can also delete folders.

The important difference between manipulating a folder and manipulating a file is that folders contain files, and potentially more folders and even more files. When you change a folder, you're changing not only that one item but also all the items contained within the folder. For example, copying or moving folders tends to confuse programs that try to remember where your files are located.

Deleting a folder removes all the folder's contents — files and subfolders. Don't use this command casually.

Never delete any folder you didn't create yourself, such as any of the Windows folders or program folders.

You can recover a deleted folder from the Recycle Bin. ***See also*** Part VII for information on recovering a deleted file; the same directions can be used to restore a deleted folder.

The Root Folder

The main folder on a hard drive must have a name, and that name is "root." The *root* folder is considered the first folder, or occasionally the only folder, on a disk. It's the root because all other folders on that drive branch out from that folder, like the root of a tree.

The root folder is specified by a single backslash character: \.

Don't save any files directly in the root folder. Your account folder is the place where you save files, and even then those files should be saved in the proper folder — in the theme of keeping everything organized.

An exception to the no-files-in-the-root-folder rule is for removable disks, such as floppy disks, CDs and DVDs, and digital media cards. For those types of media, you can put files in the root. But for the hard drives, use folders instead.

Subfolders

A *subfolder* is merely one folder inside another folder. So, when you create a folder named Work inside the Documents folder, the Work folder is said to be a subfolder of the Documents folder.

The opposite of a subfolder is a *parent* folder. In the preceding example, the Documents folder is the parent folder of the Work folder.

The root folder has no parent folder, technically speaking. In the Windows hierarchy of things, though, the Computer "folder" is the root folder's parent. The desktop is the parent of the Computer folder.

Part IX

Printing

The final step to most computer projects is printing, or getting that vital digital information out of the computer and onto paper. The key to making that happen is perhaps the most popular and long-lived computer peripheral of all time, the printer.

Like other parts of the computer, printing has come a long way since the early days of the PC. Printers are now fast, smart, and cheap — attributes not normally applied to electronic devices. (Well, the printer itself may be cheap, but the ink definitely is not!). If everything is set up, happy, and ready to run, your experience with the computer's printer will be a jolly one.

In this part . . .

- Adding a Printer
- Envelopes
- Ink and Toner
- Paper
- Printing
- Types of Printers

Adding a Printer

The printer is a peripheral device, living outside the central computer console. Like other peripherals, it's attached to the console with a cable and controlled via software. Therefore, printer setup involves both hardware and software duties.

Finding a home for the printer

Place the printer relatively close to your computer — within arm's reach so that you can pull out any paper, easily add paper, access the printer's control panel (if it has one), or add ink or toner.

Despite the printer's small size, remember that it may need extra space in front or behind to make room for paper trays that pop out or slide open. Some printers even require space on top to add or retrieve paper.

Don't place the printer in direct sunlight. That may heat up the printer and make it woefully unhappy.

Printers don't come with cables! You must buy a cable separately. ***See also*** Part II.

See also "Adding paper to the printer" and "Ink and Toner," later in this part.

Connecting the printer

Printers plug into the wall, which is how they get their power. Furthermore, the printer must be connected to the computer so that the computer can talk with the printer and tell it what to print.

A printer can connect with a computer in two ways: directly or over a network.

The direct printer connection involves a cable stringing between the computer and the printer. This cable is usually a USB cable, although older printers used a specific cable called (brace yourself) a *printer* cable. Nerds call it a *Centronics* cable, but it's still a printer cable.

Both types of cable used in the direct printer connection have two unique ends, so you cannot plug the cable in backward.

When you use a traditional printer cable to attach a printer to your computer, ensure that both the printer and computer are off. You can keep either the printer or computer on when using a USB cable.

Printers can also attach directly to a network. The network cable plugs into the printer's rump, or into a special *print server* gizmo attached to the printer's cable connector. The printer is then available to all computers on the network, if they're configured to access the network printer.

Network printers may also be USB printers, which connect directly to a router or wireless networking hub. In that case, you need to use the program that controls the networking device to help set up the printer for use on your computer network.

See also "Turning the Printer On and Off," later in this part.

Printer software setup

Printers generally come with a CD containing software that lets your computer use the printer, plus maybe a few bonus programs. The question to be answered here is whether you need to install the software from the CD before or after you connect the printer to the computer. If you must install the software first, do so. Otherwise, connect the printer to the PC first, and then install the software.

On *and* selected?

Some printers have both an On switch and a select or online switch. There's a difference between the two.

The On switch supplies power to the printer. Turning it on means that the printer is powered up and working.

The select switch, or on-line switch, opens up communications between the printer and the computer. For the printer to print, it must be both on and selected or on-line.

You can deselect the printer, or take it off-line, when you need to use the printer's control panel to make adjustments. After making the adjustments, remember to put the printer back on-line or make it selected by pressing the appropriate button.

Setting up a USB printer

Before you can use a printer, it must be recognized by Windows. Then Windows makes the printer available to any software program that prints via the Print dialog box. First things first! Heed these steps:

1. Set up the printer according to its instructions: Remove packing material, add paper, add toner or ink, and so on.
2. Plug the printer into the wall socket.
3. Ensure that the printer is off.

   If you cannot turn it off (some printers are on all the time), that's okay.
4. Plug the printer's USB cable into the console.

5. Turn the printer on.

   At this point, Windows should recognize the printer and complete the setup process for you automatically. You may hear a musical tone. You may see an animated icon in the notification area. Otherwise, you may see little confirmation, so you need to double-check that the printer was properly installed.

6. Open the Control Panel.

7. Open the Printers icon.

8. Peruse the window, looking for a printer icon that has the same name as your printer.

   For example, on my screen, I see the Epson Stylus COLOR 900 printer listed, which matches the name of the USB printer I just attached to my PC.

9. Close the Printers window.

When you don't see your printer listed, you may have goofed and forgotten to install the software first; refer to the preceding section. Otherwise, keep reading in the following section for information on forcing Windows to recognize a printer.

Forcing Windows to recognize the printer

For those rare times when Windows doesn't recognize a printer right away, you have to lead it by the nose a bit. This isn't that scary. Just follow these steps:

1. Open the Control Panel.

2. Open the Printers icon.

3. Click the Add a Printer button on the toolbar.

   This step starts the Add Printer Wizard.

4. Choose whether the printer is local or networked.

   A local printer is connected directly to your PC, through either a USB or traditional printer cable.

   A network, wireless, or Bluetooth printer isn't directly connected to your PC. It exists on the network (connected either directly to the network or to a computer on the network), or it exists on its own yet connects to your PC via the wireless networking or Bluetooth wireless adapter.

   The rest of the steps in this section assume that the printer is directly connected (a local printer). Refer to the next section for information on network printer connections.

5. Choose the proper printer port.

   For example, choose LPT1 for the computer's first printer port. That's probably the one you want.

6. Click the Next button.

7. Select your printer's manufacturer from the scrolling list on the left, and then select the specific printer from the scrolling list on the right.

   If you cannot find your printer, try to locate the manufacturer on the Web. From that Web page, download the proper printer drivers for Windows Vista so that you can use the manufacturer's printer.

8. Click the Next button.

9. Optionally, type a new name for the printer.

10. Click the Next button.

11. Optionally, click the Print a Text Page button to ensure that everything is working.

12. Click the Finish button.

In a few seconds, you can observe the test page that's printed. If the test page doesn't print, check the connection and ensure that the printer is on-line or selected and ready to print. Try again. Or, start the Troubleshooter to begin a troubleshooting session.

Adding a network printer

Windows is very smart about networking and shared printers. If any printers are available for use on the network, they automatically show up in the Printers window. Software to control those printers is also automatically installed on your computer. But that's not necessarily true for all network printers.

To add a network printer that isn't automatically added by Windows, heed these steps:

1. Open the Control Panel.

2. Open the Printers icon.

3. Click the Add a Printer button on the toolbar.

   This step starts the Add Printer Wizard.

4. Choose Add a Network, Wireless or Bluetooth Printer.

   Windows scours the network for obvious network printers, which includes mostly those printers attached to other computers in the workgroup.

5. Select one of the found printers.
6. Click the Next button.
7. Optionally, type a name for the printer.
8. Click the Next button.
9. You can click the Print a Text Page button to check the printer's operation.
10. Click the Finish button.

When the printer isn't listed in Step 5, you must manually install it. This involves obtaining the printer's network name or IP address. When you have that information, choose the option labeled The Printer That I Want Isn't Listed, and proceed to the next screen by selecting whichever option matches the information you have: either the printer name or IP address.

Oftentimes, the software that comes with a networked printer automatically installs that printer for you. If you're so lucky as to have such software, you need to follow its directions, not those steps listed in this section.

Adding more than one printer to a single PC

Windows allows you to use any number of printers, either printers directly connected to your computer or printers on a network. Variety is good! For example, you may have a color printer, a fast printer, and a printer stocked with letterhead — as many printers as you need.

To physically add a second printer to a single PC, simply connect the printer to an open USB port, or, if it's available, use a second printer port, LPT2. There's no limit on how many printers can be connected to a single PC.

The Default (Favorite) Printer

Which printer is your favorite? Which one of the many potential printers that your computer can access is the one you prefer to use most often? Windows refers to that printer as the *default printer.*

Yeah, I dislike the word *default* as well. I prefer *favorite,* but I'm not in charge. (Not in this universe.)

To choose a default printer, observe these steps:

1. Open the Control Panel.

2. Open the Printers icon.

3. Click to select the printer you want to automatically use whenever you choose to print something.

4. Click the Set As Default Toolbar button.

The default printer is identified in the Printer window with a white check mark in a green circle, as shown in the margin.

You can have only one default printer at a time, but you can change the default printer at any time.

You don't have to use the default printer. You can choose to print on any printer whenever you use the Print dialog box. ***See also*** "Printing," later in this part.

Envelopes

Your computer's printer can print envelopes just as it can print any other piece of paper. The trick is to think of the envelope as nothing more than a specially sized sheet of paper. When you get that concept down, printing on an envelope is easy.

Configuring your document as an envelope

To set up a document as an envelope, you use the Page Setup dialog box, shown in Figure 9-1. This dialog box is used in most Windows programs to set paper size, orientation, and margins.

Figure 9-1

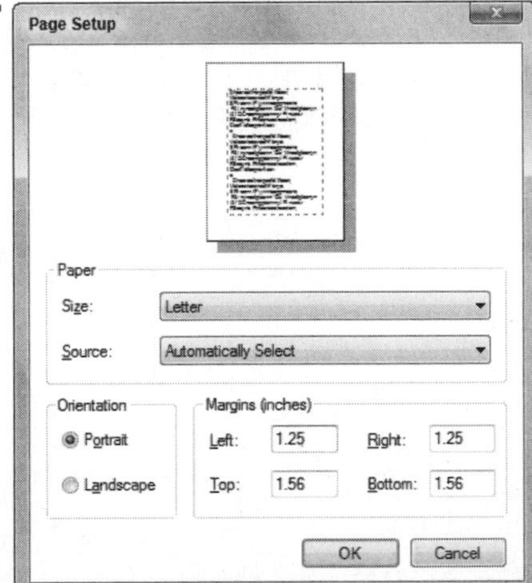

In most programs, the File⇨Page Setup command summons the Page Setup dialog box. In Office 2007, on the Page Layout tab, the Page Setup group contains paper size, margin, and orientation commands.

To print on an envelope, set these options:

Paper Size: Choose Envelope #10 as the paper size.

Orientation: Choose Landscape.

Margins: I prefer custom margins. On the top, set 1.75 inches. On the left, set 3 inches.

Use the Preview window in the Page Setup dialog box to help fine-tune the margins.

Printing on an envelope

Most printers have a special location to insert an envelope, a metaphorical envelope mouth where the printer eats envelopes.

On some printers, envelopes are fed into a special slot. Most printers, however, require that you simply adjust the standard paper input guides to account for the narrow envelope's breadth. Or, perhaps the envelope slides in all the way to the left or right of the standard paper-feed mechanism. Regardless, do know how your printer eats envelopes.

Another important thing to note is the envelope's orientation as it enters the printer. Because it's easy to improperly insert an envelope, I recommend doing a test printing first. That way, you can determine whether to insert the envelope face up or face down, and which edge of the envelope goes in first — long or short.

When you have determined which way to insert the envelope, I recommend that you attach a note to the printer or draw on the printer directly with a Sharpie or other pen, to remind you of which way the envelope goes. You can use one of the icons in Figure 9-2 as a guide.

Choose an icon to represent how your printer accepts envelopes, and then draw something similar in the proper location on your printer (if such a thing doesn't already exist).

Figure 9-2

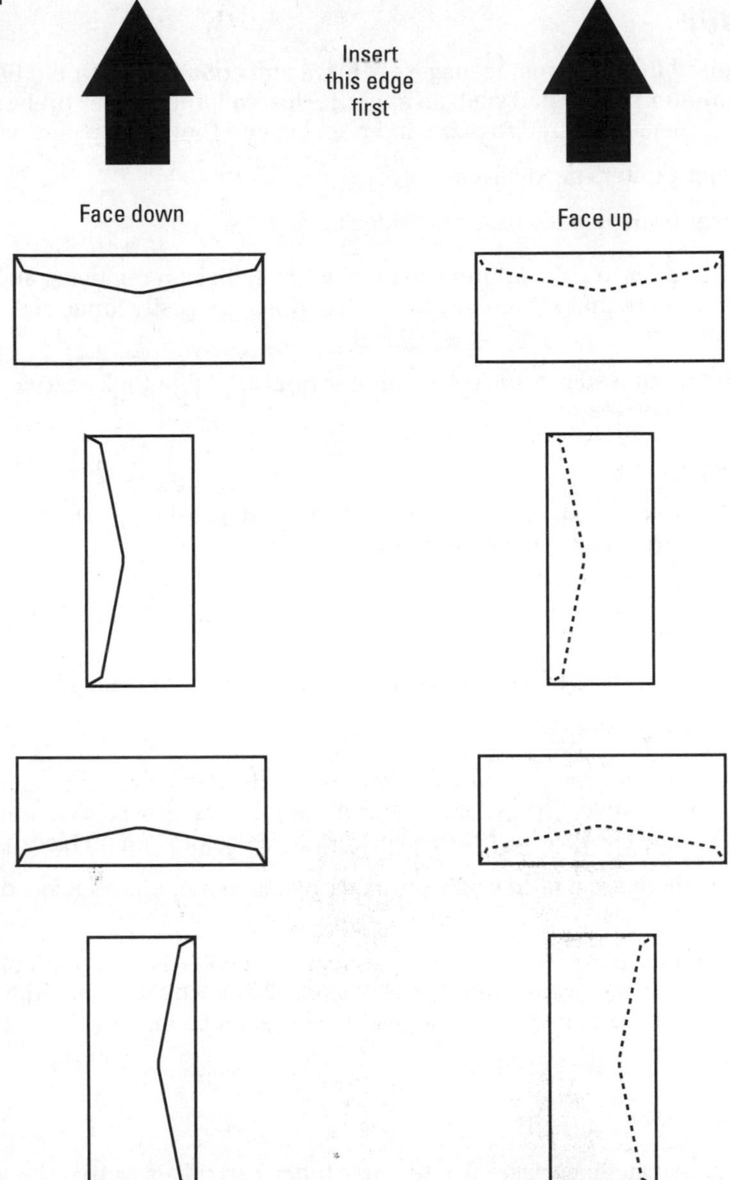

Ink and Toner

The required food for most teenagers is pizza and soda pop. It would be nice if your computer printer had such an appetite. Instead, the printer prefers to dine on ink or toner. Compared to pizza and pop, ink and toner are expensive.

- Inkjet printers need ink cartridges.
- Laser printers need toner cartridges.

You have to refer to your printer's manual for specifics on removing and adding ink or toner. Note that sometimes the instructions are easily found right under the printer's lid.

A pencil without lead is a stick. A computer printer without ink or toner is an expensive paperweight.

Ink cartridges

Inkjet printers use from one to six ink cartridges, depending on the type of printer. Ink cartridges come in these types:

- Black ink only
- Multicolor: yellow, blue, and red ink
- Multicolor: two yellow inks, two red inks, and blue or cyan ink
- Individual colors

How your inkjet printer uses ink cartridges depends on the printer's price and purpose. For example, professional color-photo printers use six ink colors (including black). Some cheaper ink printers just use three colors and no black ink.

Sometimes there are multiple inks per cartridge, and sometimes inks come in separate cartridges.

When a color cartridge is empty — even if just one color is in a multicolor cartridge — the entire thing must be replaced. That's why you should buy an ink printer that has separate cartridges, one for each color.

Yes, ink cartridges are expensive!

Toner

Just like copy machines, laser printers use toner cartridges as their inky substance. The toner cartridges aren't cheap! Fortunately, you can get more pages of paper from a single laser printer toner cartridge than an inkjet printer gets from a single thimble of ink.

Color laser printers require up to five toner cartridges, one each for black, magenta, cyan, and yellow, plus an extra toner cartridge to print in colors beyond what humans can see. (That's just a guess. Honestly, I don't know why some color laser printers need five toner cartridges.)

Ink and toner tips

- Remember the cartridge or toner part number for your printer! Not all ink or toner cartridges are alike; they're not interchangeable.
- I recommend buying the brand-name ink cartridges, despite their extra cost.
- Keep spare toner or ink cartridges available. Whenever I buy a new cartridge, I buy two. That way, when I run out, I don't need to rush to the store right away.
- Change the ink or toner when it gets low. Do not delay. Do it at once. Failure to do so can damage your printer.
- When you first see the toner-low signal from your laser printer, you can squeeze a few more pages from it (an exception to the preceding rule). Remove the toner cartridge from the printer and gently rock it back and forth to redistribute the ink powder. Reinsert the cartridge into the printer. The next time the toner-low signal appears, however, you must replace the toner; this trick works only once.
- Yes, you can use those toner-recharging places, which is cheaper than buying new toner from the manufacturer. Ditto for ink refilling, but ensure that you're getting quality stuff.
- You don't always have to print in color. You can save ink on an inkjet printer by printing test images in grayscale rather than full color all the time.

Paper

After ink, the second replaceable item you need in order to keep your printer happy is paper. Printers eat paper. You need to be sure that you buy your printer the proper types of paper to keep it happy — and there are several types of paper you can use, and many types to avoid.

Buying paper

The best kind of paper for your printer is sold with the printer type right on the paper package. For example, inkjet printer paper says "Inkjet printer paper" right on the package. Ditto for laser printer paper, although for a laser printer, any photocopier paper does just as well.

Multipurpose paper can be used in either inkjet or laser printers.

Specialty papers abound for computer printers, from high-quality ink paper that really absorbs inkjet printer ink to photo and glossy photo paper to transparencies and even iron-on transfers. Always ensure that the specialty paper works with your printer. For example, some photo-quality papers work only with inkjet printers.

Adding paper to the printer

Computer printers accept paper in one of two ways: The paper is either stacked up inside a tray, similar to a copy machine, or set in a feeding bin.

When the printer runs out of paper, it lets you know, either via a message on the computer screen or some message on the printer's control panel.

Yes, there's a face-up and face-down way of inserting paper into a printer. This distinction is important only when the paper manufacturer recommends that you print on one side of the paper first, or when you're printing on both sides of a sheet of paper. Directions on the printer should tell you which side of the paper is printed first. If not, feel free to borrow the icons in the nearby figure.

Paper tips

- Keep your printer supplies, including the paper, near your printer for easy access.
- Buy plenty of paper for your printer! Stock up! Paper is cheaper by the box. Try to find a discount, bulk-paper dealer near you.
- Be careful to note which side of the paper needs to be printed on first — if that's the case.
- Note how paper is fed into your printer: either face down or face up, or top in first. This is important to note when you're printing on letterhead or printing both sides of a page. Draw an image similar to what's shown in Figure 9-3, illustrating how paper needs to be fed into your printer.
- Not all inkjet printer paper works in laser printers. For example, if the photo paper says that it's for a color laser printer, it probably works just fine. But, if the paper doesn't say that it's okay for a color laser printer, it doesn't work.

- Avoid using powdered or erasable bond paper in your computer printer. The powder gums up the works.
- Paper stock that's too thick may not be able to wend its way through your printer's internals. I generally stick with 25-pound stock as the thickest paper to use in a computer printer.

- For the best printing on a laser printer, get laser paper.
- That continuous fanfold paper you may have seen in old movies or photos is for older impact (dot-matrix) printers that you will probably never use.
- Some printers are capable of handling larger-size paper, such as legal or tabloid. If yours can use these sizes, make sure that you load the paper properly and tell Windows or your software application that you're using a different size of paper.

Figure 9-3

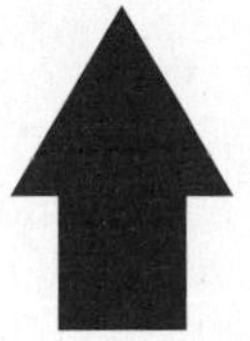

Insert
this edge
first

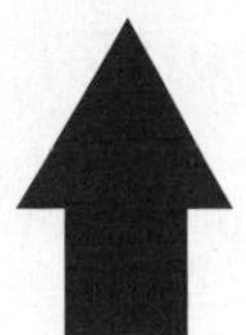

Face down

Face up

Top

Top

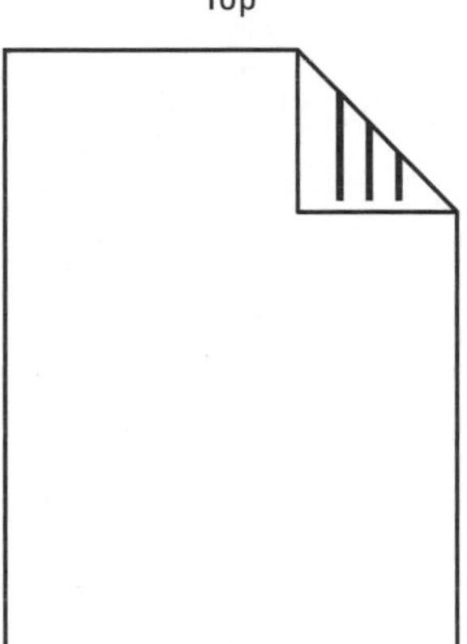

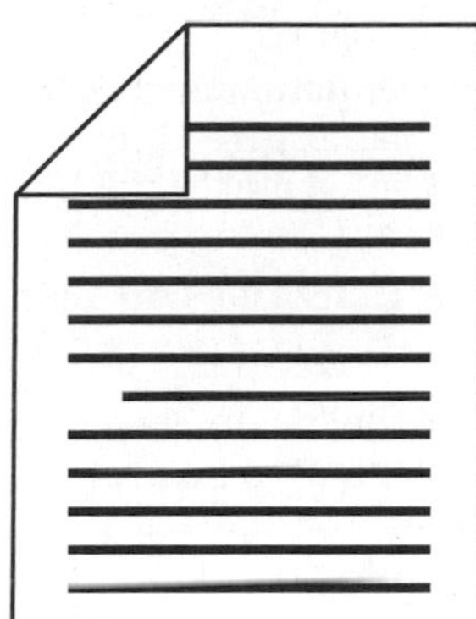

Bottom

Bottom

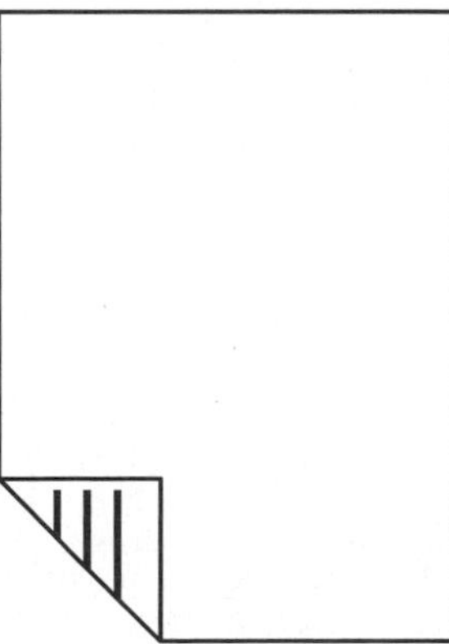

The Printer's Control Panel

The printer is really a computer all its own. Some printers have full-on microprocessors and their own memory. Other printers — cheap ones — use the computer for most of the computing horsepower, but printers still remain complex and interesting gizmos. As such, each printer has a control panel.

On some printers, the control panel is a small LCD screen with buttons to scroll through various menus and select options. Other printers may have just one or two buttons that control everything — beyond the basic power button.

Here are a few key things to locate on the printer's control panel:

- **Power button and light:** When the printer is on, the light is on. Easy.
- **Paper-out light:** This may also appear as a warning on the printer's LCD screen.
- **Ink/Toner Out/Low light:** This message may also appear on the LCD screen. You may see different lights for the different ink cartridges.
- **The on-line, or select, button:** Some printers require that an on-line or select button be pressed before the printer communicates with the computer. This button isn't used to turn the printer off and on, but, rather, to open or close communications with the printer. For example, you deselect the printer or take it off-line to change ink cartridges or eject a page or fix a misfeed.
- **Stop or Cancel:** This button is used to immediately halt printing. Consider yourself fortunate if your printer sports one of these babies.
- **The form-feed button:** This button ejects a sheet of paper from the printer.
- **Menu button:** The Menu button is used to activate a menu display on the printer's LCD. Other buttons nearby may help you navigate and choose items from the menu.

Print Preview

To help save paper, and to give you a good idea of what the printed document will look like, most applications come with a Print Preview command. Print Preview shows you on-screen exactly what the printed document looks like, all the way up to the edge of the paper.

The Print Preview command is commonly found on the File menu. In Office 2007, it's on the Office button menu, on the Print submenu. Oftentimes, a Print Preview toolbar button can also be used.

Most applications don't let you edit text or modify your document in Print Preview mode. You must first close the Print Preview window or somehow return to editing mode to continue working on the document.

Printing

In the computer world, printed material is called *hard copy,* and it's often the last step in creating something with the computer. The hard copy is pass-around proof of your efforts, the paper you turn in, a list to take shopping, sheet music for others to play, pictures to look at — you name it. Getting it on paper is what the printer is all about.

The Print command

Printing is the same in nearly every Windows application. Here are the steps I recommend that you take to print your creation:

1. Save your stuff!

   Always save before you print. It's a good habit.

2. Turn on the printer (if necessary).

   Or, take whatever steps are necessary to ensure that the printer is on-line and ready to print.

3. Access the Print command, which summons the Print dialog box.

   In most programs, the Print dialog box is brought forth by choosing File⇨Print from the menu. In Office 2007, the Print command is chosen from the Office button menu. Either way, the keyboard shortcut is Ctrl+P.

4. Make any necessary adjustments in the Print dialog box, as shown in Figure 9-4.

   The majority of these adjustments are covered in the remainder of this section.

5. Click the Print button to print the document.

6. Remove the document from the printer.

You can also print by clicking a Print toolbar button. Note that the button often just prints the document immediately without first displaying a Print dialog box.

Figure 9-4

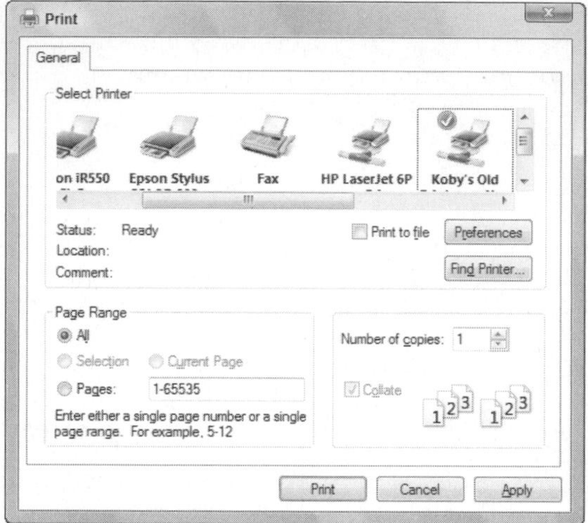

Choosing a printer

When your computer is connected to multiple printers, such as printers on a network, you select a printer inside the Print dialog box. There, you see either a list of icons or a drop-down list of printer descriptions.

When you don't choose a printer, such as when you click the Print toolbar button, Windows uses the *default printer.*

Printing multiple copies

Normally, clicking the Print button directs the printer to make only one copy of your document, photo, or whatever you're printing. When you want multiple copies, use the Number of Copies gizmo in the Print dialog box. Set the gizmo to the number of copies you want.

When printing multiple copies of a document, the oddball question of collation rears its ugly head. When you choose to collate, Windows prints each copy of a document, from first page to last. When you don't collate, windows prints several copies of page one, and then page two, and so on.

Printing a single page or range of pages

Some Print dialog boxes allow you to specify which pages of a document to print. You may click buttons to select all odd pages, all even pages, or the entire document. Or, you may see a text box where you can enter individual pages or a range of pages.

To print an individual page, simply specify that page in the text box:

5

To print a range of pages, use the hyphen to separate the first and last pages in the range:

```
2-10
```

To print a smattering of pages, separate them with commas:

```
+5, 13-15, 19, 23-30
```

Printing the Screen

It's possible to get a printed copy of what you see on the screen, or of a single window. This trick is complicated, but it can be done. Pay close attention:

1. Arrange the screen so that it looks the way you want to see it printed, or ensure that the single window you want to capture is "on top of" all other windows.
2. Press the Print Screen key to capture the entire screen, or press Alt+Print Screen to capture just a window.

   The image is now copied into the Windows Clipboard. From there, you can paste it into any program that accepts graphics.
3. From the Start button's menu, choose All Programs⇨Accessories⇨Paint to start the Windows Paint program.
4. Choose Edit⇨Paste.

   The screen image is now pasted into the Paint program, from which you can print.

   You can optionally save the image at this point, if necessary.
5. Choose File⇨Print.

   Make necessary adjustments in the Print dialog box, and ensure that the printer is ready to print.
6. Click the Print button to print the screen.
7. Quit Paint when you're done.

Printing a Test Page

One way to ensure that the printer is working and on speaking terms with the computer is to print a test page. This is done initially when you set up any printer for the first time, but Windows lets you print a test page again, just to ensure that everything is working:

1. Open the Printers window.

   Access this window from the Printers icon in the Control Panel.

2. Right-click the printer's icon.
3. Choose Properties from the pop-up menu.
4. Click the button labeled Print Test Page.

Stopping the Printer

In those moments when your patience flits away, or when something trots off to the printer before its time, you need to stop printing before paper spews all over the place.

The technical thing you're stopping is a printing *job*. Each time you print, you send a *job* to the printer. Sometimes, you want to stop all the jobs, and sometimes you need to pluck out only the one job that offends you.

The easiest way to stop printing is to locate a Cancel or Stop button on the printer's control panel. That stops the printing by canceling the current page from printing and halting any further information from coming into the printer.

If your printer lacks a Cancel or Stop button, or if you're printing a large document and you want to ensure that it's fully purged from memory, take these steps:

1. Double-click the tiny printer icon in the notification area.

   If you can see this guy, great. Otherwise, you have to do this:

   A. Open the Control Panel.

   B. Open the Printers icon.

   C. Open your printer's icon, the icon representing the printer you want to stop.

   No matter how you get there, the next thing you see is the Printers window, which displays a list, or *queue,* of jobs printing.

2. Choose Printer⇨Cancel All Documents.

   This step stops everything. That's probably what you want. Fix the problem, and then print again.

You can also select an individual document in the queue and then choose Document⇨Cancel from the menu.

Printers are often so fast now that you can't catch a job fast enough to stop it from printing.

It is impossible to cancel a job sent to a network printer unless a computer is connected to that printer, and then you can follow the preceding steps on that computer.

Turning a printer off may not cancel the job. Some larger printer jobs sit inside the computer and are fed to the printer one chunk at a time. This process is known as *spooling.* When a print job is spooling, it continues to flow to the printer when you turn the printer on again. That's why I recommend that you follow the preceding steps and not just turn a printer off.

Turning the Printer On and Off

Like many computer peripherals, printers have an on–off switch. In fact, like the console, the printer may sport a *power button* and not a true on–off switch. Sometimes, pressing the power button turns the printer off, and sometimes it activates a cooling-down period, and then the printer turns off. And I'm sure that there's a printer out there that has an on–off button just for show.

Most modern printers can be left on all the time. They have a special sleep, or standby, mode, just like computers do. After a while, a printer enters this mode, where it uses little or no power and essentially turns itself off. When the signal comes in to start printing, the printer automatically wakes itself up and prints. Then, it goes back to sleep after a period of inactivity.

You can turn your printer off, if you like. Just flip the switch. But, remember to turn the printer on again before printing.

Types of Printers

All printers serve the purpose of giving you a hard copy. Specifically, two popular types of computer printers are available on the market: inkjet printers and laser printers.

A third popular type of printer that's available is the *all-in-one.* It's basically an inkjet printer, but with the ability to act as a scanner, fax machine, and copier in addition to a computer printer. For the sake of discussion, I lump that gizmo into the inkjet category because, at its core, it's really just an inkjet printer.

You can still find the old dot-matrix, or impact, printers. They're used for high-speed operations, such as printing invoices or filling in forms. Individual computer users don't need those, mostly because they're very slow when printing graphics, and everything in Windows is graphics.

Inkjet printers

The *inkjet* printer uses literally a jet of ink to create an image on paper. A tiny ink ball is lobbed from the inkjet nozzle directly onto the paper. The ball is small enough that it's nearly instantly absorbed by the paper (although better paper absorbs the ink more efficiently).

Inkjet printers take advantage of several different inks, up to six in a single printer. The more ink, the more realistic the images. For example, special color-photo ink printers use up to six ink colors to create near-photographic-like quality in their output.

The chief advantage of using inkjet printers is that they're relatively inexpensive and they generate cheap color output.

The main disadvantage of inkjet printers is that the replacement cost of the ink cartridges is *not* cheap. In fact, it's often said that manufacturers give away the printer and make up the cost by selling you ink.

Laser printers

The technology behind the *laser* printer is the same as in a photocopier. But, rather than create an image by reflecting light off an original, a laser beam etches the printed image on a magnetic drum, which then sucks up toner dust and literally fuses the toner dust to the paper to create an image.

Laser printers are generally more expensive than inkjet printers, but then again, they're the workhorses of the modern computerized office. They're faster than inkjet printers, and their quality is higher.

Although color laser printers are available, the quality and cost of ink printers make them more attractive for individuals.

Uninstalling a Printer

Removing a printer from your computer system involves both hardware and software duties.

On the hardware side, simply disconnect the printer from the console; unplug the printer or USB cable.

On the software side, open the Printers window. Select your printer's icon and then, from the toolbar, click the Delete This Printer button. (You may need to click the Show More button to see more of the toolbar and access the Delete This Printer button.)

If you're prompted, I recommend that you leave the printer's software installed on your computer. That way, if you need to use the printer later, you don't have to reinstall the software.

Part X

Networking

Once upon a time, a network was something you didn't need to bother with. Mere mortals didn't need to concern themselves with either the software or hardware side of networking. It was something someone else did for you. But that was then! Today's computers come with networking gear preinstalled for a reason: Networking is as much a part of using a PC as the monitor, keyboard, mouse, and printer. When you have a high-speed Internet connection, networking is part of your computer life.

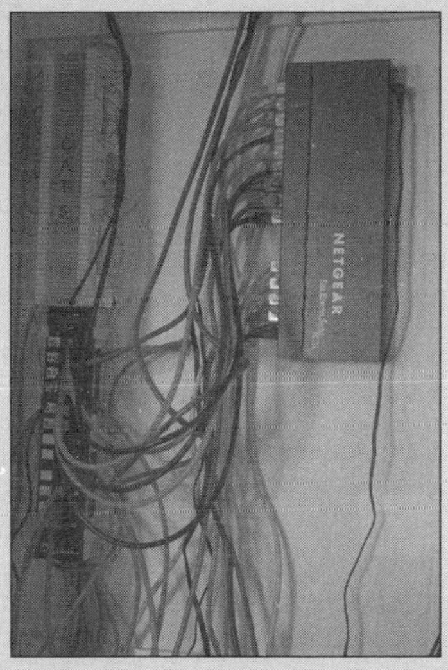

In this part . . .

- Accessing a Wireless Network
- Adding a Shared Folder to Your Disk System
- The Network and Sharing Center
- The PC's IP Address
- The PC's Network Name
- The Public Folder
- Sharing a Printer
- Workgroups

About Networking

Computer networking is about sharing resources — such as files, printers, and modems — between several computers.

Like everything else in a computer, networking involves both hardware and software.

The network hardware connects all the computers, either through wires or wirelessly.

Networking hardware requires a NIC, or network information card, also referred to as an Ethernet adapter. The NIC comes as either an expansion card or part of the motherboard. Most new PCs, and all laptops, come with networking hardware.

The network software coordinates everything so that making the connection and sharing the resource is simple. (Or so the theory goes.) Windows provides all the networking software you need.

Accessing a Shared Folder

To use a folder shared by another computer, you must first find the shared computer and then locate the shared folder. Here's what I do:

1. Open the Network window.

   The list of network resources is displayed.

2. Open the icon for the computer on which the folder is shared.

3. Open the icon representing the shared folder.

   Shared folder icons appear with "plumbing" beneath them.

After opening the icon, the files and folders available on that shared folder appear in a Windows Explorer window and are available to you just as though you were using them on your computer.

Some shared folders may require password access.

Some shared folders may limit your interaction to read-only status: You can open or copy files, but you cannot change, modify, or delete anything on the shared folder itself.

You must configure Windows Vista for *network discovery* if you want to browse other computers on the network. ***See also*** "The Network and Sharing Center," later in this part, for information on turning on network discovery.

See also "The Network Window," later in this part, for more information.

Accessing a Wireless Network

Wireless networking is all the rage. As long as your PC is equipped with a wireless networking adapter and a broadcast networking signal is available, you too can do the networking thing without wires.

To home in on any available wireless network, heed these steps:

1. Pop up the Start menu.
2. Choose Connect To.

   The Connect to Network window appears.
3. Choose a wireless network from the list.

   When the list is empty, no compatible wireless networks are in range.
4. Click the Connect button.

   Public wireless networks are commonly unsecured. Windows warns you about this situation, and it's a legitimate security concern, but also one that you have no control over on a public network: Choose the Connect Anyway option.
5. Enter the network password, if prompted to do so.
6. Choose whether the network is public or private.

   The public/private question has to do with security: Public networks exist out in the open, at a public library or cybercafé. Private networks exist in an office or in your home, where you know things are secure.
7. Save the network's connection information.
8. Click Close.

   If you're prompted with a User Account Control security warning, click the Continue button.

You're now connected to and using the network; a pop-up bubble from the notification area may alert you to various trivia about the connection, such as the network's name, connection speed, and wireless signal strength.

A wireless computer is said to have an *ad hoc* network connection. Unlike peer-to-peer or other network connections, an ad hoc network connection is up and running only for the time the wireless computer is connected to the network.

Many wireless network adapters come with their own, special network connection software. If such software is available on your PC, I recommend that you use it rather than the Windows Vista method just described.

Adding a Shared Folder to Your Disk System

Often, you may find yourself repeatedly using a shared folder on the network. When that happens, I believe that you'll find it easier to just *map* that folder into your computer's disk system. By mapping the folder, and assigning it a disk drive letter, you make accessing the folder as easy as accessing any disk drive on your computer. Windows even remembers which folders are mapped, so that every time you start the computer, the folder is again given the same, local drive letter.

Mapping a folder to a disk drive

To add a shared folder on the network to your PC's disk drive system, follow these steps:

1. Open the Computer window.
2. On the toolbar, choose Map Network Drive.

   The Map Network Drive dialog box appears. (See Figure 10-1.)

Figure 10-1

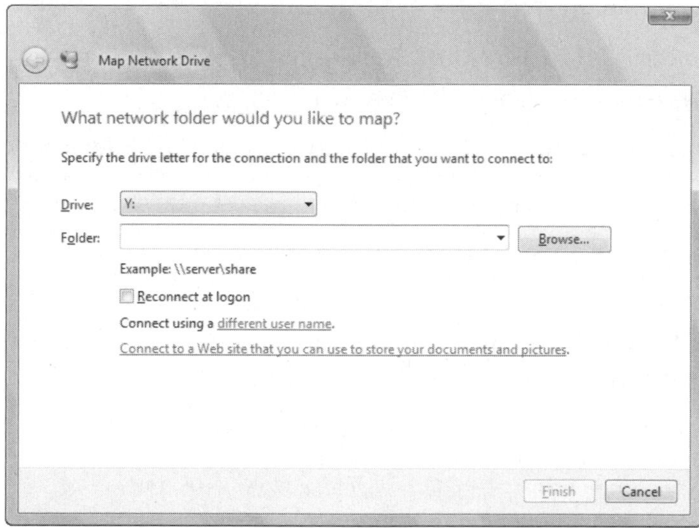

3. Choose a drive letter from the Drive drop-down list.

   Try to make the letter memorable, such as drive R for an a*r*chive folder, drive M for shared *m*usic, or drive P for shared *p*hotos.

4. Click the Browse button to locate a shared folder on the network.

The folders appear in a tree structure, listing each found computer on the network.

5. Open a computer "branch" to reveal which folders are available on that computer for sharing.

6. Click to select the folder.

7. Click the OK button.

   The folder's officially cryptic network pathname appears in the Folder box.

8. Click to put a check mark by the box labeled Reconnect at Logon.

   By completing this step, you ensure that Windows remembers to remap the network folder to a disk drive letter whenever you restart Windows.

9. Click the Finish button to add the folder as a mapped disk drive.

   The shared folder or disk drive window then appears. (You can close it.)

The mapped drive appears in the Computer window with its own, special icon, but listed along with other disk drives that are part of your computer system. When you're viewing the Computer window, mapped disk drives appear in the section labeled Network Location.

Some firewalls disable access to folders shared on the local network. If you're using a firewall, be sure to allow access through the firewall (both in and out) from computers on your network.

Unmapping a folder

When you tire of having the convenience of a network drive, you can unmap it. It's cinchy:

1. Open the Computer window.
2. Right-click the network drive you want to unmap.
3. Choose the Disconnect command from the pop-up menu.

You may be warned if the connection is still active. If so, stop using the mapped drive, and then try again.

Checking the Network Connection

There are several ways you can confirm that your PC is actively connected to the network and things are set up properly.

Checking the Network window

Opening the Network window displays a list of shared resources that are accessible over the network. If you open that window and it's empty, it means that either networking isn't working or there just aren't any resources to be shared.

Checking the Network and Sharing Center window

The Network and Sharing Center window is the central location for computer networking in Windows Vista. The main display graphically illustrates whether your computer is connected to a network and connected to the Internet. ***See also*** "The Network and Sharing Center," later in this part.

Using the little networking guys

When your PC is actively connected to a network, the little networking-guys icon appears in the notification area. They dwell down there primarily to tell you that the networking is happening.

If just seeing the network guys isn't enough, point the mouse at them for a second. You see a pop-up balloon, shown in Figure 10-2, indicating the network's current status.

Figure 10-2

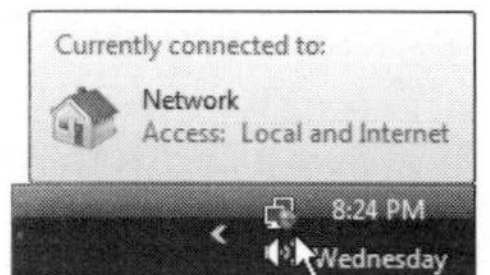

See also Part V, the section about controlling the notification area, to ensure that the little networking guys show up in the notification area.

Connecting to a Network

The only good news about connecting to a computer network is that after you get it right, you never really have to do it again. It's getting to that point that causes the most frustration among PC users.

See also "Accessing a Wireless Network," earlier in this part.

The NIC

On the hardware side of connecting the network, your PC needs a NIC, or network interface card. The NIC hardware is incorporated into the motherboard on modern PCs, although traditionally the NIC was added as an expansion card. Either way, the NIC sports an RJ-45 jack, or network hole, on the console's rump.

The network cable

Physically connecting the network is networking cable, also known as *Cat-5 cable.* This cable connects each computer on the network to a central router, switch, or networking hub.

The ends of the cable are RJ-45 jacks, one of which plugs into the NIC on your PC and the other of which plugs into the router, switch, or hub.

You can also network two PCs directly, by connecting a network cable between each computer's NIC.

Configuring the network

After making the hardware connection, your next step is to properly configure Windows to understand and obey the network. Do this by running the Network Setup Wizard:

1. Open the Control Panel.

2. Open the Network Sharing Center icon.
3. From the left side of the window, choose the task labeled Set Up Connection or Network.
4. Answer the questions that are given, and click the Next button after each choice.
5. Click the Finish button when the wizard is done.

For creating a peer-to-peer network, each computer on the network must belong to the same workgroup. ***See also*** "Workgroups," later in this part.

The Network and Sharing Center

The central location for network control in Windows is the Network and Sharing Center window, shown in Figure 10-3. You get there by opening the Network and Sharing Center icon in the Control Panel.

The left side of the window lists various networking tasks and activities. On the right is information about the current network setup and options.

At the top of the right side of the Network and Sharing Center, you see a graphical depiction of the current network setup. Click the View Full Map link to see a graphical layout of your entire PC network (although it works best when all the computers are running Windows Vista).

The Network section lists current network connections. You can change the network name and icon, as well as whether it's a public or private network, by clicking the Customize link on the right.

Figure 10-3

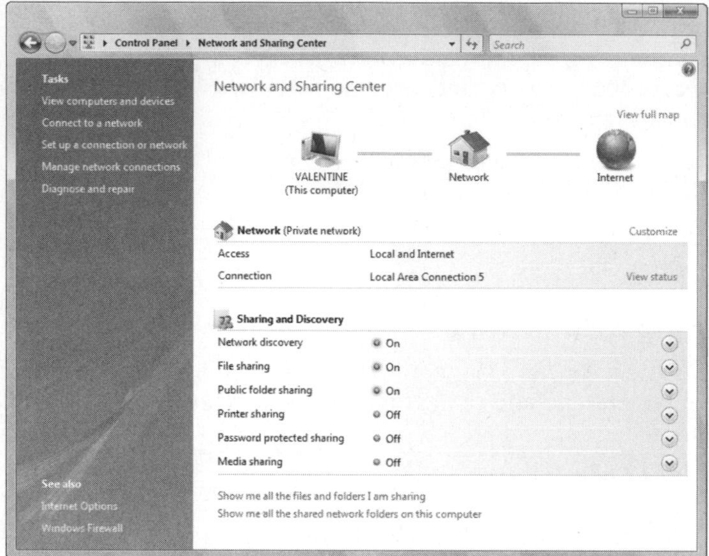

The Sharing and Discovery section is where you control how much you want your computer to use the network as well as how much you want the network to use your computer. The status of various settings is shown as either On or Off. To view more information or change the status, click the downward-pointing chevron to the right of any item:

Network Discovery: When network discovery is on, your computer can view and access other computers on the network. Likewise, other computers on the network can see your computer and access any shared resources. This option must be on if you plan on sharing resources on a network.

File Sharing: When file sharing is on, other users on the network can access shared files and folders on your computer. Only those folders you have marked as "shared" can be shared.

Public Folder Sharing: When this option is off, it prevents others from accessing the Public folder on your PC. There are two "on" settings: The first allows for read-only access to your computer; others can only open files or copy them from your PC. The second option allows for full access to the files in the Public folder; others can create new files or copy files into the Public folder, rename, delete, move, or otherwise manipulate files in the Public folder.

Printer Sharing: When printer sharing is on, it allows others on the network to use any printer attached to your computer and available for sharing.

Password Protected Sharing: When this option is on, only users with a password-protected account on your PC can access the Public folder, other shared folders, and shared printers on your computer. Those users must log in remotely to use any shared resources on your PC.

Media Sharing: When media sharing is on, other users on the network can access any shared music, videos, or pictures you make available on your PC. Media programs such as Windows Media Player or iTunes do this kind of sharing; it's not simply sharing files, which can be done through the Public folder.

After changing any item in the Sharing and Discovery list, you may be confronted with a User Account Control warning. Because you initiated the action, feel free to click the Continue button.

Various other sections in this part describe details in the Network and Sharing Center window, as well as how and when to set various options.

Your computer's network name, as well as the name of any workgroup or network the computer is attached to, is set in the System Properties dialog box. ***See also*** "The PC's Network Name," earlier in this part.

The Network Connections Window

Windows Vista puts all the network information you need to know in the Network and Sharing Center window, covered in the preceding section. But, if you're an old hand who needs to use the Network Connections window, it's still available: Open the Network and Sharing Center window and choose the task Manage Network Connections.

The Network Connections window lists the available networking hardware as well as other connections, divided into different areas, similar to how the Computer window lists storage devices in categories. But little can be done here that cannot be done elsewhere in Windows Vista. For specific information, refer to the various sections in this part.

The Network Window

Windows lists all shared resources available on the local network in the Network window, similar to what's shown in Figure 10-4. You can open this window by clicking the Network icon on the desktop, by choosing Network from the Start menu, or from the first triangle's menu on the far left end of the Address bar.

The Network window lists available computers and other resources on the network. Specifically, it lists computers belonging to the Workgroup. ***See also*** "Workgroups," later in this part.

Figure 10-4

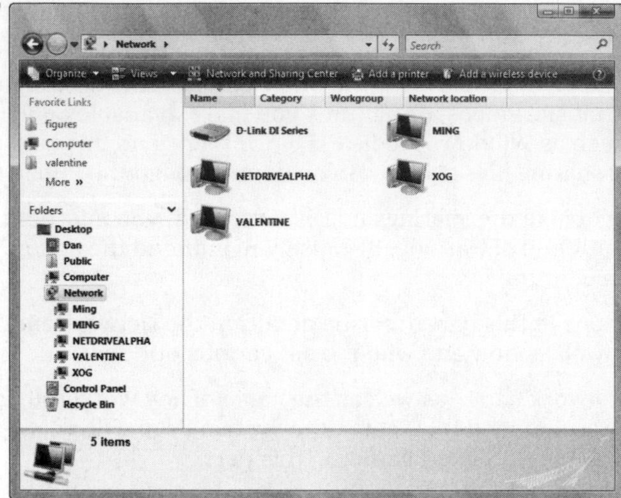

When a computer is turned off, disconnected from the network, or not a member of the workgroup, it doesn't show up in the Network window.

When the Network window is empty, it means that your computer is the only member of its workgroup. Otherwise, you have misspelled the workgroup name or have some other network problem.

To see specific resources associated with a computer, open that computer's icon. ***See also*** "Accessing a Shared Folder," earlier in this part.

In previous versions of Windows, the Network window was named *My Network Places* or the *Network Neighborhood.*

The PC's IP Address

Every computer on the network has its own, unique network ID number, known as an *IP address.* IP stands for Internet Protocol, the same rules and directions for connecting computers on the Internet. It's pronounced "I pee," as in "I am urinating."

You may be asked to report your PC's IP address for troubleshooting purposes or to tech support. When asked, here's how you can report that information:

1. Open the Control Panel.

2. Open the Network and Sharing Center icon.
3. Click the View Status link on the right side of the window.

   The link appears on the left side of the Network area.

   The Local Area Connection Status window displays lots of trivial information about the computer's network connection. Sadly, it doesn't display the IP address. For that, you have one more step.
4. Click the Details button.

   Ah! There in the Network Connection Details dialog box is a list of even more trivial aspects about your computer and its networking abilities. The fifth (or so) item in the list is the IP address.

Most networks assign IP addresses to all the computers on the network. They do this by using a networking program named DHCP. If your network uses a router or one computer is using Internet Connection Sharing, it provides the IP addresses to all other computers on the network by using DHCP. If not, IP addresses must be manually assigned.

DHCP stands for Dynamic Host Configuration Protocol, if that makes you feel any better.

Most IP addresses for the local network start with either 10.0.*x*.*x* or 192.168.*x*.*x*.

The currently popular IP address is known as the IPv4 Address. The IPv6 address will soon take over as the new standard. In fact, you can see your computer's IPv6 address listed toward the bottom of the Network Connection Details list. Unlike the IPv4 number, the IPv6 number is far longer, contains letters A through F, and is a lot less memorable!

The PC's MAC Address

The MAC address is a unique number given to your PC's Ethernet hardware. It's different from the IP address in that the MAC address is encoded in hardware and cannot be changed. Many wireless networks use the MAC address as a form of security; no two MAC addresses are identical, and it's difficult to fake a MAC address.

To discover your PC's MAC address, follow the steps in the preceding section. The MAC address appears as the first item on the list, labeled Physical Address.

If your PC has more than one NIC, each one has its own, distinct MAC address.

MAC stands for Media Access Control. Say "mack" — don't spell out the letters.

The PC's Network Name

All PCs connected to the network make themselves known in various ways:

- The computer's IP address
- The networking hardware's MAC address
- The computer's networking name
- The computer's description
- Any shared resources on the computer

The computer's networking name is used by Windows to name the computer system as well. So, if Windows knows your computer as Daisy, it also appears on the network as Daisy. You change this nonsense, along with the computer's description, in the System Properties dialog box:

1. Open the System icon in the Control Panel.

   The System window lists all sorts of interesting information about your computer, most of which is designed to look impressive. Under the heading Computer Name, Domain, and Workgroup Settings, you find various network information.

2. Choose Change Settings, found in the Computer Name, Domain, and Workgroup Settings area.

   Because changing the network information could be a security breach, a User Account Control may appear at this point.

3. Click the Continue button in the User Account Control window.

   The System Properties dialog box appears.

4. To change the computer's name, click the Change button.

5. Type the name in the Computer Name text box.

   Try to keep the name to fewer than 15 characters, with no spaces. No two computers on the network can share the same name.

6. Click OK to set the new computer name.

   The name appears in the Network window by any shared folders. It also becomes the root name of the computer in a network pathname.

7. Click OK to close the System Properties dialog box and accept your changes. Close any other open windows as well.

   Restart Windows if you're prompted to do so.

The Public Folder

Windows Vista designates a special account as *public* on your computer. This public account is available for sharing files, either between users on the same computer or with other users on the network. The main folder for those public files is the Public folder.

You can access the Public folder from the Windows Explorer window. Choose Public from the folder tree (at the bottom of the Navigation pane), or click the first triangle on the Address bar and choose Public from the drop-down menu.

The Public folder (see Figure 10-5) is considered an account folder in Windows Vista, although, unlike other accounts, its contents are open to anyone else using the computer. As with other account folders, the Public folder comes populated with subfolders to help with organization.

Figure 10-5

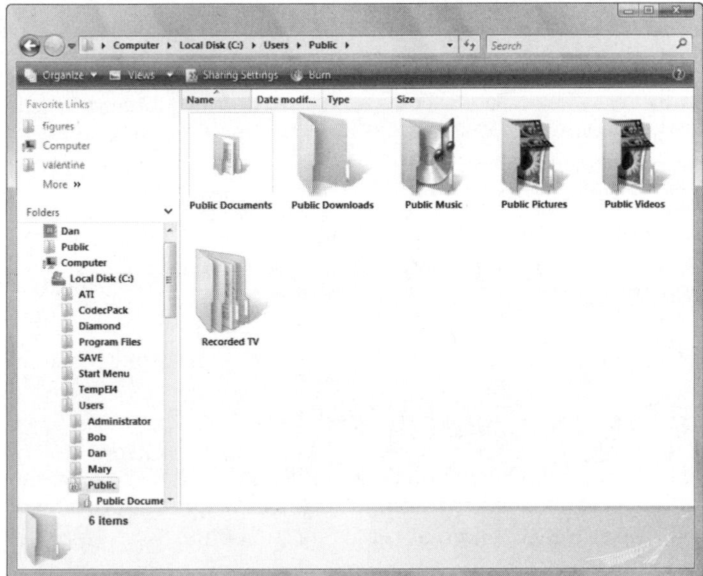

To use the Public folder to share files with other users on the same computer, simply copy the files you want to share to the Public folder or one of its subfolders.

The pathname to the Public folder is `\users\public`.

Sharing the Public folder on the network

To make files in the Public folder available to others on the network, obey these steps:

1. Open the Network and Sharing Center window.
2. Turn Network Discovery on.
3. Turn File Sharing on.
4. Turn Public Folder Sharing on.

When prompted by a User Account Control security warning (after Step 4), answer by clicking the Continue button.

In Step 4, you have a choice between giving others read-only or full access. When you want merely to share files and not have others add to or change the files in the Public folder, choose the first option, Turn On Sharing So Anyone with Network Access Can Open Files. Otherwise, choose the second option, Turn On Sharing So Anyone with Network Access Can Open, Change, and Create Files.

You can further limit who on the network has access by activating password-protected sharing in the Network and Sharing Center window. That way, you limit access from the network to only those who have password-protected accounts on your computer. For example, someone on the network who wants to access your PC's Public folder is greeted with a dialog box prompting for a username and password.

Unsharing the Public folder

To make the files in the Public folder private again, restricting network access, open the Network and Sharing Center window and change the Public Folder Sharing option to Off.

Repairing a Network Connection

Networking isn't perfect. Occasionally, you may think that you're connected to a network, but for some reason the computer is being ignorant or slow. To remedy the situation, you can take a stab at repairing the connection. Here's how:

1. Open the Network and Sharing Center icon in the Control Panel.
2. In the Network and Sharing Center window, choose the task on the left labeled Diagnose and Repair.

   Windows attempts to remedy the situation.
3. Read the (dismal) results, and then click the Close button.

Most of the time, I find that Windows can handily repair a broken wireless connection or a fouled-up wire-based connection. Sometimes, the process just poops out. As an alternative solution, consider restarting Windows. ***See also*** Part IV.

Sharing a Folder

I don't recommend sharing folders on the network in Windows Vista, primarily for security reasons. You should copy things to the Public folder, which can easily be shared, rather than make a single folder in your account area shared on the network.

Making a folder on your PC available to the network

When you're desperate to ignore my advice and share any folder in your account, follow these steps to do so:

1. Right-click the folder.

   That folder and its contents — including any and all subfolders and their contents — are shared on the network.

2. Choose Properties from the shortcut menu.
3. Click the Sharing tab.
4. Click the Advanced Sharing button.

   If warned by a User Account Control message, click the Continue button.

5. Put a check mark by Share the Folder.
6. Optionally, type a share name for the folder.

   I tend to keep my folder names short and in context with their parent folders. When a folder has an ambiguous or short name on my computer, I typically give it a more descriptive share name.

7. Click the Permissions button.

   You must instruct Windows Vista in who is allowed to access the shared folder. Not every bum on the network can just walk right in, don't ya know.

   The Permissions window should specify Everyone. That's fine. Put check marks next to Full-Control to give everyone full access. Otherwise, the Read option presets read-only access.

8. Click OK to dismiss the Permissions dialog box.
9. Click OK to close the Advanced Sharing dialog box.
10. Click the Close button to close the folder's Properties dialog box.

I don't recommend that you share the root folder of any hard drive; likewise, don't share any of Windows own folders or folders containing programs you installed on your computer. Such a thing proves to be a major security risk. (Windows warns you when you try.)

Shared folders appear with the "we're buddies" icon in the lower-left corner.

You can also share individual files, although I believe that you'll find it easier to copy them to the Public folder instead.

To privately share a folder, select the folder and click the Share button on the toolbar. Work through the wizard, adding users and permissions for the folder. Be sure to e-mail or copy the shared address because the folder you share doesn't appear on other computer's Network window. Only by typing the shared folder's network pathname can others get access.

Unsharing a folder

To unshare a folder, repeat the steps from the preceding section, but in Step 5, remove the check mark by Share This Folder. Click OK and then Close to clean up any open dialog boxes.

You're duly warned if anyone else on the network is using that folder when you unshare it.

Sharing a Printer

To share a printer attached to your PC, and make it available for use by others on the network, pursue these steps:

1. Open the Printers icon in the Control Panel.
2. Right-click the printer you want to share.
3. Choose Sharing from the shortcut menu.

   The printer's Properties dialog box appears.
4. Click the Change Sharing Options button.
5. Click the Continue button in the User Account Control dialog box.
6. Put a check mark by Share This Printer.
7. Optionally, enter a share name.

   This step helps folks identify the printer on the network. Oftentimes, renaming the HP4500n to "Color Laser in Dan's Office" can help network users choose which printer they need.
8. Click OK.

Printers you're sharing appear with the "we're buddies" icon in their lower-left corner, just like shared folders on your computer.

To unshare a printer, repeat these steps, but in Step 6, remove the check mark by Share This Printer.

Using a Network Printer

See Part IX for more information about printing over the network.

Which Folders Are You Sharing?

To help you keep track of which folders your PC is sharing on the network, Windows provides a handy summary: Open the Network and Sharing Center window, and from the bottom of the right side, choose the Show Me All the Shared Network Folders on This Computer link. Windows displays a search results window, listing all the folders plus any shared printers.

Workgroups

The simplest type of network is the *peer-to-peer* network. In this setup, the network lacks a central powerful computer, such as a file server. Instead, each computer can access any other computer on the network directly. To help keep the network organized, it can further be broken up into smaller units, called workgroups.

A *workgroup* is nothing more than a collection of computers on the network. By isolating larger networks into workgroups, it makes accessing other computers with similar needs and resources easier. But, on a small-office or home-office system, workgroups are still necessary, even though the system doesn't have that many computers.

Your computer must belong to a workgroup so that you can easily access other computers in the workgroup. For a small office or home office, I recommend that all computers belong to the same workgroup.

Only resources from the workgroup appear in the Network window.

To join a workgroup, simply specify its name:

1. Open the System icon in the Control Panel.
2. Choose the Change Settings link located in the Computer Name, Domain and Workgroup Settings area.

   Click the Continue button if you're prompted with a User Account Control security warning.

3. Click the Change button to display the Computer Name/Domain Changes dialog box.
4. In the Member Of area, choose the option labeled Workgroup.
5. Type the name of the workgroup.

   Either enter the name of an existing workgroup, or create a new name for your workgroup here. For example, my computers are on a workgroup named CAT. All the computers specify CAT as the workgroup name; therefore, they all belong to that workgroup.

   The workgroup name should be short, with no spaces.
6. Click OK to close the Computer Name Changes dialog box.
7. Click OK to dismiss the welcome message.
8. Click OK to acknowledge the restart message.
9. Click the Close button to dismiss the System Properties dialog box, and, optionally, close the Control Panel window.
10. Restart Windows.

I recommend using a workgroup name other than WORKGROUP, which is the standard name used on most computers. It's just more secure to choose a unique workgroup name and not run the risk of some bad guy guessing that you didn't change the name and are still using WORKGROUP.

To view all computers belonging to the workgroup, open the Network window. See "The Network Window," earlier in this part.

Part XI

Creating Your Own CDs and DVDs

When the CD originally brought mass, removable storage to the PC in the early 1990s, users immediately wanted to write to the discs. Alas, they were told that the CD was ROM — Read Only Memory. The same sadness darkened the PC kingdom with the dawn of the DVD and its immense storage capacity. The time during which mere users were unable to create their own CDs or DVDs, however, is but a brief chapter in the PC's cosmic history.

Most PCs now are blessed with drives that can read CDs and DVDs *and* create them, and in a variety of formats. You can write whatever information you want to a CD or DVD, use the disc for backup, create a musical CD, or do a variety of wondrous things.

In this part . . .

- CD Types
- Creating a Musical CD
- Enabling a CD-R/RW Drive
- Erasing a CD-RW
- Importing Music
- Using a CD-R/RW in Windows

Checking to See Whether You Have a Recordable Drive

There are four different types of drives that your PC can have for working with the shiny media:

- **CD-ROM drive:** This drive can only read CDs — data CDs, musical CDs, or CDs created on someone else's computer.
- **CD-ROM recordable drive:** This drive can read from CDs *and* create CD-R discs. Most of them also say "Rewriteable," which means that they can use CD-RW discs.
- **DVD drive:** This drive can read both DVDs and CDs. It cannot record either format.
- **DVD combo or super drive:** This type of drive can read DVDs and CDs, and it can also create both CDs and DVDs, and in a variety of formats.

Knowing which type of drive you have can be tough because there's no standard logo or moniker for each drive type. Some drives do say "Rewriteable" or "Recordable" on them. Some drives say "R/RW" or something similar. Some drives say nothing!

See also Part VI, the section about CD-ROM and DVD drives.

Creating a Musical CD

Programs that let you collect and play music on your PC are the same ones you can use to create musical CDs. Many programs do this, although the information here is specific to the Windows Media Player program.

Music is collected in a program like Windows Media Player either over the Internet or by inserting a CD into your computer and ripping music from the CD. (*Ripping* is the hip term for copying music from the CD onto your PC's hard drive.) After it's in your computer, it's simply a matter of making a list of songs you want to *burn* to a CD.

In Windows Media Player, the easiest way to burn a CD is as follows:

1. Click the Burn tab.
2. Insert a blank CD-R.
3. If you're prompted with an AutoPlay dialog box, click the X button to close the box.
4. Drag songs from the center part of the window to the right side of the window, where it says Drag Items Here to Create a Burn List. (See Figure 11-1.)

Figure 11-1

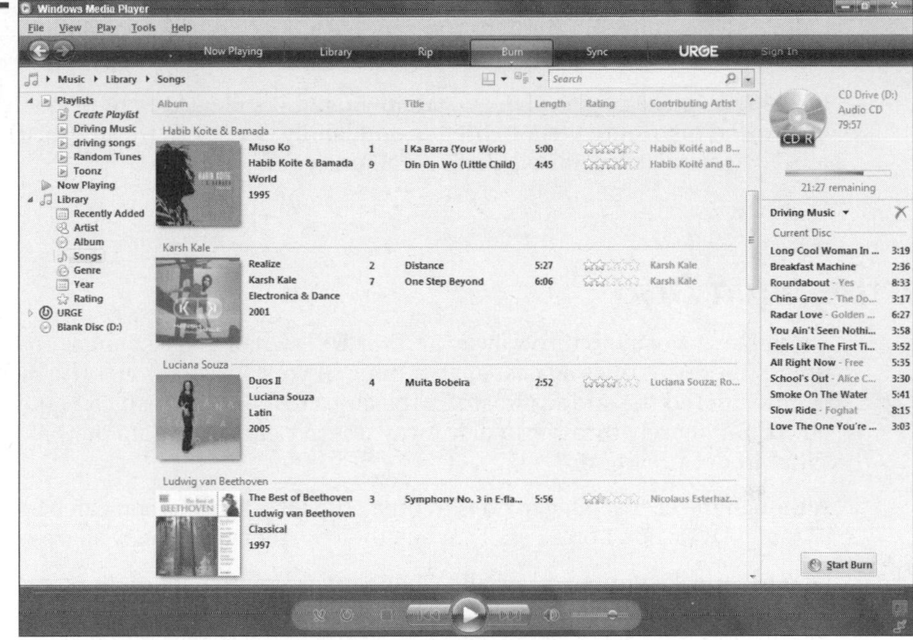

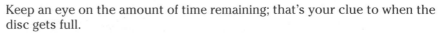

To add an entire album, drag the album's icon over to the burn list.

To add a *playlist* (a list of favorite tunes), drag the playlist over from the far left side of the window.

5. Repeat Step 4 over and over to build your CD.

Keep an eye on the amount of time remaining; that's your clue to when the disc gets full.

To remove a song from the burn list, right-click the song and choose Remove from List from the shortcut menu. (This command doesn't remove the song from the library.)

6. To create the music CD, click the Start Burn button at the bottom of the burn list.

Sit back and watch. The speed at which the songs burn to the CD-R depends on the CD/DVD drive's speed. Most drives can write music eight times faster than the music takes to play. But at least the screen is interesting to watch.

The disc may eject automatically when it's done burning. If not, choose Burn➪Eject Disc After Burning.

Label the disc after it's burned! You can use a Sharpie to write on the disc itself, or you can go all fancy and create a peel-and-stick label.

It's okay to make copies of music you own, but it's illegal to create copies of music and distribute them to friends and family. Yes, even those "Christmas mix" discs are illegal. Please don't steal music.

Destroying a Disc

I suppose it's okay to throw away a CD or DVD when you're done with it — unless there are rules against such a thing in your jurisdiction. (The discs may be considered "hazardous waste.") Tossing a disc into a trash can takes little effort. But merely throwing a disc away doesn't erase the data on that disc. What to do, what to do?

Although the casual thing to do is to break the disc, this method can be dangerous. CDs and DVDs don't break easily. When they do, they have many sharp edges.

One practical solution, especially when you deal with a lot of discs, is to invest in a CD shredder. Just like a paper shredder, the CD shredder carefully rips a CD or DVD into tiny, harmless pieces. If the price of a CD shredder is out of your range, look in the newspaper for a recycling center or local financial institution (or law office) that may offer shredding services.

Finally, don't burn your old CDs or DVDs. Burning discs emit a toxic smoke, and you risk getting burned from molten disc material, or perhaps you could burn down your house. That's a bad thing.

Disc Formats

When referring to computer discs, *format* describes the way information is written to the disc. It's a technical thing, and the details would bore you. But it helps to know the differences between the two types of disc formats so that you can best choose which one to use when you create a disc:

Live File System: When using the Live File System, you can freely write files to a CD or DVD at any time. Eject the disc, reinsert the disc, and add more files. The Live File System is flexible, but discs written in this format may not be compatible with all computer CD and DVD drives.

Mastered: The Mastered disc format writes all data to a CD or DVD at once. The files waiting to be copied to the disc sit on the hard drive until you're ready to create the disc. When the disc is finally created, it's *burned* all at once and then closed; the disc can no longer be written to. The Mastered format is more compatible with other computers' CD and DVD drives.

I recommend using the Live File System for everyday activities, such as backing up files at the end of the day or swapping files between two computers. Use the Mastered format when you're creating a data CD or DVD to send to a friend or when doing large-scale backups or archiving.

Disc Types

Two types of shiny discs are used in a PC:

- CD, the Compact Disc
- DVD, the Digital Versatile (or Video) Disc

Right away, the most important thing to remember here is that it's redundant to say "CD disc" or "DVD disc." The "disc" is already part of the acronym.

Without saying otherwise, both types of disc are *read-only,* the RO in ROM. So, you can say CD or CD-ROM, DVD or DVD-ROM. But most folks drop the "ROM" part. Either way, the ROM discs cannot be written to; you can only read information from a read-only disc.

To write to a CD or DVD, you need a recordable disc:

- CD-R, or CD recordable
- DVD-R, DVD+R

To write to a CD or DVD multiple times, erasing and rewriting, you need a rewritable disc:

- CD-RW, or CD rewriteable
- DVD-RW, DVD+RW, DVD-RAM

A typical CD holds 600MB of computer data or 74 minutes of music. Higher capacities are available on some CDs.

A typical DVD holds 4.7GB of data.

In addition, you can use the DVD DL types of discs, where the DL stands for Dual Layer. These discs can record twice as much information as non-DL discs, or about 8.54GB as opposed to 4.7GB. Only when you have a DVD drive that can handle these discs should you concern yourself with this format. Also, the DL format isn't fully compatible with older DVD drives.

Some DVDs are sold in an 8-centimeter diameter. This type is for use primarily in DVD cameras. Computers use 12-centimeter discs.

Some CD-Rs are sold as Music CDs. These are usually of lower quality than other CD-Rs. That's fine for music, where teeny, tiny errors don't affect the quality for most people. But, for data CD-Rs, the lower quality doesn't cut it.

This reference book doesn't cover the newer Blu-ray discs or HD DVDs, which are not yet standard on the PC.

The CD-R, DVD-R, DVD+R

You can write information only once to a CD-R, DVD-R, or DVD+R. After the disc is full, it cannot be written to again, although it can be read from. Nearly all computers recognize the recordable format and can read from that type of disc, even if the drive is a standard (not recording) CD or DVD drive.

Data is *burned* to the CD-R before the disc is ejected. But, in Windows, that doesn't mean that you're done with the disc. You can reinsert the disc and continue to add information until it's full.

Information can be written to the CD-R in short spurts or in one long burst, depending on the format. See "Disc Formats," earlier in this part.

The DVD-R format is more compatible with other DVD players than the DVD+R. The DVD+R format, however, is more efficient. The only time the difference comes into play is when your software requests one format or the other. For example, my DVD-creator program uses only DVD-R as its disc of choice to create DVD movies. Most DVD recordable drives, however, eat both the -R and +R formats. These drives are often called ± drives.

The CD-RW, DVD-RW, DVD+RW, DVD-RAM

RW discs work just like their R sisters. At any point, however, you can elect to erase the entire disc and start over. Note that the entire disc is always erased; you cannot erase small chunks of a disc at a time.

CD-RW discs aren't the best choice for recording music. Not all audio CD players are compatible with the CD-RW format. (Those that are usually say so somewhere on the drive.)

The difference between DVD-RW and DVD+RW is the same difference between DVD-R and DVD+R; refer to the preceding section.

RW discs are more expensive than R discs, which is another reason not to use them for music. Some users find it cheaper, for example, to buy a spool of DVD-Rs, use them, and then throw them away as opposed to reusing a handful of DVD-RWs.

The DVD-RAM format is the oldest recordable DVD format available. Few PCs use this format, although it's quite efficient and more reliable than the newer formats. The DVD-RAM format is incompatible with standard DVD drives and video players.

Erasing an RW Disc

The only advantage of an RW disc over the standard recordable discs is that the RW disc gives you the option of completely erasing the disc and starting over. Yes, erasing the disc utterly deletes any files, folders, programs, and whatnot on that disc. But you get to start over again, with a fresh, blank disc, which is the selling point.

To utterly zap an RW disc, heed these steps:

1. Open the disc's window.

   You can also open the Computer window and click to select the CD/DVD RW drive.

2. Click the Erase This Disc toolbar button.

   An informative yet misnamed window appears.

3. Click the Next button.

   It takes a while for Windows to utterly zap the disc.

4. Click the finish button.
5. Eject the disc.

The last step is optional; you can also try to open the disc, which is the same as initializing it all over again, preparing it for first-time use.

Writing to a Disc in Windows

Windows is keenly aware of, and understands, how to create both CDs and DVDs. When you have the right hardware, Windows lets you add files to those discs in a simple, straightforward manner. Generally, the steps go like this:

1. Insert the disc into the drive.
2. Direct Windows to open the disc for burning (writing).
3. Copy files to the disc.
4. Burn/eject the disc.

The specifics for Steps 3 and 4 vary, depending on how the disc is formatted. The following sections explain the details.

Initializing a recordable or rewritable disc

Recordable and rewritable discs come ready to use. No preparation is involved; you don't have to preformat them, like floppy disks. In fact, the disc is formatted as you write data. But that happens later. To start using the disc, follow these steps:

1. Stick the disc into the drive.

   Windows recognizes the disc, thanks to Autoplay, and asks you what to do. (See Part VI.)

2. Click the button labeled Burn Files to Disc.

3. Name the disc.

   As when you name anything, be brief and descriptive, such as what's shown in Figure 11-2.

Figure 11-2

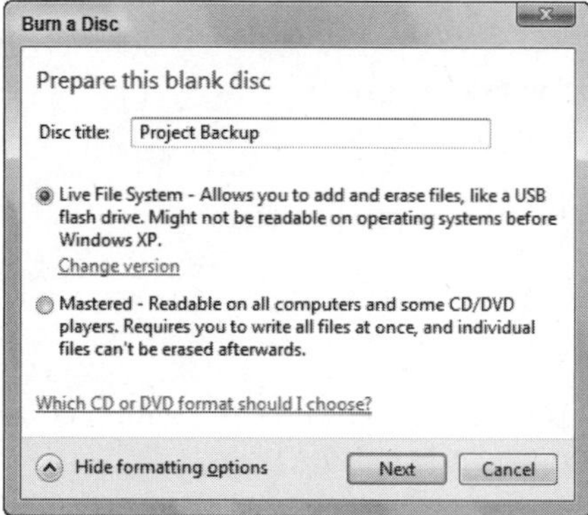

4. Click the chevron to show formatting options.

5. Choose Live File System or Mastered.

   See "Disc Formats," earlier in this part.

   You may see a warning when formatting a CD-RW disc with the Live File System. I must admit that using the Mastered format with CD-RW discs is more efficient.

6. Click the Next button.

   If you choose Live File System, Windows claims that it's formatting the disc, but really it's just preparing the disc to receive data. When you choose Mastered, the disc is immediately made available for use.

   A Windows Explorer window appears, showing the contents of the disc. Yes, it's empty.

7. Start using the disc.

   The disc is ready for writing.

If Windows doesn't recognize the disc or an error occurs, toss out the CD-R/RW. Bum discs happen. There's nothing you can do, other than throw the turkey away and start over.

Working with a Live File System disc

Live File System discs have the advantage that they're used just like any other disk drive in your computer system: Copy or move files or folders to the disc's window. You can even create new folders on the disc.

A quick way to copy one or more files to the disc is to use the Burn button on the toolbar. Select the files to copy and click the Burn button, and the files are burned onto the disc.

Copying files to a Live File System disc takes longer than copying them to a Mastered disc. The reason for the delay is that the files are being written to the disc as you copy them. Remember: *Live* File System.

I do not recommend saving files directly to a disc. Save files to your hard drive, and then copy them to the disc.

When you're done with the disc, eject it as you would any CD or DVD. This process takes a bit longer as Windows works to finalize a few things, but eventually the disc spits out of the drive.

You can reuse the Live File System disc at any time: simply reinsert the disc. Files can be copied to the disc as long as there's room. Eject the disc when you're done.

It may seem like it's possible to delete files from a recordable disc. This is only partially true: Although the file you delete from the disc no longer shows up, its data is still on the disc. Rather than delete the information, Windows merely covers it up, like burying your little brother in the sand. The room that the file occupied isn't gone, and the file's data can be recovered by clever nerd types. But as far as what you see, it looks like the file is gone. My advice is simply to be more careful about what you put on a recordable disc in the first place.

Working with a Mastered disc

When you choose the Mastered disc format, nothing is written to disc until you direct Windows to do so. Until then, files you copy to the disc sit in a special folder — a sort of waiting room.

Files and folders copied to the Mastered disc have a special download icon on them, as shown in the margin. This icon is your clue that the file is waiting to be written to the disc.

A quick way to copy files to the disc is to use the Burn button on the toolbar. Clicking the Burn button doesn't burn the files to the disc, but, rather, copies them there for eventual writing — a lot faster than other ways to copy the file.

Nothing is written to the disc until you direct Windows to burn the disc. If you want to remove a file from the disc, delete it as you would any file.

To purge the entire disc before it's written, open the disc's window and click the Delete Temporary Files toolbar button.

When you're ready to create the disc, and all the files you want to put on the disc have been chosen and copied to the waiting room folder, follow these steps:

1. **Open the disc's window.**
2. **Click the Burn to Disc toolbar button.**

   A Burn to Disc window appears.
3. **Give the disc a name or title.**
4. **Optionally, choose the recording speed.**

   I don't know why they put this option here, because most people think faster is better.
5. **Click the Next button.**

   The disc is formatted and ejected.
6. **Click the Finish button.**

The disc can now be read by any computer with a CD drive.

You cannot write any more information to a Mastered CD. After you choose to burn the files, the disc is *closed.* When you want to keep using a disc, choose the Live File System instead, or use an RW disc.

Part XII

The Keyboard

Yell all you like, but the computer doesn't hear anything you have to say unless you go through the proper channels. The keyboard is one of your PC's primary input devices, right along with the mouse. In a way, the keyboard acts as the computer's ears, listening to your input. Based on what you type, the computer then diligently goes off and obeys your commands, right or wrong. This makes the keyboard one of the most important gizmos attached to your computer system.

In this part . . .

- Accessing Menus with the Keyboard
- Controlling a Window with the Keyboard
- The Help Key
- Keyboard Basics
- Keyboard Shortcuts
- Keys for Editing Text
- Setting the Repeat Delay and Repeat Rate
- Special Keys

Accessing Menus with the Keyboard

Although a casual user may plod through menus with a mouse, the power user eschews the mouse and employs the keyboard. By using keyboard shortcuts, or accelerator keys, power users can get at the various menu commands faster and more efficiently than by using a mouse.

A *keyboard shortcut* is merely a key combination assigned to a specific command, such as Ctrl+S for the Save command. See "Keyboard Shortcuts," later in this part, for a list.

Accelerator keys are key combinations that activate and choose commands from menus. To activate a menu, begin by pressing the Alt key. Depending on the program, pressing the Alt key activates the first menu, displays underlines on the menu names to indicate additional shortcut keys, or displays an otherwise hidden menu.

After pressing the Alt key, use the underlines that appear in the menu names and commands to activate those menus and commands. The underlines indicate which keys on the keyboard activate those menu items. From that point onward, it's a matter of pressing the proper keys to match the menu commands.

For example, to access the File⇨Page Setup command in Microsoft Word, you press Alt, F, U. That's Alt to activate the underlines, F for File, and U for Page Setup.

Some manuals and documentation even underline the commands for you, to help identify the keys: File⇨Page Setup.

The first step can also be combined: Alt+F, U. In this case, pressing Alt+F immediately accesses the File menu.

The Alt key technique can also be used in applications employing the Ribbon interface. Pressing Alt in an Office 2007 application, for example, displays the keys necessary to access various tabs, groups, and command buttons visible on the screen.

The F10 key can also be used to show a hidden menu.

Press the Esc key to cancel and back out of the menus.

The Any Key

The Any key is more of a relic from the computer's text-based past. Oftentimes, a program would prompt you (in what the programmer believed to be a friendly manner) to "Press any key to continue." The idea was to give you a choice: Press any old key on the keyboard, just like a rap on the door to know that things are okay.

Sadly, many beginners would scour the keyboard in futile frustration for a single key labeled Any. There is no such key.

Today, such a message is often more precise: “Press the Enter key to continue.” The Enter key *is* the Any key. (Well, so is the spacebar.)

Controlling a Window with the Keyboard

The key to using the keyboard to manipulate a window is understanding the Control menu. All windows have a Control menu, flagged by a tiny icon in the window's upper-left corner. Clicking that icon with the mouse, or pressing Alt+spacebar, displays the Control menu, shown in Figure 12-1.

Figure 12-1

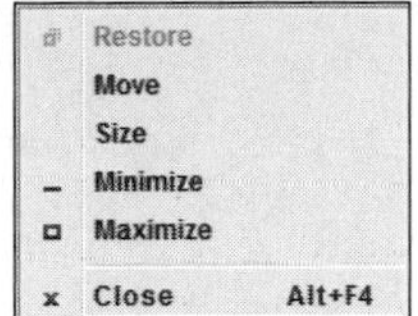

Not all Control menus are the same. Some programs sport special items on their Control menus. Sometimes, programs you install on your PC may add new Control menu commands. But the common commands found on the Control menu are those that let you use the keyboard to manipulate the window:

Restore: Alt+spacebar, R. The window is restored to its previous size and location after being maximized.

Move: Alt+spacebar, M. The window can be moved by using the four arrow keys on the keyboard. Simply press an arrow key to move the window in that direction. Press Enter or Esc when you're done moving the window.

Size: Alt+spacebar, S. The window's size can be changed. First, press an arrow key to indicate which side of the window you want to move: right, left, top, or bottom. Then press the corresponding arrow keys to move that side of the window in or out. Press Enter or Esc when you're done.

Minimize: Alt+spacebar, N. The window is minimized and becomes a button on the taskbar.

Maximize: Alt+spacebar, X. The window is maximized to fill the entire screen.

Close: Alt+spacebar, C, or Alt+F4. The window is closed. If the window is a program, the program quits.

Dead Keys

Certain legacy keys are left over on the PC's keyboard from days gone by. Although some programs may use these, most don't. They exist on the PC's keyboard for compatibility with older programs:

SysRq: The System Request key was once considered *the* important operating system key. Sadly, that time never came to pass, although the key has remained on the keyboard, albeit tucked under the Print Screen key.

Pause: This key can still be used to pause the text display, but has no purpose in Windows. Some games may use the Pause key to pause the action, but this key has otherwise lost its function.

Break: This key was used to cancel a command, often in conjunction with the Ctrl key. Today, it hides below the Pause key, out of sight and out of mind.

The Help Key

No Help key is on the PC's keyboard. Instead, in Windows the F1 key is used to summon help. Press F1 in most applications or in Windows itself to bring up a Help window, often specific to whatever action you're doing in a program.

(Help keys were once common on computer keyboards. In fact, the Macintosh computer keyboard sports a key labeled Help.)

Keyboard Basics

Computer keyboards have evolved through the years, from primitive teletypes to terminals to the standard PC keyboard of today. Even then, the current PC keyboard model, the 104-key keyboard, shown in Figure 12-2, is only a few years old. And, variations on that keyboard exist from manufacturer to manufacturer, especially on laptop PCs.

Keyboard layout

Keyboards include these four main areas:

- **Function keys:** These keys, on the top row of the keyboard, are labeled F1 through F12.
- **Typewriter keys:** These are the alphabet and number keys, plus a smattering of punctuation and other symbols — the main part of your computer's keyboard.

- **Cursor-control keys:** Just to the right of the typewriter keys, these keys are used to move a cursor or insertion pointer on the screen, and to do general editing. The keys are duplicated on the numeric keypad. Some manuals refer to these as the *arrow keys.*
- **Numeric keypad:** This area contains duplicates of the number keys, 0 through 9, along with a period and various mathematical symbols. This area is designed for quick number entry. Also, the numeric keypad doubles as a secondary location for the cursor-control keys. The Num Lock key determines which set of keys — numeric or cursor — are in use. When the Num Lock light is on, the numeric keys are used.

Figure 12-2

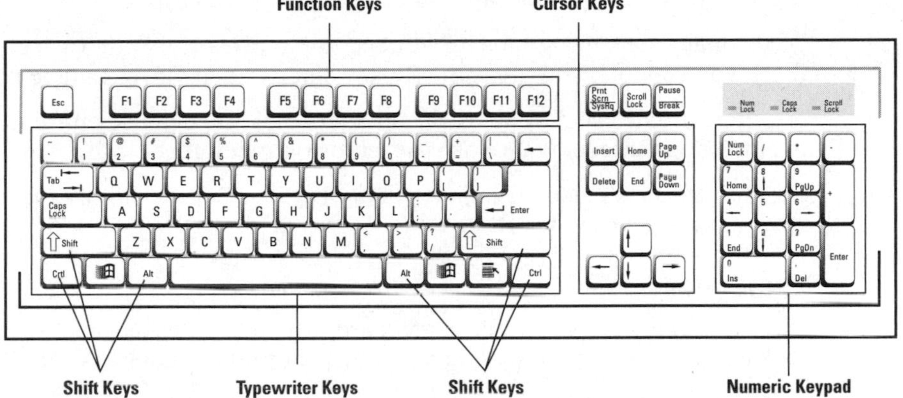

Note that the mathematical symbols surrounding the numeric keypad aren't exactly the ones you learned about in grammar school. Here's a quick translation:

- + is for addition.
- – is for subtraction.
- * is for multiplication.
- / is for division.

Shift keys

Unlike a typewriter, the computer keyboard has three sets of shift keys. These keys are used in combination with other keys to display interesting characters on the screen, control the cursor, or give commands to the computer:

- **Alt:** Short for Alternate Shift key, this key is used in combination with other shift keys or with letter keys to carry out commands or functions in Windows.

- **Ctrl:** Also called the *Control* key, this key is used in combination with various letter keys to issue command shortcuts, such as Ctrl+P ("control pee") to print.
- **Shift:** This key works just like the Shift key on a typewriter. Shift is used primarily with the letter keys to produce uppercase text. Shift can also be used with other keys and in combination with other shift keys.

When these keys are used in combination with other keys, a plus sign joins them. For example, Shift+S means to press the Shift and S keys, to yield a capital S on the screen. Ctrl+S is the Save command in many programs. And, a command can even use multiple shift keys, such as Ctrl+Alt+Q.

The Win, or Windows, key can also be used as a shift key.

Occasionally some programs may direct you to press the Shift, Ctrl, or Alt key alone. For example, you press the Alt key alone to activate the menu bar.

Yes, there are two sets of Alt, Ctrl, and Shift keys. You can use either one unless an application directs you to use the left or right key specifically.

The shift keys may also be called *modifier* keys, as in they modify the function of other keys when used together.

Lock keys

Three Lock keys are on the PC's keyboard, which are also associated with three Lock lights, either above the numeric keypad or on the Lock keys themselves:

- **Caps Lock:** Used like Shift+Lock on a typewriter. When this key is active and the Caps Lock light is on, all alphabet keys on the keyboard generate uppercase letters. But, note that unlike a typewriter, Caps Lock doesn't shift the number keys to their symbols.
- **Num Lock:** When this key is active, and the Num Lock light is on, the numeric keypad generates numbers. Otherwise, the numeric keypad is used as a cursor keypad.
- **Scroll Lock:** This locking key isn't used in Windows. Only a few spreadsheet programs use it. When Scroll Lock is on, and its light is on, using the cursor keys moves the entire worksheet, not just the cell selector.

Another key found on some specialty keyboards is the F Lock key, also known as the Function Key Lock. The F Lock key allows the function keys to be used in two ways. When F Lock is on, the function keys behave like the standard function keys. When F Lock is off, the function keys take on specific characteristics as written on the keyboard or programmed into the keyboard by using special software.

It's often frustrating to many folks not used to using the F Lock key to use a keyboard with such a feature. For example, when you press F1 and expect to get help, but none appears, check to see whether the keyboard sports an F Lock key.

See also "Special Keys," later in this part.

Keyboard Shortcuts

One of the joys of using a PC keyboard is taking advantage of all the various shortcut keys in Windows because your hands are often resting on the keyboard anyway:

Press This Key	*To Do This*
In a dialog box	
Alt+↓	Drop down a list.
Alt+*letter*	Switch to gizmo identified by the underlined *letter.*
Ctrl+Tab	Switch to next tab (multitab dialog boxes).
↓	Adjust a value down, or choose next item in a list.
Enter	Click the OK button.
Esc	Click the Cancel button.
F1	Display dialog box help (if available).
F4	Display list or drop-down list.
Shift+Ctrl+Tab	Switch to preceding tab.
Shift+Tab	Switch to preceding input field or dialog box gizmo.
Space	Switch check mark off or on.
Tab	Switch to next input field or gizmo.
↑	Increase a value or choose preceding item in a list.
Window shortcuts	
Alt+F4	Close window.
Alt+spacebar	Display Control menu.
Ctrl+Shift+Tab	Switch to preceding pane.
Ctrl+Tab	Switch to next pane.
F6	Switch between panes.
Windows desktop shortcuts	
Alt+Enter	Display selected item's Properties dialog box.
Alt+Esc	Cycle through open programs.
Alt+Shift+Tab	Switch to preceding program.

cont.

Press This Key	*To Do This*
Windows desktop shortcuts	
Alt+Tab	Switch to next program.
Application	Display shortcut menu for selected item.
Ctrl+Esc	Pop up Start button's menu.
F3	Open the Search command.
Win	Pop up Start button's menu.
Win+Break	Display System Properties dialog box.
Win+D	Show the desktop (hide windows).
Win+E	Open Windows Explorer window.
Win+F	Open Search Companion (Find).
Win+L	Lock Windows.
Win+M	Minimize all windows.
Win+R	Display Run dialog box.
Win+Shift+M	Restore minimized windows.
Win+Tab	Flip between open windows and the desktop.
Win+U	Open Utility Manager window.
Windows Explorer shortcuts	
Alt+Enter	Display selected item's Properties dialog box.
Backspace	Go up one level in folder hierarchy.
Ctrl+A	Select all files.
Ctrl+C	Copy selected file or files.
Ctrl+E	Activate Search text box.
Ctrl+F	Display Search window.
Ctrl+V	Paste cut or copied files.
Ctrl+X	Cut selected file or files for a move.
Delete	Delete file.
F2	Rename file.
F5	Refresh window contents.
Shift	Prevent inserted CD or DVD from playing automatically.
Shift+Delete	Permanently delete file.

Press This Key	*To Do This*
Common application shortcuts	
Alt	Activate menu.
Ctrl+A	Select All.
Ctrl+B	Apply bold type.
Ctrl+C	Copy.
Ctrl+D	Unselect / Find dialog box.
Ctrl+F4	Close document window, but not program.
Ctrl+I	Apply italics.
Ctrl+N	Create new document.
Ctrl+O	Open.
Ctrl+P	Print.
Ctrl+S	Save.
Ctrl+U	Underline.
Ctrl+V	Paste.
Ctrl+W	Close window.
Ctrl+X	Cut.
Ctrl+Y	Redo.
Ctrl+Z	Undo.
Delete	Clear.
F10	Activate or display menu.

Keyboard Types

There's really only one type of keyboard for the PC: the standard 104-key keyboard. It's called 104-key because it really does have 104 keys. That's three more keys than the old 101-key keyboard, which was a standard for about 15 years. (Before that, the original IBM PC used an 83-key keyboard.)

The extra three keys on the 104-key keyboard are the two Windows keys and the Application key. ***See also*** "Special Keys," later in this part.

You can find variations on the standard keyboard, including wireless keyboards, ergonomically designed keyboards, and keyboards with specialty buttons on them for doing tasks such as send e-mail, search the Web, scan documents, and set the speaker volume. Note that those keyboards and their special buttons are nonstandard.

Keys for Editing Text

Windows uses a common set of keyboard commands to edit, change, or modify any text just about anywhere in Windows:

Press This Key	To Do This
←	Move the text cursor left (back) one character.
→	Move the text cursor right (forward) one character.
↑	Move the text cursor up one line.
↓	Move the text cursor down one line.
Ctrl+←	Move the text cursor left one word.
Ctrl+→	Move the text cursor right one word.
Home	Move the text cursor to the beginning of the line.
End	Move the text cursor to the end of the line.
Delete	Delete the character immediately to the right of the text cursor.
Backspace	Delete the character immediately preceding the text cursor.
PgUp	Move the text cursor up one screen.
PgDn	Move the text cursor down one screen.
Ctrl+PgUp	Move the text cursor up one full screen in the document.
Ctrl+PgDn	Move the text cursor down one full screen in the document.
Ctrl+↑	Move the text cursor to the preceding paragraph.
Ctrl+↓	Move the text cursor to the next paragraph.
Ctrl+Delete	Delete characters from the cursor's position to the end of the line.
Ctrl+End	Move the text cursor to the end of the document.
Ctrl+Home	Move the text cursor to the beginning of the document.
Insert	Insert characters in a line of text. Pressing the Insert button again types over the current text.

Names for Funky Keys

Symbols unusual abound on the PC keyboard — things that would mortify the standard eighth-grade typing teacher. Here are the common names for these unusual symbols:

Symbol	Name
!	Exclamation point, bang
#	Hash, pound sign
*	Asterisk, star, splat
.	Period, dot
/	Slash, forward slash
@	At
[ ]	Square brackets
\	Backslash
^	Circumflex, hat, control
_	Underline, underscore
`	Accent grave
{ }	Curly brackets, braces
|	Pipe, vertical bar
~	Tilde ("till-duh")
< >	Angle brackets, less-than, greater-than

Setting the Repeat Delay and Repeat Rate

Yes, there's a Keyboard icon in the Control Panel. The icon doesn't do much, however, unlike the Mouse icon (see also Part XIII). But the Keyboard icon does let you control two important keyboard settings: the repeat delay and the repeat rate.

The *repeat delay* is the length of time the keyboard waits while you press a key before that key starts repeating. So, press and hold the D key, and eventually the computer repeats the letter: DDDDDD. The pause before it goes nuts like that is the repeat delay.

The *repeat rate* is how quickly the characters appear after the repeat-delay time has elapsed.

You use the Keyboard icon in the Control Panel to set the repeat delay and the repeat rate. There's a text box where you can check your settings before clicking the OK button to lock them in.

Special Keys

A few keys carry more weight than others. These keys are important to know:

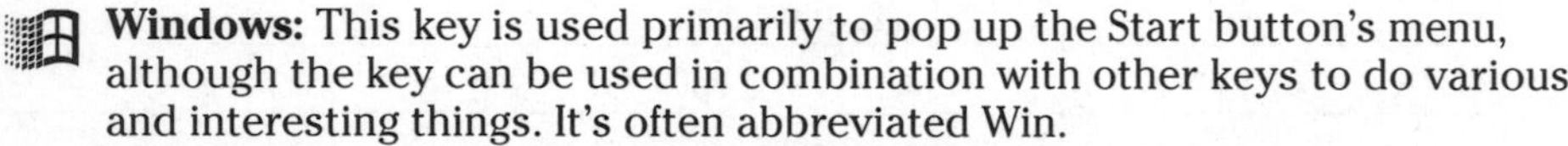

Windows: This key is used primarily to pop up the Start button's menu, although the key can be used in combination with other keys to do various and interesting things. It's often abbreviated Win.

Application: This key exists to the left of the second Windows key on the standard 104-key PC keyboard. This key is rarely used, although when you select an icon or item and press this key, that item's Properties dialog box is displayed. Yawn.

FN: This key is found mostly on laptop PCs. It's used in combination with other keys on a laptop to produce key combinations not normally available on the smaller, laptop keyboard.

Enter: This key must be important because two of them are on the keyboard. Relax! Both Enter keys do the same thing. Enter is commonly used as a command key to signal to Windows that you're done typing a command or have finished making selections in a dialog box. It's also used when writing text to mark the end of a paragraph.

Tab: In Windows, you press Tab to move between fields in a dialog box. Remember this point because pressing the Enter key is like clicking the OK button.

Esc: This key, also called *escape,* is used to cancel certain operations. It can also be used to close some windows.

Print Screen: This key is used to take a snapshot of the desktop (***see also*** Part IX). Note that the key may also be labeled PrtSc or Pr Scr or some other cryptic combination. They're all Print Screen keys.

Part XIII

The Mouse

The computer mouse has been included in the standard PC configuration for about 20 years now. You can thank all those graphics up on the screen for the necessity of a computer mouse. The mouse makes working with graphics — and even manipulating text — much easier. After all, computers don't live by keyboard input alone.

In this part . . .

- Basic Mouse Activities
- Changing the Double-Click Rate
- Connecting a Mouse
- Extra Mouse Buttons
- Increasing the Mouse Pointer Visibility
- Left-Handed Mouse
- The Mouse Pad
- Mouse Pointers
- Mouse Types

Basic Mouse Activities

You can do only a few things with a computer mouse. Basically, you can roll it around and click the buttons. But doing that in various ways and in various combinations gives it specific terms and jargon:

Point: The most basic mouse command is *point,* as in "Point the mouse at the circle." This instruction requires you to move the mouse around on your desk, which controls the mouse pointer on the screen by moving it in a similar manner. You move and maneuver the mouse until the mouse pointer on the screen is pointing at some specific or interesting object.

Click: Pressing and releasing the mouse's button is known as clicking. But — aha! — the mouse has more than one button. Therefore, the plain click is a quick press (and release) of the mouse's main button, the one under your index finger. For right-handed people, that's the left mouse button.

You click the mouse in combination with pointing.

Clicking may also be done in combination with pressing a shift key on the keyboard: Shift, Ctrl, Alt, or a combination of these. Using the Ctrl key with a mouse click, for example, is known as a Ctrl+click, or "control click."

Clicking the mouse does indeed make a clicking noise. The computer may also be programmed to play a sound when you click the mouse, such as a squishing noise or painful little yelp.

Right-click: Pressing and releasing the right mouse button — the one not normally pressed — is a right-click.

A regular click is a click of the left button, and a right-click is specifically the right button.

Double-click: Two quick clicks in a row is a double-click. For example, a single click may merely select an object, to make it ready for manipulation. But a double-click does something more powerful, such as open an item or just cause it twice as much pain as a single click.

Double-clicking must be done quickly; if you take too long, the computer assumes that you have made two single clicks and not a double click. ***See also*** "Changing the Double-Click Rate," later in this part.

You can also triple-, quadruple-, and quintuple-click, depending on the program.

Drag: The drag operation involves pointing the mouse at some object and then pressing and holding down the mouse's (left) button. You then move the mouse while keeping the button held down. Releasing the mouse button ends the drag operation.

Dragging is used to select groups of objects, an area, or a swath of text, or to move things around. The key is to keep the mouse button down.

Select: The mouse is often used to select an object or text on the screen. You do this by using a number of mouse techniques, depending on what is being selected.

For example, to select a graphical object or icon, you click the mouse on the object. That highlights the object, indicating that it's selected and ready for action.

To select a group of items or a span of text, you drag the mouse over the items or text. You can also select text by double-clicking the mouse on the text, or by triple-clicking or using a shift key while clicking. (It depends on the application.)

Selected objects and text appear highlighted on the screen.

The best way to get familiar with using the mouse is to play one of the many games included with Windows, such as Solitaire, FreeCell, or Minesweeper. These games help you practice the basic mouse movements just described, as well as kill some time and have fun.

Changing the Double-Click Rate

A *double-click* is defined as two clicks in rapid succession at the same location. The location can vary slightly; the mouse programming forgives a few pixels on the screen one way or the other. But the "rapid succession" part can vary, and can be controlled:

1. Open the Control Panel.

2. Open the Mouse icon to display the Mouse Properties dialog box.
3. Click the Buttons or Activities tab.

   The tab sports a different name depending on which type of mouse is attached to your PC; not every Mouse Properties dialog box is alike.
4. Use the slider in the Double-Click Speed area to adjust the double-click speed slower or faster. Test the speed by double-clicking the mouse in the Test Area display.
5. Click OK to set the new double-click speed.

Connecting a Mouse

Connecting a mouse to the console is easy: Basically, you just plug the thing in.

For a mouse plugged into the console's mouse port, first turn off the console and then plug in the mouse. Turn the computer on after the mouse is connected.

Likewise, turn off the console when you're disconnecting the mouse from the mouse port.

For USB and serial mice, you can connect or disconnect the mouse while keeping the console on.

Serial mice traditionally plug into the COM1 port. (COM2 is used internally by the dialup modem.)

See also Part II.

Extra Mouse Buttons

The standard PC mouse has three buttons:

- The left button, which is the main button
- The right button
- A center wheel, which is also a button

The wheel button has multiple purposes: It can roll up or down, which normally scrolls text in a window but can also be used to zoom in or out in some applications (usually in combination with the Ctrl key). The wheel button can also be pressed. In some applications, pressing the wheel button and dragging the mouse "pans" data in a window. Finally, newer mice have a wheel button that tilts from side to side, also panning data in a window.

Some mice have even more buttons. Windows doesn't officially use those buttons for anything, so you can use the Mouse icon in the Control Panel, on the Buttons tab, to assign functions to those extra buttons.

For example, the IntelliMouse Explorer has two bonus buttons on the left side, which can be manipulated with your right thumb. These buttons can be *mapped* to any key combination or assigned commands that do things in Windows. For this to work, you must install the specific software that comes with your computer mouse.

Increasing the Mouse Pointer Visibility

It's easy to lose the mouse pointer on the Windows desktop. To help find the wayward little guy, you can activate some bonus pointer features:

1. Open the Control Panel.

2. Open the Mouse icon in the Control Panel to display the Mouse Properties dialog box.
3. Click the Pointer Options tab.

   Several options are available to increase mouse visibility, depending on the type of mouse you have. The two common options are

   - **Pointer Trails:** This option causes multiple pointers to "comet tail" after the mouse pointer.
   - **Show Location:** This option causes a ring of concentric circles to appear around the pointer when either Ctrl key is pressed.
4. Make your selection, and then click OK.

You can also increase the pointer's size by choosing a larger pointer, or an animated pointer, or even an inverse color pointer. ***See also*** "Mouse Pointers," later in this part.

Left-Handed Mouse

Various efforts throughout history to eliminate left-handed people have happily failed. There's hope for the happy southpaws among us, as well as for other folks who prefer to hold the mouse in their left hands. Windows lets you reassign the mouse buttons, left and right, so that you can use the right mouse button with your left hand — which makes sense and is quite a kind gesture to the left-behind part of the population:

1. Open the Control Panel.

2. Open the Mouse icon in the Control Panel to display the Mouse Properties dialog box.
3. Click the Buttons tab.
4. Change the function of the left button to Right-Click.

   Use the drop-down list to assign the new button function.
5. Change the function of the right button to Click.
6. Click OK.

Remember that you have a left-handed mouse! Most computer documentation assumes that the mouse is right-handed. So whenever you see a "right-click" instruction, remember to click your *left* mouse button.

The Mouse Pad

A *mouse pad* is merely a small piece of foam rubber on which a computer mouse can roll very well. This item is optional to purchase for a computer; in fact, optical mice don't need a mouse pad, although mechanical, or *ball,* mice can really benefit from the textured surface a mouse pad offers.

Mouse pads are often covered in special designs or with pictures of something pleasing or inspiring.

Just about anything can be used as a mouse pad, but textured surfaces work best. Avoid slick mouse pads.

A mouse pad also ensures that you have at least one clean area on your desk to roll the mouse around!

Mouse Pointers

The graphical doohickey that the mouse manipulates on the desktop is the *mouse pointer.* Some may call it a *mouse cursor* or just *cursor,* but that's easy to confuse with the text cursor. To avoid confusion, and because the thing looks like a pointer anyway, I use the term mouse pointer.

Making the pointer go faster or slower

The mouse pointer can be geared to go faster or slower, which is controlled from the Mouse Properties dialog box, on the Pointer Options tab:

1. Open the Control Panel.

2. Open the Mouse icon in the Control Panel to display the Mouse Properties dialog box.
3. Click the Pointer Options tab.
4. Adjust the pointer speed slider slower or faster.
5. Click OK.

A faster pointer is easier to use when you have a larger screen or high screen-size setting. Slower pointers are better when you're working with graphics or other things that require precise mouse movement.

If the Mouse Properties dialog box sports an acceleration option for the mouse pointer, I highly recommend that you use it. The acceleration option directs the pointer to move in greater distances when you move the mouse faster, and to move the pointer more precisely when the mouse is moving slowly.

Choosing a new pointer

The mouse pointer can be replaced with just about any graphical image, from a real arrow to a pointing hand to a tomahawk. You do this by using the Pointers tab in the Mouse Properties dialog box:

1. Open the Control Panel.

2. Open the Mouse icon in the Control Panel to display the Mouse Properties dialog box.
3. Click the Pointers tab.
4. In the scrolling list of pointers, click to select the Normal Select pointer.
5. Click the Browse button.

   A special type of Open dialog box appears, listing a cartload of various pointers available in Windows. Notice the special preview area in the lower-left corner of this dialog box.
6. Click to select a new pointer from the many options listed.

   The files beginning with the name `arrow` are all pointing arrows, although you're not limited to that selection for replacing the Normal Select pointer.
7. Click the Open button to choose the highlighted pointer.
8. Click OK.

You can use these steps to replace any of the various mouse pointers. Note that there are different pointers for different activities. There are no rules for what is or isn't a proper pointer — but keep in mind that all Windows documentation assumes that you're using the standard set of pointers.

Yes, it's okay to have fun here.

Using an animated pointer

Many of the optional mouse pointers are animated. For example, you can use spinning barber polls, lumbering dinosaurs, and snapping fingers. To select one of these animated cursors, after Step 5 in the preceding subsection, choose Animated Cursors (*.ani) from the Files of Type drop-down list in the Browse dialog box.

Loading a set of pointers

Windows comes with preset groups, or *themes,* of mouse pointers. You can choose one of these themes by using the Scheme drop-down list at the top of the Pointers tab in the Mouse Properties dialog box. By choosing a theme or scheme, you can quickly replace the whole set of mouse pointers at one time.

Saving your own set of pointers

After customizing your mouse pointers, you can save your collection as a scheme, which saves time in case you need to reset all the mouse pointers at some later point. To save a scheme on the Pointers tab of the Mouse Properties dialog box, first set each individual mouse pointer, and then click the Save As button. Use the Save As dialog box to save your scheme just as you would save any file.

Mouse Types

There's really no such thing as a standard PC mouse. All mice have left and right buttons, and most of them now have a wheel button or similar gizmo between the buttons. But that's where the similarities stop.

This section covers various mouse options. Some mice may have most or all of the options, and some may have none. The variety is endless.

Air mouse

The very peculiar *air* mouse can be held up, off the desktop. In a way, it kind of works like a TV remote control. That's good for demonstrations and perhaps some games, but, otherwise, mice work best next to the keyboard, where they remain handy and accessible.

Mechanical, or ball, mouse

The traditional computer mouse uses a round ball on its underside to detect movement. In fact, the very first mouse, pioneered in the 1960s, used such a ball to detect movement, although today the balls (and the mouse) are much smaller. This type of mouse is known as a *mechanical* mouse.

Optical mouse

The *optical* mouse uses a special light sensor to detect movement. This mouse has, aside from the buttons, no moving parts, which makes it extremely reliable. Also, unlike the mechanical mouse, the optical mouse doesn't require a mouse pad or textured surface — although it doesn't work on smooth, reflective surfaces.

Trackball mouse

The *trackball* is often called the upside-down mouse. With a trackball, the mouse is stationary, and the mouse pointer is moved by rotating a large ball atop the mouse with your fingers. The mouse also sports buttons and, often, a *scroll ring* around the ball, used like the wheel button on a regular mouse.

Wireless mouse

A *wireless* mouse requires no wires to connect to the desktop, which is great if you have a cluttered desk already. There are two types of wireless mice:

- **Radio frequency (RF):** This mouse uses an electronic signal to connect to the base station.
- **Infrared (IR):** This mouse uses an infrared light to connect to the base station. The path between the mouse and the base station must not be obscured, or else the IR mouse doesn't work.

Wireless mice require batteries, which I recommend that you keep on hand in abundance. Either that, or the mouse must be recharged. I recommend getting a rechargeable mouse base station, which not only keeps the wireless mouse in a convenient place, but also recharges the mouse when it's docked.

Eventually, wires come into play with wireless mice. The base station, or receiving unit, must be connected to the console somehow, either directly to the mouse port or into a USB port.

Glossary: Tech Talk

802.11: The current wireless networking standard, typically followed by a letter, such as **b**, **g**, or **n**. For wireless gizmos to communicate, they must share the same standard or a compatible standard.

ad hoc: The type of wireless network you may join in a wireless café or wherever wireless networking is available. An ad hoc network is typically joined for short periods, generally as long as the laptop's battery lasts.

AGP: Acronym for Accelerated Graphics Port, a special type of expansion slot into which you can plug high-speed video adapters. The PCI-Express and PCI-X standards have surpassed AGP as the graphics port expansion slot of choice.

All Programs menu: The main program menu branching from the Start button's menu. Pretty much every program installed on your computer appears somewhere on the All Programs menu or on one of its ubiquitous submenus.

Alt: A special shift key on the PC keyboard, often used in combination with some other key, although it can be used by itself.

application: Another name for a computer program, although usually describing a major software category, such as word processing, spreadsheet, or e-mail.

Apply button: Used like the OK button in a dialog box in that it accepts any changes. Unlike clicking the OK button, clicking the Apply button doesn't close the dialog box.

arrow keys: Another term for the four basic cursor keys on the keyboard: up, down, left, and right.

asterisk: The * symbol on the keyboard. Used to represent multiplication in many programs. Also, the multiple-character filename wildcard.

background: 1. A multitasking term indicating a program that is running a task you aren't currently working with or don't have visible on the screen. Most printing takes place in the background. 2. An image on the desktop, also known as wallpaper.

backspace: 1. The key on the keyboard that has the word *Backspace* on it. This key may also have a left-pointing arrow on it. 2. To press the Backspace key, which deletes something. In a word processor, the Backspace key erases the character immediately to the left of the cursor.

bold: In word processing or desktop publishing, the attribute applied to text that *darkens* it.

boot: 1. To start a computer. 2. To load a specific operating system.

boot disk: The disk used to start your computer. Most often, the boot disk is the hard drive, although you can start a computer with a floppy, CD, or DVD.

broadband: Another term for a high-speed Internet connection. Broadband can be DSL, cable, satellite, or some other zippy form of access.

bug: A problem that prevents a program from working properly. Typically unexpected, bugs are something that nearly every program has.

burn: To write information to a CD, either data or music. This is the final step in using the CD-R or CD-RW disc.

button: Either a physical button on the keyboard or console or the graphical representation of a button appearing on the screen. You "press" graphical buttons by using the mouse.

byte: A single storage location, either in computer memory or on disk. A byte can store one character of information.

cable: A wire or bundle of wires used to connect devices inside or outside of a computer. Cables are used for communications between the computer and the device. It's that old I/O thing, made famous in all those songs that kids once sang around the flickering monitors of computer camp.

cable modem: The fastest type of modem. However, you must live in an area where a cable company offers cable modem access.

Cancel button: Used to dismiss a dialog box and ignore any changes that were made. Pressing the Esc key is the same as clicking the Cancel button.

CD-R: A CD that can have information written to it. The R stands for *r*ecordable.

CD-ROM: Acronym for Compact Disc–Read-Only Memory. CD-ROMs are discs that contain megabytes of information.

CD-RW: A CD that can have information written to it, and can also be erased and used again. RW stands for *rew*riteable.

Celeron: Another popular type of microprocessor for the PC; similar to the Pentium but not as powerful or as expensive.

central processing unit (CPU): The computer's microprocessor. Often used incorrectly to refer to the console.

character: Any letter, number, or symbol. Most keys on a PC's keyboard are adorned with characters, which are displayed on the screen when the keys are pressed.

child folder: Another name for a subfolder, but specifically with reference to the containing folder. For example, any folder inside the Documents folder is a child folder of the Documents folder.

chipset: A collection of circuits used together inside a PC for basic functions or to provide basic hardware, such as graphics or networking.

clear: To erase or delete.

Clipboard: A temporary storage area for items that have been cut or copied using either the Edit⇨Cut or Edit⇨Copy command. The Edit⇨Paste command is used to dump the Clipboard's contents into the appropriate location or program. The Clipboard can hold only one item at a time.

close: To remove a window from the screen or a document from an application's window. Can also mean to exit a program.

compressed folder: A special type of folder that can store files and folders just like a regular folder, although the contents of the compressed folder take up less space on the hard drive. ***See also*** Zip.

Computer: An icon representing the contents of your PC in Windows — all the disk drives, printers, and other folders.

connector: One end of a computer cable; matches a plug-in or hole on the console or computer peripheral to which it attaches.

console: The main computer box; the thing that all other parts of your computer plug into. Sometimes mistakenly referred to as the CPU.

Control Panel: The place to go to customize various aspects of Windows and your PC.

CRT monitor: The traditional glass-screen computer monitor. CRT stands for *c*athode *r*ay *t*ube, the doodad inside the monitor that displays the image.

Ctrl: A special shift key, called Control, on the PC's keyboard. This key is often used in combination with other keys to carry out commands or do other cool things.

cursor: A blinking underline, block, or vertical line on the screen that shows where new text appears in a window or document. Also mistakenly used to refer to the mouse pointer. *Cursor* is from the Latin word for *runner.*

cursor keys: Another term for the arrow keys on the keyboard. The keys are called cursor keys because they manipulate the cursor. Unlike the arrow keys, cursor keys also include Insert, Delete, Home, End, Page Up, and Page Down.

data: The computer term for organized stuff or information.

default: An ugly word meaning "the setting selected for you when you don't make any other choice." For example, the default printer is the printer Windows chooses to use when you don't specify a printer.

delay rate: The rate at which the PC waits before redisplaying a character on the screen when its key on the keyboard has been pressed and held.

delete: To remove a file from a disk; to erase or kill the file or a chunk of text or any selected thingy.

desktop: The main screen displayed by Windows. The desktop is home to various icons, the taskbar, the Start button, plus an optional pretty picture.

DIMM: Acronym for Dual In-line Memory Module, a small expansion card on which memory chips are placed.

disk: The part of the disk drive on which information is written. It can be a removable disk, such as a floppy disk or CD, or a nonremovable disk, such as the disk inside a hard drive.

display: The monitor or computer screen — specifically, the information shown on the screen.

Documents: A folder window used as the primary location for where you save stuff on your computer.

double-click: To press the left (or primary) mouse button twice in rapid succession without moving the mouse between clicks.

drag: To move an onscreen object with the mouse. Also, for a man to dress in women's clothing.

drive: A disk drive in the computer system, usually described by the type of drive it is: CD-ROM drive or flash memory drive, for example.

driver: The software program that controls some piece of hardware. For example, a printer driver is used to control how the printer prints information. You can have modem drivers, graphics display drivers, network drivers, women drivers, and more.

DSL modem: A type of high-speed modem used with a phone company's DSL, or Digital Subscriber Line, connection.

DVD: Acronym for Digital Versatile (or Video) Disc, a high-capacity form of read-only computer storage. A DVD disc can store as much as 4.7 gigabytes of information per side.

DVD recordable: One of several types of DVD disc used to record information. The variety includes DVD-R, DVD+R, DVD-RW, DVD+RW, DVD-RAM, and probably a few others that I don't really care to write about just now.

eject: To remove a disk from a disk drive.

Enter key: A special key on the keyboard used to end input or a paragraph of text, or as a substitute for clicking the OK button in a dialog box. The PC keyboard has two Enter keys: one in the typewriter key area and the second on the numeric keypad. Both Enter keys work the same.

erase: To remove a file from a disk.

error message: A cryptic note the computer displays to let you know that the program isn't working right or that you screwed up.

Ethernet: The type of networking system PCs use.

expansion card: A circuit board that plugs into expansion slots on the motherboard and is used to add new features to your PC.

expansion slot: A slot into which expansion cards are plugged, on the PC's motherboard. There are three types of expansion slots: AGP, ISA, and PCI.

file: The basic chunk of information stored on a computer disk. Files can be programs, text, raw data, graphics, or other stuff.

fixed disk: Another term for a hard drive. The disk is fixed as in *not removable,* not as in *repaired.*

F-key: A function key.

floppy disk: A removable disk, traditional for PCs but rarely used these days because their capacity is too low to hold today's larger files.

floppy drive: A disk drive designed to read from and write to floppy disks.

folder: A container for files as well as other folders. Folders are used to help organize the information you collect or create on your computer.

font: A collection of characters with predefined sizes and styles. Most word processors and desktop publishing programs let you choose different fonts to make your writing prettier.

function keys: The keys labeled F1 through F12 on your keyboard. Each key does a specific task or can be programmed to do certain tasks.

gigabyte (GB, G): One billion bytes, or 1,000 megabytes. Used to measure computer storage — usually, hard drive storage.

glitch: A problem (sometimes temporary) that causes a program to work erratically or not at all.

graphics: Artwork; anything nontext on a computer.

hard copy: Printed information.

hard disk: The physical disk used to store information inside a hard drive. The thing you use in a computer is the *hard drive;* hard disk is a technical term.

hard drive: The main device for long-term storage in a PC.

hardware: The physical part of a computer; anything you can touch and see.

Help system: The program used to display (helpful) information in Windows.

icon: A tiny picture used to represent something else, such as an image used to represent a file on disk.

ink cartridge: The small container used to supply inkjet printers with ink. Different cartridges have different colors of ink, or sometimes multiple colors are put in separate compartments of single ink cartridges.

inkjet printer: A type of printer that sprays ink on paper rather than smacks an inked ribbon against the page, as an impact printer does. Inkjet printers are quieter than dot-matrix printers and produce better-quality printing (but not as good as laser printers).

insertion pointer: The cursor, on the screen, used in a program to mark where new text appears.

I/O: Input and output. At its core, input and output are what the computer does. Input is information going into the computer, and output is the stuff the computer produces, modified or mangled by the computer itself.

IP: Acronym for Internet Protocol, a set of rules for sending and receiving information over a network as well as over the Internet (which is just a big network anyway).

IP address: An ID number given to computers on the network according to various rules and protocols. IP stands for Internet Protocol. The IP address is a group of four numbers, each from 0 to 255, separated by dots, as in 192.168.0.1.

ISA: Acronym for Industry Standard Architecture, the name given to the traditional, old-fashioned expansion slots found inside PCs. These slots are kept around for compatibility reasons.

italic: In word processing or desktop publishing, the attribute applied to text that *slants* it — like the leaning tower of Pisa in Italy!

jack: Another term for a hole or connector on the console, into which cables plug for connecting external devices.

key: A button on the keyboard.

keyboard: The device you use to communicate with the computer. You mostly interact with the computer by typing on the keyboard.

keyboard shortcut: A single key or combination of keys that activates a command. Specifically, this term refers to the shortcut shown on a menu, such as Ctrl+V, the keyboard shortcut for pasting something from the Clipboard into a document.

kilobyte (K, KB): One thousand bytes of storage, either on disk or in RAM. It's exactly 1,024 bytes, but who really cares?

Landscape mode: Printing that goes the long way on a sheet of paper — wide rather than narrow.

laptop: A computer small enough to fit on your lap without crushing your kneecaps.

laser printer: A type of printer that uses a laser beam to generate an image and electronically transfer it to paper.

LCD monitor: The thin, flat-screen monitor used with a laptop; now trendy to have with a desktop computer.

Live File System: A method for writing to a recordable or rewriteable CD or DVD where information is burned to the disc as it's copied to the drive. The live file format is more interactive than the mastered format, although it consumes more disk space.

MAC address: The physical address, or serial number, given to the networking hardware in your PC. The MAC address is often used for security purposes when networking — specifically, wireless networking.

map: To assign a drive letter to a folder or a shared disk drive or folder on the network.

Mastered: A method for writing to a recordable or rewriteable CD or DVD. In the Mastered format, information written to disk sits in a special folder on the hard drive. The disc is then burned only once, placing all the files and folders waiting to be burned on the disc in one action. This method is more efficient than the live file system.

Maximize button: The button in the upper-right corner of a window that is used to make the window fill the entire screen.

megabyte (M, MB): Approximately 1 million bytes of computer storage.

memory: Information storage inside a computer — specifically, RAM.

menu: A list of commands or options available within a program. Menus show you options on a list.

microprocessor: The main processing chip inside a computer, specifically dwelling in the console. Also called the CPU or just "the processor."

Minimize button: Used to turn an open window into a button on the taskbar. The Minimize button is located in the upper-right corner of the window.

minitower PC: A type of computer that sits tall and squat, usually on top of the desktop but often beneath.

modem: The device that enables your computer to connect to other computers using standard phone lines. Modems are now used primarily to connect with the Internet.

monitor: Another name for the display. It's that thing you stare into for hours on end when using your computer.

motherboard: The main circuit board of a computer, located inside the console.

mount: To add a disk drive to your computer system. Windows does this automatically whenever you insert a removable disk.

mouse: A pointing device used to provide input as well as to manipulate graphical objects on the screen.

mouse pointer: The graphical representation of the mouse on the screen — usually, a pointing arrow. The mouse pointer, manipulated by using the mouse, mimics the mouse's movements on the desktop.

network: A system of computers connected to each other for sharing information and computer resources, such as hard drives and printers.

Network: A window where various computers on the network are displayed and from which those computers and their resources can be accessed. In Windows Vista, the Network window replaces the older My Network Places and Network Neighborhood windows.

networking: Connecting twoor more computers to share resources, such as disk drives, printers, and high-speed modems.

NIC: Acronym for *n*etwork *i*nformation *c*ard (also known as an Ethernet card), the adapter or circuitry on the motherboard responsible for networking in a PC.

Notepad: The text editor program that comes with Windows.

notification area: Another term for the *system tray.*

numeric keypad: The portion of the keyboard that contains the number keys, usually all grouped into rows and columns by themselves.

online: Another way of saying that two devices are connected, such as the modem connected to the Internet.

open: To access a program or file, just as you open a book if you want to read it.

operating system: The main program that controls the PC hardware, runs your programs, and interacts with you to help control the computer.

parent folder: A folder in which a subfolder dwells. The parent folder is one level up in the folder hierarchy.

pathname: The full name of a file. The pathname includes the drive where the file lives, the folders in which the file is saved, and then the file itself. The drive letter is followed by a colon and a backslash that separate the folder names: for example, `C:\My Documents\kids\Jordan\2006`.

PC: Acronym for personal computer — specifically, a computer designed to run the Windows operating system.

PCI: Acronym for Peripheral Component Interconnect, a type of expansion slot on the PC's motherboard.

PCI-Express/PCI-X: The next-generation expansion slot standard for adding circuitry to a PC's motherboard. Express and X are two different standards, each more advanced than basic PCI (and AGP), but with their own, unique features and advantages.

peer-to-peer: A type of network where all computers can access and share information equally. No central computer controls the network or acts as a *server* for other network computers.

Pentium: The name given to the popular line of PC microprocessors developed by Intel.

Portrait mode: The tall mode, versus the wide mode for a rectangular image or sheet of paper. Normally, the printer prints on paper in Portrait mode. The other mode is *Landscape* mode.

power button: The real name of the PC's on–off switch. As a power button, the switch can have its function changed. Pressing the power button can turn off the PC, put it to sleep, hibernate it, or do nothing.

power strip: A device containing several power sockets, designed like an extension cord and used to plug in myriad devices surrounding your computer.

printer: A device for putting information on paper.

Public: A folder in Windows Vista that can be used to share information between multiple users on the same PC or made available for access by others on a network.

RAM: Acronym for Random-Access Memory, the computer's memory or primary form of temporary storage.

repeat rate: The rate at which a character is displayed on the screen after its key has been held down for a given length of time.

resource: Something that is used by a computer; a necessary component or vital piece of equipment. Examples of resources are memory (RAM), disk storage, and the printer.

Restore button: A button used to reposition a window to its previous size and location after the window has been maximized or minimized. This button appears in the upper-right corner of the window.

rip: To copy music from a CD onto the computer's hard drive.

ROM: Acronym for Read-Only Memory, a type of computer memory that cannot be erased. Normally, only computer instructions for the hardware are stored in ROM.

save: To store data in a permanent form, such as a file on a disk drive.

screen: Another term for the computer monitor; specifically, the front part of the monitor where information is displayed.

screen saver: A special program that periodically blanks out the screen and replaces it with utter darkness or, often, some form of graphical or entertaining images.

shared: A disk drive or printer that is available for use by other computers on the network.

Shift key: A modifier key used primarily to produce uppercase letters on the keyboard, or used in combination with other keys to do amazing things.

software: The brains of the computer. Software tells the hardware what to do.

SSID: Acronym for Service Set Identifier, a special code used in wireless networking; also, slang for the name of the wireless network.

Start button: The big button! The Start button lives on the taskbar and is used to start a number of activities in Windows. Clicking the Start button displays the Start menu and various options or places to go.

Start menu: The main menu in Windows; displays locations, important and recently opened programs, help information, other commands, and the All Programs menu.

subdirectory: An older term for a subfolder.

subfolder: A folder inside another folder.

submenu: A menu that appears after you choose an item from the primary menu.

surge suppressor: A special type of power strip that helps fight irregularities in the electrical supply. It's more expensive than a plain power strip.

system tray: The location on the taskbar for a group of tiny icons, the time, and the volume control. Also referred to as the *notification area.*

taskbar: One of the main Windows components, with the Start button on one end and the system tray on the other, plus buttons representing open windows and programs in the middle. The taskbar can also be home to various toolbars.

terabyte (T, TB): A huge amount of computer storage; 1 trillion bytes or 1,000 gigabytes or 1 million megabytes.

text: Stuff you type into a document. Letters, numbers, and other characters or symbols on your keyboard create text.

toner cartridge: The source of ink for a laser printer.

toolbar: A collection of buttons, plus other tools and gizmos. A toolbar is often a long, skinny palette that holds those buttons and controls. Toolbars are found in programs, and some even dwell on the taskbar.

tower PC: A desktop computer on its side, but really a computer that was made to stand vertically (up and down). These computers have more room and tend to be more powerful than mere mortal desktop models.

UAC: See User Account Control.

undelete: To put something back the way it was before you deleted it.

underline: In word processing or desktop publishing, the attribute applied to text that makes it look like it has a line under it.

undo: To retract the last action you did, whether it was adding or deleting text or applying bold or italics.

unmount: To remove or eject a disk from a computer system. To unmount the disk is to remove it from the file system, which also ensures that the files on the disk are no longer in use.

UPS: Acronym for uninterruptible power supply, a standby power device used to keep the computer running during brief power outages, or to give you enough time to shut it down during power outages.

User Account Control: A warning dialog box in Windows Vista, alerting you that something is attempting to change the system. If you're presently not doing any activity that changes the system, click Cancel. Otherwise, if you're modifying the system or making a change in Windows, it's okay to click the Continue button.

User Profile: The main folder for storing files in Windows Vista. It's your account folder, the one you see when you open your account name from the Start button's menu.

utility: A category of software that includes tools and programs specifically designed to fix, diagnose, automate, or do other amazing things in a computer. Unlike applications, utilities don't help you create things on the computer.

wallpaper: An older term for the background image on the desktop.

window: An area on the screen that displays data, programs, or information. A window can be moved, resized, opened, and closed, allowing you to organize the data on your computer screen.

Windows: An operating system, currently the most common one used to control a PC. The current version of Windows is Vista.

wireless networking: Connecting to a network without a physical connection. With wireless networking, the network information is sent and received using radio signals.

Zip: A type of file compression where one or more files can be placed into a single file archive, which is digitally compressed to take up less room on the hard drive. In Windows Vista, Zip files are also known as Compressed Folders.

zoom: To enlarge or reduce an image — typically, a document displayed in a window.

Index

Symbols and Numerics

A

B

C

D

H

I

J

K

L